CAFÉ CUISINE

CAFÉ CUISINE

LINDA
GLICK
CONWAY

HOUGHTON
MIFFLIN
COMPANY

BOSTON

Library of Congress Cataloging-in-Publication Data

Conway, Linda Glick.
  Café cuisine.

  Includes index.
  List of author's works: p.
  1. Cookery.   2. Restaurants, lunchrooms, etc. —
United States — Guide-books.   I. Title.
TX715.C7589   1987   641.5'0973   87-10037
ISBN 0-395-43025-9
ISBN 0-395-45391-7 (pbk.)

Printed in the United States of America

HM   10   9   8   7   6   5   4   3   2

To Jim

ACKNOWLEDGMENTS

My primary thanks go to the restaurant owners and chefs named throughout the text, whose work this book is. Over and over I was impressed with their talent, their willingness to combine creativity with back-breaking physical labor, and their cheerful and friendly response to my request for recipes and time.

For help before and after the recipes were compiled, I am grateful to my friends Frances Tenenbaum and Luise M. Erdmann, my editor and manuscript editor, whose advice and skills (and hospitality!) have greatly improved the collection. Thanks also to the people who played chef for a day (or more) and helped with the recipe testing — Helena Bentz, SusanMary Broadbent, Susan Clark, Sylvia Davatz, Wendy Hawkes, David Paisner, Susan Riecken, Jean Smith, Ruth Whitney, and Wendy Withington.

As I traveled throughout the country, friends and acquaintances often provided lodging, transportation, and valuable tips and information. For that help I thank Jim Burnett, Henrietta Humphreys, Jordan Irwin, Liz Johnson, Mimi Luebberman, Sally and Dave Ricci, and Deen Terry.

CONTENTS

INTRODUCTION

When I was growing up in the Midwest, the word *café* held a mysterious fascination. In the next town was the Vogue Café, enticingly off-limits, and on the other side of the world were the chic sidewalk establishments of Paris. Several decades later, cafés of more general appeal are thriving throughout the country, all catering to a new informality in eating out. "Café cuisine" can be found not only in restaurants that call themselves cafés but in bars, bistros, and diners throughout the United States.

The idea is flexibility — being able to eat as simply or as elaborately as you like at almost any time of day. If you prefer ordering several appetizers instead of an entrée, then you already know what I mean by "café cuisine." This trend has been well observed by an attentive food press, which refers to it variously as small meals, light fare, grazing, noshing — even modular eating.

At many cafés, the day begins with breakfast, a time that is growing in popularity for meeting friends or doing business. Others open in the late morning and serve continuously until late evening. Some feature live music; others offer the latest magazines and newspapers. The décor varies with the setting — the funkiness of a neighborhood bar, the special ambience of a museum café, the simple look of a classic bistro, where dark paneling is a backdrop for white napery.

In my travels to American cities (and, as an indulgence, in my own North Berkshire back yard), I looked for restaurants that fulfilled the criteria of interesting food prepared well, moderately priced, and served in relaxing surroundings. I have tried to include not necessarily the trendiest places but a variety of cafés from each city — from the simple natural foods restaurant to the elegant bistro. Regrettably, the number of likely choices left out far exceeds the number included.

The recipes had to be dishes that could be made at home with a minimum of time-consuming preparation (with a few worthy exceptions). The result is a collection that reflects the menu choices being made all over the country — the embellishment of the All-American sandwich, the continuing popularity of pasta and ''designer'' pizza, the ongoing influence of the Southwest in all parts of the country, a growing interest in Caribbean cooking, the simplicity of grilled fish and meat, the newly sophisticated treatment of natural foods and vegetarian dishes. You will also find clear evidence of a return to down-home cooking, often with a new twist, and to old-fashioned desserts — and lots of them.

Behind this eclectic national cuisine are talented, well-trained, and hard-working chefs who have a high regard for the ingredients this country has to offer and seek to combine them in ways that bring out their best characteristics. Although at first glance some of the ingredients may seem esoteric, not only gourmet food shops and ethnic markets but supermarkets, too, are stocking a tremendous variety of seasonings, produce, and specialty meats. An exception may be a full range of fresh and dried peppers. (A good mail order source is Casa Moneo, 210 West Fourteenth Street, New York, New York 10011; 212-929-1644.)

The goal of *Café Cuisine* is to give you the same flexibility at home that you have when you go out to eat. There are recipes for every mood and occasion, whether you are inclined to simply upgrade your soup and sandwich suppers or want to have fun experimenting with the new bistro cooking in your own kitchen or outside on the grill. Though I have arranged the recipes in somewhat predictable chapters for the sake of convenience, the categories are often interchangeable — many of the small courses make fine entrées, and several of the salads serve just as well as first courses. All of the recipes have been tested and edited for style and consistency, but I have let the recommendations of the individual chefs stand. This means there is more than one recipe for salsa, pesto, and pizza dough, for instance. Recipes for more basic stocks and sauces are given in the Café Pantry, at the back of the book.

The key to café cuisine is informality, whether you are cooking for yourself, your family, or friends. These days, when the formal dinner party no longer seems to be an option, why not present a buffet of *tapas* and small courses and a selection of desserts? Whatever your purpose, I hope *Café Cuisine* will help you recreate the diverse and imaginative cooking that has become the new American cuisine.

THE CAFÉS AND THEIR RECIPES

TAPAS AND SMALL COURSES

Cold Dishes

Hot Dishes

COLD DISHES

Eggplant Caviar with Tapenade
Marabella's Famous Sweet and Hot Peppers
Escarole Arrabbiata
Jade and Ivory Chicken
Insalata di Bistecca
Terrine of Pork and Veal
Cold Roast Pork with Marinated Papaya
Enoteca Duck Salad
Pasta with Coriander Sauce
Shrimp and Wild Mushrooms with Lemon
Salmon Tartare
Salmon Mousse with Herb Sauce
Smoked Salmon with Mozzarella and Yellow
   Tomato Sauce
Swordfish Carpaccio
Mussels Vinaigrette
Salpicon de Mariscos (Seafood Salad)
Scallops Ceviche with Mint

Not all the food served in the French Quarter is Creole or Cajun, and this new bistro is garnering high praise for its mostly Provençal French menu. Its chef, Susan Spicer, is one of the most celebrated young cooks in New Orleans. She has cooked at several restaurants in the city, most notably Savoir-Faire, and recently spent a year traveling and working in California, Greece, and the South of France. This combination of Mediterranean flavors reflects those travels.

EGGPLANT CAVIAR WITH TAPENADE

Serves 4 to 6

1 large eggplant
½ small onion, finely chopped
¼ teaspoon minced garlic
½ tomato, peeled, seeded, and patted dry
2 tablespoons olive oil
Juice of ½ lemon
2 tablespoons chopped parsley
Salt and pepper to taste
1 tablespoon chopped fresh basil (optional)
Toasted French bread slices or garlic croutons
Tapenade (recipe follows)

Prick the eggplant several times with a fork and roast directly on the rack in a 450° oven for 15 to 20 minutes, until the skin starts to blacken, the juices turn syrupy, and the pulp feels completely soft. (Place a tray or sheet of foil on the rack below the rack containing the eggplant. For some reason, this tends to enhance the flavor.)

When the eggplant is cool enough to handle, peel it and roughly chop the pulp. Add the onion, garlic, tomato, olive oil, lemon juice, parsley, and salt and pepper and mix gently. Add more olive oil or lemon juice if necessary. Serve in small crocks on individual plates, accompanying each with a ramekin of Tapenade and slices of toasted French bread or croutons.

THE BISTRO AT
MAISON DE
VILLE

—

NEW ORLEANS

Tapenade

4 ounces Greek olives, pitted
2 anchovy fillets
1 tablespoon drained capers
2 teaspoons Dijon mustard
4 tablespoons olive oil

Place the first four ingredients in a blender or food processor and turn on and off until finely chopped. Add the olive oil and stir to blend.

NOTE: To decrease the saltiness of the Tapenade, rinse the olives and capers under cold running water and drain well.

MARABELLA'S FAMOUS SWEET AND HOT PEPPERS

Serves 6

8 large green peppers
2 large sweet red peppers
2 long hot peppers
Mazola oil
Salt
Freshly ground black pepper
Granulated garlic

Cut the green and red peppers in ½-inch strips lengthwise. Cut the hot peppers in half lengthwise and then halve the strips crosswise. Coat the bottom of a sauté pan with the Mazola oil and heat. When the oil is hot, add the peppers. Sprinkle the salt in an S shape over the peppers. Do the same with the pepper and garlic.

Sauté, stirring continuously, until the peppers are soft and pliable. The colors will begin to fade. Remove from the heat. Serve the peppers and their juices with crisp, fresh bread, with or without butter.

This glitzy Italian café was an instant success when it opened in the fall of 1984, and it continues to serve about seven hundred people a day, from late morning to very late evening. The signature dish at Marabella's is these sweet and hot peppers, which are brought to each table along with crusty fresh bread. Don't be put off by the somewhat idiosyncratic way of measuring the seasonings — it works!

MARABELLA'S
—
PHILADELPHIA

A special feature of the Café Petitto — one that draws the attention of passersby on busy Connecticut Avenue — is the antipasto buffet displayed in a bay window at the front of the restaurant. The colorful daily offerings include salads, sausages, and calzones. Escarole Arrabbiata is a spicy favorite at the antipasto bar.

ESCAROLE ARRABBIATA

Serves 6

1 large head escarole
½ cup olive oil
2 cloves garlic
4 ounces pancetta (Italian bacon), coarsely diced
½ to 1 teaspoon crushed red pepper flakes
Coarse (kosher) salt

Clean the escarole, cut into bite-size pieces, and blanch for 1 minute in boiling water. Drain well and squeeze out any remaining water. Separate the leaves.

Heat a large skillet over moderate heat. Add the olive oil and garlic and sauté until the garlic browns. Remove the garlic. Add the pancetta and cook until golden. Add the escarole and crushed red pepper and sauté for 5 minutes, stirring frequently. Salt to taste. If the escarole becomes dry as it cooks, add more olive oil. Serve at room temperature.

JADE AND IVORY CHICKEN

Serves 4

1¼ pounds skinned and boned chicken breasts,
  poached lightly
1 pound broccoli, trimmed and cut in flowerets
3 tablespoons sesame seeds, roasted
1 orange, thinly sliced, for garnish

JADE DRESSING

1 clove garlic
1¼ teaspoons Chinese five-spice powder
2 tablespoons brown sugar
2 tablespoons water
2 tablespoons white wine vinegar
¼ cup soy sauce
2 tablespoons Oriental sesame oil
2 teaspoons Dijon mustard
1⅓ cup mayonnaise, preferably homemade

Prepare the dressing by combining the first six ingredients in a heavy saucepan and simmering over
moderate heat until the mixture is reduced by a
third. Strain the mixture and combine 1 tablespoon
of the reduction with the sesame oil, mustard, and
mayonnaise. Set aside.

  Cut the poached chicken breasts in strips approximately ½ inch by 3 inches. Blanch the broccoli in
boiling water until barely tender and refresh in cold

water. Drain well. Toss the chicken in a small amount of the dressing and arrange on one side of a serving platter. Arrange the broccoli on the other side and place a bowl of dressing for dipping in the center of the platter. Sprinkle the platter with sesame seeds and garnish it with twisted orange slices.

Café Spiaggia is the informal sister of Spiaggia, said to be Chicago's premier northern Italian restaurant. Flagships of the Levy Organization, the restaurants share space at One Magnificent Mile, amid the elegant department stores, boutiques, and hotels on North Michigan Avenue. A special feature of Café Spiaggia is the antipasto bar, where one may order just an appetizer or make a whole meal of antipasti.

INSALATA DI BISTECCA

Serves 6 to 8

1 eye of round (3 to 4 pounds)
½ red onion, julienne-cut
5 plum tomatoes, peeled, seeded, and coarsely
   chopped
3 ounces arugula
4 tablespoons olive oil
2 tablespoons oregano
Salt and pepper to taste

Trim any excess fat from the meat and grill or broil until medium rare. Chill.

When the beef is cold, cut it in julienne strips and place in a large bowl with the onion, tomato, and arugula. Toss with the olive oil, oregano, and salt and pepper.

CAFÉ SPIAGGIA
—
CHICAGO

TERRINE OF PORK AND VEAL

Serves 6 to 8

3 tablespoons chopped shallots
1 tablespoon butter
½ pound *each* lean pork shoulder, veal, and pork
  fat, ground together
½ cup Madeira, Port, Armagnac, or Cognac
2 cloves garlic, crushed
½ teaspoon ground thyme
Salt and pepper to taste
2 truffles, cut into fine strips (optional)
1 pound chicken livers
3 egg yolks
1 bay leaf
½ pound fatback, in strips, to line terrine
Cornichons for garnish

Sauté the shallots in the butter. In a mixing bowl, combine the shallots, ground meat and pork fat, wine or brandy, garlic, thyme, salt, pepper, and truffles.

Lightly sauté the chicken livers, then grind them in a food processor with the egg yolks. Add the liver to the meat mixture and marinate for about 2 hours at room temperature or overnight in the refrigerator.

Line the bottom and sides of a 12-by-4-by-4-inch terrine with the fatback. Spoon the meat mixture into the terrine, place the bay leaf on top, and fold

Monique's Café was one of the first restaurants to open in the Superior/Huron art gallery district — Chicago's answer to New York's SoHo. Occupying the first floor of a refurbished warehouse, the café uses one third of its space for the kitchen, and a charcuterie/ patisserie take-out counter and a cocktail/espresso bar serve as dividers in the front of the house. Exposed pipes and ducts and hanging industrial lamps contrast with white linen, fresh flowers, and white bent- wood chairs, but the overall effect is restful and somewhat feminine.

MONIQUE'S
CAFÉ

—

CHICAGO

the pork fat over the top. Cover the top with a sheet of aluminum foil and set the terrine in a pan of boiling water that comes to two thirds of the depth of the terrine.

Bake the terrine at 350° for about 45 minutes, adjusting the temperature to keep the water from boiling. The terrine is cooked through when the meat shrinks from the sides of the pan or a meat thermometer reads 130°.

Remove the terrine from the oven and the water bath and weight down the top. When the pâté is cool, remove it from the terrine, wrap in plastic, and refrigerate. Serve in slices with cornichons.

The Balboa Cafe

COLD ROAST PORK WITH MARINATED PAPAYA

Serves 6 to 8

1 2-pound boneless pork loin
1 small onion, sliced
4 cloves garlic, sliced
4 sprigs rosemary
1 tablespoon black peppercorns
¼ cup olive oil
3 papayas, peeled, seeded, and chopped
Juice of 2 or 3 limes, depending on size
¼ teaspoon ground cumin
¼ cup sour cream
Juice of 1 lime

Marinate the pork loin in a mixture of the onion, garlic, rosemary, peppercorns, and olive oil for anywhere from 2 hours to 2 days.

Marinate the chopped papaya in the juice of 2 or 3 limes and the cumin for 1 hour.

Sear the pork loin on all sides in a heavy pot on top of the stove and roast in a 350° oven for about 45 minutes, until the meat is still pink in the center. Let it cool.

Mix the sour cream and the juice of 1 lime and set aside. Carve the pork in ⅛-inch slices and place 5 or 6 pieces in a fan shape on each serving plate. Arrange some drained papaya at the base of each fan, and garnish with a dollop of lime sour cream.

Balboa Café has been in operation since 1914, and until 1975 it was continuously owned by the Carmigani family. The grand mahogany and oak bar, the etched-glass doors, and the old photographs on the walls tell the story of days past, when the café was a favorite gathering place for city politicians. Today the café has a varied clientele, including visitors to the nearby Union Street area.

BALBOA CAFÉ

—

SAN FRANCISCO

Malinda Pryde, the co-owner of Enoteca, has made good use of her combined experience as a home economics major in college and a public relations assistant at the Christian Brothers Winery in Napa, California. Her goal is not only to sell wine but to promote it and to educate her customers: "We serve the history, romance, and language, too." Nearly thirty wines are available by the glass, and they are especially popular with the Northwest tapas *offerings on the restaurant menu. This duck salad is one of the* tapas.

ENOTECA DUCK SALAD

Serves 8

1 pound smoked duck (or smoked chicken)
2 papayas
4 bunches spinach, washed twice and dried well
Freshly ground pepper
Juice of 1 lime
1 cup coarsely chopped walnuts
1 lime, quartered, for garnish

RASPBERRY-SOY DRESSING

½ cup soy sauce
⅔ cup red wine vinegar
½ cup sugar
4 tablespoons vegetable oil
4 tablespoons rice wine vinegar
4 tablespoons raspberry vinegar
Juice of 1 lime

Prepare the dressing: bring to a boil the soy sauce, vinegar, sugar, and oil. Cook until the sugar is dissolved. Add the remaining ingredients and let cool.

Cut the smoked duck into bite-size pieces. Peel and halve the papayas, scoop out the seeds, and slice; reserve a few slices for garnish. Place the spinach, duck, and papaya in a salad bowl. Grind the pepper over the mixture and squeeze over it the juice of 1 lime. Add the walnuts and dressing and toss. Garnish the salad with the remaining quarters of lime and the reserved papaya slices.

el farol

PASTA WITH CORIANDER SAUCE

Serves 8 to 10

6 quarts water
1 tablespoon olive oil
1 tablespoon coarse (kosher) salt
12 ounces dry fusilli or other spiral pasta

CORIANDER SAUCE

1 teaspoon finely minced fresh ginger
1 teaspoon finely minced garlic
¼ teaspoon finely chopped seeded fresh hot pepper
½ cup olive oil
4 cups tightly packed coriander leaves, washed and
 dried on paper towels

MAYONNAISE BASE

1 egg yolk
1 teaspoon lemon juice
1 cup vegetable oil

ASSEMBLY

¼ cup lemon juice
4 tablespoons water
1 teaspoon coarse (kosher) salt
¼ cup thinly sliced scallions

In a large pot, bring 6 quarts of water to a boil. Add
the olive oil, salt, and pasta. Return to a boil, turn

*Denise Dreszman feels that
people eat with their eyes, so
she makes sure that her tapas
bar is a feast in every way.
Platters of hot and cold tapas
alternate with pyramids of
fresh fruits and vegetables: ''I
use produce instead of flowers.
We'll use it all soon, so why
hide it in the refrigerator?''*

EL FAROL
—
SANTA FE

down the heat, and simmer for 10 to 15 minutes, until the pasta is *al dente*. Rinse the pasta under cold water to cool, drain, and set aside.

In a food processor, combine all the ingredients for the coriander sauce except the coriander. Process until smooth and, without stopping the machine, gradually add the coriander leaves until all are combined and the mixture is smooth. Pour into a small bowl and set aside.

To make the mayonnaise base, combine the egg yolk and lemon juice in a small bowl and whisk until the mixture is thick, about 2 minutes. Add the vegetable oil in a thin, steady stream, whisking continuously, until all the oil has been incorporated and you have 1 cup of thick mayonnaise base.

To assemble, combine the coriander sauce with the mayonnaise base and add the lemon juice, water, and salt. Whisk until smooth. Place the pasta in a bowl with the scallions and toss with the dressing. Taste and add salt if necessary. Serve at room temperature.

SHRIMP AND WILD MUSHROOMS WITH LEMON

Serves 6

1 pound shiitake mushrooms
2 cups olive oil
2 whole cloves
5 cloves garlic
6 bay leaves
1 small bunch fresh parsley, chopped
Salt and pepper to taste
1 cup lemon juice
¼ cup white wine
1 pound shrimp (about 25)

Clean the mushroom caps with a cloth. In a heavy casserole, heat the olive oil and add the cloves, garlic, bay leaves, and mushrooms. Stir the mixture continuously until it boils, then add the parsley and salt and pepper and cook for 2 minutes. Add the wine and lemon juice and cook for 3 to 4 minutes more. Remove from the heat and let cool.

In a separate saucepan or sauté pan poach the shrimp in salted water until they turn pink (do not overcook). Drain and let cool. When the mushrooms and shrimp are cool, add the shrimp to the mushroom mixture and marinate for 2 hours. Drain off the marinade before serving.

In recent years, many established restaurants have opened a more casual counterpart, and that is the relationship Cucina bears to the venerable Los Angeles landmark Chianti, founded by Romeo Salta in 1938. After a visit to Italy, where fellow restaurateurs invariably invited them to eat in the kitchen, Jerry Magnin and Larry Mindel decided that the sights, sounds, color, and aroma of the Chianti kitchen (cucina) would make an appealing setting for an informal dining room. Adjustments were made, and the first guests were welcomed in July 1984.

CHIANTI &
CUCINA
—
LOS ANGELES

Pacific Heights Bar & Grill is on Fillmore Street, just down the hill from the posh Pacific Heights residential area. In a gentrified neighborhood becoming heavily populated with boutiques and gourmet food in every form, owners Susan and Craig Bashel rescued a boarded-up Victorian building in March of 1984 and opened their restaurant before the end of the year. The interior is light and airy, decorated in soft colors with touches of exposed brick and etched glass, and features a long, copper-topped bar.

SALMON TARTARE

Serves 6 to 8

1½ small onions, chopped
2 pounds salmon, skinned and boned
3 scallions, coarsely chopped
2 cloves garlic, pressed
1 cup finely chopped parsley leaves
1 cup finely chopped fresh tarragon leaves
Grated rind of 1½ limes
3 tablespoons lime juice
⅓ to ½ cup olive oil
2 teaspoons coarse (kosher) salt, freshly ground if possible
1½ teaspoons freshly ground pepper

Rinse the chopped onion and press in a sieve to remove the excess water. Cut the salmon in 1-inch pieces and chop in batches in a food processor until medium fine (about ¼-inch pieces, which should be fairly spreadable). Combine with the remaining ingredients.

Serve the tartare with black bread or buttered toast points and accompany it with any or all of the following: sliced cucumbers, niçoise olives, capers, chopped egg, chopped onion.

NOTE: Norwegian salmon works best for this recipe, since it has a high fat content, which gives it a buttery flavor and makes it easier to spread.

PACIFIC
HEIGHTS BAR &
GRILL
—
SAN FRANCISCO

SALMON MOUSSE WITH HERB SAUCE

Serves 6

2 ¼-ounce packages unflavored gelatin
3 tablespoons lemon juice
⅓ cup dry white wine
Rind from 1 lemon
1 15½-ounce can red or pink salmon *or* 1 pound
  poached fresh salmon
2 eggs, separated
¾ cup heavy cream
Salt and white pepper to taste
Fresh dill sprigs for garnish

In the top of a double boiler, stir the gelatin into a mixture of the lemon juice and white wine and heat over simmering water until the gelatin is fully dissolved. Set aside. Chop the lemon rind in a food processor until it is very fine. Add the salmon, egg yolks, ¼ cup of the cream, and the gelatin mixture to the bowl of the food processor and mix until smooth. Set aside.

Whip the egg whites until stiff peaks form; whip the rest of the cream. Gently but thoroughly fold the egg whites and whipped cream into the salmon mixture and pour into an oiled 4-cup mold. Refrigerate until the mousse is set, 2 hours or less, or overnight. Serve with Herb Sauce (recipe follows), and garnish with the sprigs of dill.

One of the best reasons to plan a trip to scenic Berkshire County in western Massachusetts is to visit the Sterling and Francine Clark Art Institute, a museum built by Robert Sterling Clark to house his superb collection of paintings, silver, prints, and drawings. Since it was opened to the public in 1955, the museum collection and the space to house it have been augmented regularly, and in 1981 a summer café was added to enhance the experience of visiting the Clark.

CLARK CAFÉ
—
WILLIAMSTOWN,
MASSACHUSETTS

Herb Sauce

2 cups mayonnaise, preferably homemade (see
    page 334)
½ cup chopped fresh dill
½ cup chopped fresh basil
½ cup chopped fresh chives
¼ cup chopped fresh tarragon
2 tablespoons chopped fresh parsley

Combine the ingredients in a food processor and
blend until the herbs are finely chopped.

NOTE: Various combinations of herbs may be used,
depending on what is available and what flavor you
wish to predominate.

SMOKED SALMON WITH MOZZARELLA AND YELLOW TOMATO SAUCE

Serves 6

4 yellow tomatoes, peeled and seeded
1 shallot
1 clove garlic
1 small jalapeño pepper
2 tablespoons virgin olive oil
3 sprigs cilantro, chopped
Salt and freshly ground pepper to taste
Lemon juice (if needed)
24 thin slices smoked salmon, approximately
    1 ounce each
24 thin slices fresh mozzarella, approximately
    1 ounce each

Dice the tomatoes, shallot, garlic, and jalapeño pepper. Add the olive oil, cilantro, and salt and pepper and let sit overnight in a sealed container; there is no need to refrigerate. Before using, pass the sauce through a sieve, pressing through as much of the vegetable as possible. Taste, adding a few drops of lemon juice if the sauce is not tart enough.

Spoon the sauce onto six serving plates and arrange alternating slices of salmon and mozzarella (four of each) on top in a pattern resembling the spokes of a wheel.

Café Pacific is a classy, elegant, yet casual restaurant in the Highland Park Village shopping area — surely the world's most elegant shopping center. Black and white marble floors, dark wood, crystal chandeliers, brass ornaments, and lots of crisp white linen create a look that was once vintage San Francisco but now appears in restaurants from coast to coast.

CAFÉ PACIFIC
—
DALLAS

In addition to Petaluma, Ann Isaak (from Petaluma, California) and Elio Guaitolini own Elio's, a more elegant Italian restaurant. At Petaluma, the menu overseen by chef Pino Coladonato is a mix of California fresh and creative Italian.

Petaluma

SWORDFISH CARPACCIO

Serves 6

1 6-ounce piece fresh swordfish (at least 1 inch thick), cut horizontally into 6 1-ounce slices (see Note)
1 large carrot, julienne-cut
1 stalk celery, julienne-cut
Freshly ground black pepper
2 tablespoons chopped fresh basil
1 large tomato, peeled, seeded, and cut into medium dice
1 bunch chives, finely snipped
4 tablespoons extra virgin olive oil
Juice of ½ lemon

Place each piece of swordfish between two sheets of plastic wrap and pound flat with a mallet or the edge of a plate, being careful not to break the flesh. The fish should be almost translucent and about the size of an 8-inch plate.

Divide the carpaccio among six plates and sprinkle with the julienne of carrot and celery. Sprinkle the pepper and basil over the vegetables and top with the tomato and chives. Whisk the olive oil and lemon juice together and lightly drizzle over the top. Serve immediately.

NOTE: Unless you have a slicing machine, have your fishmonger slice the swordfish.

PETALUMA
—
NEW YORK CITY

Cold Dishes

21

MUSSELS VINAIGRETTE

Serves 8 to 12

5 pounds fresh mussels, scrubbed and beards
   removed
2 tablespoons plus ½ cup olive oil
½ cup white wine
4 sprigs fresh thyme *or* 1 teaspoon dried thyme
   leaves
½ pound new potatoes (unpeeled), cooked and
   quartered
1½ pounds ripe tomatoes, cut in bite-size chunks
½ medium onion, thinly sliced
4 tablespoons cooked green peas
⅓ cup white vinegar
⅓ cup chopped Italian parsley
1 teaspoon coarse (kosher) salt

In a 12-inch sauté pan with a tight lid, place the
mussels with the 2 tablespoons olive oil, 2 tablespoons of the white wine, and the thyme. Cover the
pan and steam the mussels over high heat for 5 to 8
minutes, until the shells open. Discard any shells
that have not opened. Remove the mussels and
allow the liquid in the pan to settle for a few minutes
so that any sediment sinks to the bottom. Carefully
strain the liquid through a sieve lined with cheesecloth into a bowl, making sure to leave any residue
in the pan.

El Farol ("the street lamp")
combines the look of the Old
West with the flavors of Ma-
drid and New York City. Denise Dreszman, who worked
with Felipe Rojas-Lombardi at
the Ballroom in New York,
has brought tapas to Santa
Fe, and the nightly display at
El Farol features more than
twenty different hot and cold
dishes.

EL FAROL
—
SANTA FE

Detach the mussels from their shells, being careful not to tear them. Remove any leftover beards. Place the mussels in the bowl containing the liquid and add the remaining ingredients. Toss gently, being careful not to damage the mussels. Serve at room temperature.

The Spanish custom of "little bites" of bar food originated in the nineteenth century in Andalusia, where a piece of cured ham or a slice of bread was used as a lid for a glass of sherry, reputedly to keep flies out of the glass. Since that time tapas *(literally, "lids") have become more varied and complex, and by now one can make a balanced meal of the cold and hot offerings at Café Ba-Ba-Reeba! and other* tapas *bars.*

CAFE BA·BA·REEBA!®

SALPICON DE MARISCOS (SEAFOOD SALAD)

Serves 6

1 pound bay scallops
½ pound monkfish, cut in cubes the size
   of the scallops
Juice of 4 limes
1 sweet red pepper, cut in ¼-inch dice
1 green pepper, cut in ¼-inch dice
½ pound cooked small shrimp, deveined
1 clove garlic, minced
½ jalapeño pepper, seeded and finely diced
¼ cup olive oil
1 tablespoon sherry vinegar
6 tablespoons lemon juice
3 tablespoons chopped cilantro
Salt and pepper to taste

Place the scallops and monkfish in a bowl and cover with the lime juice. Cover and refrigerate for 12 to 24 hours. Drain the lime juice from the seafood and add the remaining ingredients. Toss well and serve.

CAFÉ
BA-BA-REEBA!
—
CHICAGO

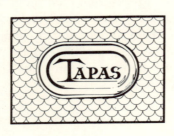

SCALLOPS CEVICHE WITH MINT

Serves 6

1 pound scallops, preferably sweet bay scallops
½ cup fresh lime juice
1 tablespoon fresh orange juice
1 tablespoon fresh lemon juice
4 tablespoons chopped fresh mint
1 or 2 fresh hot green chili peppers, seeded and
    finely chopped
2 tablespoons olive oil
Salt to taste
1 small red onion, chopped
1 medium tomato, peeled, seeded, and chopped
1 ripe avocado, peeled, pitted, and cubed
Lemon or lime wedges and fresh mint leaves
    for garnish

Combine the scallops with the citrus juices, mint, peppers, olive oil, and salt. Cover and refrigerate for about 4 hours, until the scallops are opaque.

Drain the scallops and combine with the onion, tomato, and avocado.

Serve on a lettuce leaf or in a scallop shell, garnished with citrus wedges and mint leaves.

Polly Guggenheim and her husband, Glenn Matsuura, dared to open Tapas on Friday the 13th, in April 1984. They chose the name, not because they intended to serve authentic Spanish tapas, but because when they went out to eat they always seemed to order a whole meal from the appetizer section of the menu. Actually, ceviche is typically Spanish, though the addition of mint makes a refreshing difference.

TAPAS
—
CAMBRIDGE,
MASSACHUSETTS

HOT DISHES

Fried Cheddar and Monterey Jack with
   Roasted Tomato Salsa
Roasted Garlic
Buffalo Wings
Slats
Pigs in Blankets
Quesadillas Fritas
Duck and Spinach Turnovers with
   Spiced Pear Sauce
Caribbean Lamb Turnovers
Sweetbread, Shrimp, and Shiitake Sauté
Alcachofas con Jamón (Artichokes with Ham)
Pappardelle of Zucchini
Grilled Red Potatoes with Rouille
Stuffed New Potatoes with Three Cheeses
Ouisie's Spud
Mezzo Ditale with Eggplant
Spaghetti Squash Pancakes with
   Chipotle Pepper Sauce
Vegetable Strudel
Risotto with Celery and Sweet Fennel Sausage
Mykonos Plate
Grilled Prawns with Black Beans, Chili, and Garlic
Prawns in Brandy Sauce
Baked Smoked Mussels with Spinach
Sea Scallops with Mint, Montrachet, and Cappelini
Hot and Spicy Scallops
Grilled Oysters with Creole Mustard Vinaigrette
Oriental Oysters
Oyster and Corn Fritters with Rémoulade
Smoked Trout Fritters

USA CAFE

AT THE COMMISSARY

FRIED CHEDDAR AND MONTEREY JACK WITH ROASTED TOMATO SALSA

Serves 6

4 cups vegetable oil, for deep frying
2 eggs
2 cups half-and-half or milk
1 teaspoon salt
12 2-by-1-inch sticks Cheddar cheese, about
   1 pound
12 2-by-1-inch sticks Monterey Jack cheese,
   about 1 pound
Flour for dredging
3 cups breadcrumbs

ROASTED TOMATO SALSA

6 large ripe tomatoes, peeled
½ cup finely chopped onion
Juice of 1 lemon
1 tablespoon chopped cilantro
1 tablespoon chopped jalapeño peppers
Salt and pepper to taste

Prepare the salsa by first roasting the tomatoes in a 400° oven for 15 minutes; let cool. Chop the tomatoes in a food processor or blender, being careful not to overblend (small pieces of tomato should remain). Add the remaining ingredients and mix well. Set aside.

USA Café is a part of the group of highly successful Philadelphia restaurants masterminded by Steven Poses. Frog was the first, City Bites is the most recent, and the Commissary complex, including USA Café, is somewhere in between. The Commissary is a cafeteria par excellence, with a line of office workers reaching way down the street at lunchtime; upstairs, USA Café offers table service and the best in regional American cuisine.

USA CAFÉ
—
PHILADELPHIA

Place the oil in a large saucepan and heat to 350°. Whisk the eggs, half-and-half, and salt until blended. Dredge the cheese sticks in the flour, then dip them into the egg mixture. Coat the sticks evenly with breadcrumbs and fry in the hot oil until golden brown. Drain on paper towels and serve immediately with the salsa.

ROASTED GARLIC

Serves 6

6 whole large garlic heads
¾ cup virgin olive oil
1½ teaspoons dried thyme leaves

Peel off the loose paper skin of each garlic head. Place each head on a square of aluminum foil large enough to completely surround it. Spoon 2 tablespoons of the olive oil over each head and sprinkle each with ¼ teaspoon of the thyme. Wrap each head in the foil, to resemble a Hershey Kiss. Place on a baking sheet and bake in a 350° oven for 40 to 45 minutes. Serve with crusty fresh bread.

MARABELLA'S
—
PHILADELPHIA

North Star Bar

casual drinking & dining

Few barroom menus are without this dish; even Craig Clai-
borne admits that buffalo
chicken wings are one of his
favorites among the culinary
inventions of the past ten
years. Originated by Teresa
Bellissimo of the Anchor Bar
in Buffalo, the recipe has been
widely adapted all over the
country. North Star's rendi-
tion is labeled "spicy."

BUFFALO WINGS

Serves 6

4 pounds chicken wings
3 bay leaves
3 cups peanut oil
1 cup Tabasco
¼ cup fresh lemon juice
Celery sticks for accompaniment

DRESSING

8 ounces cream cheese, softened
4 ounces Danish blue cheese
2 tablespoons finely chopped red onion
2 tablespoons finely chopped parsley
¼ cup safflower oil
¼ cup white wine
1 tablespoon cider vinegar
1 teaspoon salt
1 teaspoon freshly ground pepper

Put the chicken wings and bay leaves in a large pot
with 3 quarts of water. Bring the water to a boil, let
it boil for 3 minutes, and then turn off the heat; leave
the wings in the pot for 5 minutes. Split the wings at
the joint. This may be done a day ahead.

Prepare the dressing by blending all the ingredients in a food processor until smooth. Set aside.

Heat the peanut oil to 350° in a pan suitable for

NORTH STAR
BAR
—
PHILADELPHIA

deep frying. Deep-fry the wings for 1½ minutes and drain on paper towels.

Combine the Tabasco and lemon juice in a small bowl. Using tongs, dip the wings into this mixture and serve immediately with the dressing and celery sticks.

Garlic bread with tomatoes and basil (bruschetta con pomidore) has always been called ''slats'' in Rome, and the dish is listed with a small trademark symbol in the specialties section of Café Petitto's menu. Although it is available year-round at the café, the best time to make Slats is in the summer, when garden tomatoes are on hand.

SLATS

Serves 6

4 medium over-ripe tomatoes, peeled, seeded, drained, and chopped
1 cup fresh basil leaves, torn into small pieces
¾ cup olive oil
Coarse (kosher) salt
Freshly ground pepper
3 cloves garlic, peeled and halved
6 thick slices Italian bread

Place the tomatoes, basil, and ½ cup of the olive oil in a small bowl. Add salt and pepper to taste. Mix well and let stand at room temperature for 1 hour.

Heat the remaining ¼ cup olive oil in a skillet. Add the garlic and cook until it browns; remove the garlic. Brush one side of each slice of bread liberally with the garlic oil. Top with the tomato mixture and put under the broiler until the edges brown (about 4 minutes).

EMPIRE

PIGS IN BLANKETS

Serves 6

12 ounces puff pastry, homemade or frozen
6 all-beef hot dogs
½ cup grated Swiss cheese
½ cup Dijon mustard
2 tablespoons heavy cream

On a lightly floured surface, roll out or unfold the puff pastry. Lay one hot dog across the sheet and cut it just wide enough to hold the hot dog end to end. Without sealing the pastry, roll it around the hot dog, leaving a ¼-inch overlap, and cut; unroll the pastry from the hot dog. Using this first rectangle as a guide, cut five more pieces of pastry to the same size.

Sprinkle the cheese over the pastry, place a hot dog on each piece, and roll up. Seal the seam with cold water. Cut each rolled hot dog crosswise into four segments. Place the pieces, seam side down, on a parchment-lined baking sheet. Refrigerate for 1 hour. Meanwhile, combine the mustard and cream.

Bake the pigs in a 450° oven for 12 to 15 minutes, until they are golden brown. Place on a serving platter or individual plates, spear with fancy toothpicks, and serve with a small bowl of the mustard cream.

Unlike many ''new wave'' diners that have been moved to their present location from a roadside along a truck route, the Empire has always been on Tenth Avenue. The present owners spotted the empty shell in 1975, introduced a sleek black and white color scheme, hired a pianist, and added candles to the long black-glass counter. Now twelve years old, the Empire was definitely in the vanguard of a highly popular trend.

EMPIRE DINER
—
NEW YORK CITY

The Egg and the Eye is some-
thing of an institution in Los
Angeles. It all began in 1965
when a restaurant called The
Egg shared a building on Wil-
shire Boulevard with a craft
shop called The Eye. In 1973
the shop became the Craft and
Folk Art Museum and the res-
taurant became the Egg and
the Eye. The present owner,
Ian Barrington, began work-
ing at The Egg as a waiter in
1971 and has been part of the
scene off and on ever since.

QUESADILLAS FRITAS

Serves 6

1 cup diced pimientos
1 cup diced green Ortega chilies
1 cup grated mild Cheddar cheese
1 cup grated Monterey Jack cheese
Salt and pepper to taste
6 10-inch flour tortillas
Oil for deep frying
Salsa, guacamole, sour cream for garnish

Mix the pimientos, chilies, cheeses, and salt and pepper in a medium-size bowl. Warm the tortillas over
a direct flame or on a griddle to make them pliant.

Place ⅙ of the cheese mixture on the lower third
of each tortilla, at least an inch from the edge. Make
the tortilla into an envelope, folding the sides into
the center to form a rectangle. Secure the package
by threading a long toothpick or a short skewer
through the "back flap" of the envelope. Heat 2 to 3
inches of oil in a deep heavy skillet to a temperature
of 375°, and fry the quesadillas until they are golden
brown.

When they are cool enough to handle, cut each
quesadilla in half and up-end to make little cups.
Place two cups on each plate and spoon your choice
of salsa, guacamole, or sour cream — or all three —
next to the quesadillas.

THE EGG AND
THE EYE
—
LOS ANGELES

BAY WOLF

RESTAURANT & CAFE

DUCK AND SPINACH TURNOVERS WITH SPICED PEAR SAUCE

Makes 12

2 pounds puff pastry
1 egg, beaten

FILLING

1 red onion, finely diced
3 cloves garlic, minced
1 sweet red pepper, finely diced
¼ cup extra virgin olive oil
½ cup pine nuts
¼ cup currants
1 cup dry sherry
2 cups cooked duck meat, finely diced
1 10-ounce package frozen chopped spinach,
    thawed, drained, and squeezed dry, *or* 2 large
    handfuls fresh spinach, cooked, squeezed dry,
    and chopped
Salt and pepper to taste

In a sauté pan, cook the onion, garlic, and red pepper in the olive oil until the onions are translucent. Add the pine nuts and sauté for 1 minute. Add the currants and sherry and cook until the sherry has evaporated, stirring frequently. Let the mixture cool. Mix with the duck meat and spinach and add salt and pepper.

Roll out the puff pastry to a ⅛-inch thickness and cut into 3-inch squares. Place 1 tablespoon of filling on each square and fold over on the diagonal. Seal the edges, using a little cold water. Brush the tops of

The name Bay Wolf has something to do with geography, something to do with the fact that Oakland was the home of Jack London, and something to do with co-owner Michael Wild's previous incarnation as a professor of comparative literature. The restaurant occupies a Victorian house that has had several additions but still maintains a comfortable feeling. The interior is simple and soothing, with an abundance of natural wood, fresh flowers, and well-placed pieces of art.

BAY WOLF
—
OAKLAND,
CALIFORNIA

the turnovers with the beaten egg and chill before baking. Bake at 450° for 10 minutes. Serve immediately, with Spiced Pear Sauce.

Spiced Pear Sauce

2 pounds pears, peeled, cored, and quartered
1 cup dry sherry
1 cup sherry wine vinegar
1 stick cinnamon
6 cloves garlic, sliced
3 shallots, sliced
1 tablespoon minced fresh ginger
1 teaspoon dry red chili flakes

Combine all the ingredients in a nonreactive pan. Simmer for 30 to 45 minutes, until the pears are tender. Remove the cinnamon stick and purée the mixture, using a food mill or food processor.

CARIBBEAN LAMB TURNOVERS

Makes 12 turnovers

PASTRY

5 cups self-rising flour
Pinch of salt
About 1½ cups ice water
¾ cup vegetable oil

Combine the flour and salt in a large bowl. Make a well in the flour and pour in 1 cup of the water and the vegetable oil. Incorporate the liquids with your fingers (if needed, add the remaining water), turn the dough out onto a floured board, and knead several times (the mixture will be sticky). Shape the dough into an oval, dust with flour, cover with plastic wrap, and chill 2 to 3 hours or overnight.

FILLING

¾ pound ground lamb
¼ cup chopped parsley
2 whole scallions, chopped
1 Anaheim pepper, finely diced
1 cup coarsely shredded red cabbage
¼ cup diced onion
1 Fresno pepper, finely diced
½ green pepper, diced
½ sweet red pepper, diced
1 teaspoon chili powder
¼ teaspoon Tabasco

This highly popular 1986 addition to the roster of Atlanta restaurants has been called ''campy and Caribbean,'' even though the coastal dishes extend pretty much from New England south, and around to the Gulf of Mexico. Alix Kenagy Carson and her husband and partner, Dan Carson, came by their theme naturally. Alix grew up in New England and Dan's family lives in the Florida Keys. These spicy turnovers, a favorite Indigo appetizer, need to be started early in the day.

INDIGO COASTAL
GRILL
—
ATLANTA

½ teaspoon Worcestershire
Pinch each of cayenne, coarse black pepper, white
  pepper
½ cup cooked black beans, seasoned with salt and
  pepper
1 tablespoon red wine vinegar

2 eggs, beaten, for egg wash
Vegetable oil

Sauté the lamb in a skillet and add all the vegetables and seasonings but the black beans. Simmer for about 10 minutes. Add the black beans, simmer for a few minutes, taste, and add salt and vinegar as needed. Cool and chill the filling.

To assemble the turnovers, turn the pastry dough out onto a floured board and roll out to a thickness of ¼ to ⅛ inch. Cut sixteen 4-inch rounds with a large biscuit cutter or glass. Place eight of the rounds on a baking sheet covered with plastic wrap and brush with the egg wash. Cover with the filling to within ½ inch of the edge. Roll the remaining eight rounds slightly larger, place one over each filled round, and crimp the edges with a fork. Cover the tray with plastic wrap and chill for 2 hours or freeze for later use.

To cook the turnovers, fry them in vegetable oil that has been heated to 350° for 9 or 10 minutes, until golden brown. Drain on paper towels and serve immediately with Mint Yogurt Sauce.

NOTE: Any leftover filling makes a good omelette.

Mint Yogurt Sauce

1 pint plain yogurt
½ cup chopped fresh mint leaves (or more, to taste)
2 tablespoons freshly squeezed lemon juice

Mix all the ingredients and chill.

SWEETBREAD, SHRIMP, AND SHIITAKE SAUTÉ

Serves 6

1 tablespoon butter
½ teaspoon Oriental sesame oil
Salt and pepper to taste
1 pound veal sweetbreads, blanched in salted water, trimmed, peeled, and broken into 18 pieces
18 large shrimp, peeled and deveined
18 large shiitake mushrooms, stems removed and halved
1½ teaspoons chopped fresh rosemary
4 green onions, trimmed and sliced thinly on the diagonal
Watercress and radicchio for garnish

MUSTARD SAUCE

1 tablespoon jaggery (palm sugar) *or* half light brown sugar and half molasses
1 teaspoon honey
1 tablespoon Chinese mustard powder
½ teaspoon cracked black pepper
¼ teaspoon salt
1 teaspoon Chinese black vinegar
1 teaspoon lemon juice

At Star Top, what has been called a hyper-relaxed atmosphere (TV at the bar, a juke-box featuring everything from The Doors to fifties bop) is balanced by an intensely creative and highly acclaimed menu. Chef Michael Short uses a great many Oriental ingredients and combines them with other ethnic flavorings in imaginative ways.

STAR TOP CAFÉ
—
CHICAGO

To make the mustard sauce, combine all the ingredients in a nonreactive bowl. Stir until blended and set aside.

In a large cast-iron skillet, melt the butter with the sesame oil over high heat until the butter browns and just begins to smoke around the edges of the pan. Sprinkle salt and pepper on the sweetbreads and shrimp and add all at once to the pan (do not crowd or the pan will cool, preventing the sweetbreads and shrimp from browning; if necessary, use two pans). Sauté quickly until well browned but not more than medium rare on the inside.

Remove the sweetbreads and shrimp from the pan and add the mushrooms. Sauté until three-quarters done and then return the sweetbreads and shrimp to the pan. Toss with the rosemary, mustard sauce, and scallions. Divide among six plates and garnish with the watercress and radicchio or other colorful bitter greens.

CAFE BA·BA·REEBA!®

ALCACHOFAS CON JAMÓN (ARTICHOKES WITH HAM)

Serves 4

¼ cup olive oil
2 teaspoons minced garlic
4 cooked artichokes, choke removed and quartered
4 ounces Spanish serrano or prosciutto ham, julienne-cut
1 large tomato, peeled, seeded, and diced
1 teaspoon chopped parsley
Salt and pepper to taste

Heat the oil in a skillet over medium-high heat. Add the garlic and sauté until limp (do not brown). Add the artichokes, ham, and tomato and sauté until heated through. Sprinkle with parsley, season to taste, and divide among four individual plates. Serve hot or warm.

Richard Melman and his Lettuce Entertain You Enterprises have brought a bit of Spain to North Halsted Street's restaurant row by opening what must be one of the world's liveliest tapas bars. There is nothing intimate about this café. Every evening, more than three hundred people fill three dining areas with spirited conversation and conviviality, as waiters dressed in costumes left over from Carmen weave their way through the crowd with arms full of tiny plates. As Melman says, "Chaos is part of the charm of the place."

CAFÉ
BA-BA-REEBA!
—
CHICAGO

Union Square Café is restaurateur Danny Meyer's version of the sophisticated yet casual French bistro or Italian trattoria. The menu is rustic northern Italian, with grilled seafood and an oyster bar significant sidelines. In this dish, chef Ali Barker, formerly chef poissonier at La Côte Basque, substitutes zucchini for the traditional wide pappardelle noodle.

PAPPARDELLE OF ZUCCHINI

Serves 4

3 tablespoons extra virgin olive oil
2 medium to small zucchini, peeled and sliced
    vertically in strips 1½ inches wide and ¼ inch
    thick
1 clove garlic, minced
2 shallots, minced
¼ cup dry white wine
¾ cup heavy cream
4 medium plum tomatoes, peeled, seeded, and
    diced
¼ teaspoon chopped fresh oregano
¼ teaspoon chopped fresh marjoram
1 teaspoon chopped fresh basil
3 tablespoons freshly grated Parmesan cheese,
    preferably Parmigiano Reggiano
1 teaspoon chopped parsley for garnish

In a sauté pan over medium heat, sweat the olive oil, zucchini, garlic, and shallots without allowing them to color. Add the white wine and reduce until the zucchini is wilted (be careful not to overcook or the zucchini will fall apart, no longer resembling a noodle). Add the cream, tomatoes, oregano, marjoram, and basil. Reduce for 2 minutes, until the sauce thickens. Stir in 2 tablespoons of the Parmesan cheese. Serve in soup plates, garnished with the parsley and the remaining Parmesan cheese.

UNION SQUARE
CAFÉ
—
NEW YORK CITY

GRILLED RED POTATOES WITH ROUILLE

Serves 6

6 red potatoes, 1½ to 2 inches in diameter, washed
  and dried well
Olive oil

ROUILLE

5 cloves garlic
1½ teaspoons salt
18 fresh basil leaves, roughly chopped
4 ounces pimiento, drained and chopped
½ cup breadcrumbs
2 egg yolks
1½ cups olive oil
5 drops Tabasco
Freshly ground pepper to taste

Rub each potato with the oil and bake in a 425°
oven until almost done (the centers should remain
firm). The time will vary according to the size of the
potato. Let cool until ready to serve.

To prepare the rouille, first purée the garlic with
the salt in a food processor. Add the basil and purée
until smooth. Add the pimiento and purée again.
Stir in the breadcrumbs. Add the egg yolks and blend
until well mixed. Add the olive oil in a steady
stream, then add the Tabasco and pepper.

To serve the potatoes, cut them in half and lightly
brush the cut sides with olive oil. Place, cut side

*The menu at Pacific Heights
Bar & Grill is basically the
same for lunch and dinner,
and there is always a lengthy
list of offerings in the Fresh
Starts/Light Entrées section.
The Provençal rouille used in
this dish also makes a spicy
and colorful addition to fish
soups and stews.*

PACIFIC
HEIGHTS BAR &
GRILL
—
SAN FRANCISCO

down, on a grill to heat through. If no grill is available, reheat the potatoes in the oven or sauté in a bit of oil. Place two halves on each serving plate and top with an ample spoonful of the rouille.

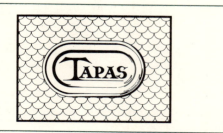

STUFFED NEW POTATOES WITH THREE CHEESES

Serves 4

12 new potatoes, preferably red bliss, about 2
    inches in diameter
2 ounces Swiss cheese
1 ounce Havarti cheese
2 tablespoons grated Parmesan cheese
2 tablespoons heavy cream
1 egg yolk
Salt, pepper, and nutmeg to taste
Dash of Tabasco
Heavy dash of Worcestershire sauce
Sour cream and snipped fresh chives for garnish

Cook the potatoes in salted water until they are just tender (15 to 20 minutes). Run under cold water to cool quickly. When cool enough to handle, cut off the tops and scoop out the centers.

Grate the Swiss and Havarti cheeses. Rice or mash the potato meat and add all the cheeses, the cream, egg, and seasonings. Spoon or pipe the mixture into the potato shells. Heat the stuffed potatoes in a 350° oven until the tops brown (10 to 15 minutes). Serve with a dollop of sour cream topped with chives.

Alison Ring, the chef at Tapas and a part owner of the restaurant, describes her international menu as the company best of housewives all over the world. The 3- or 4-ounce portions, instead of the standard 4- to 6-ounce size, make it possible for people to make a meal out of two or three dishes.

TAPAS

—

CAMBRIDGE,
MASSACHUSETTS

OUISIE'S SPUD

Serves 6

3 medium baking potatoes, wrapped in foil and
   baked until tender
Extra virgin olive oil
Fresh cracked black pepper
¾ cup sour cream
3 green onions, chopped fine
6 tablespoons black lumpfish caviar or Beluga (as
   much as you can afford)
2 cloves garlic
Dill sprigs, lemon wedges, and parsley sprigs for
   garnish

When the potatoes are still slightly warm, slice each
one crosswise into six ½-inch circles. Drizzle the
olive oil over the cut surfaces and sprinkle with the
pepper. Arrange the slices on a serving platter or
place three on each of six plates. Spoon the sour
cream on top of each slice and sprinkle with the
chopped green onions.

Top each serving with 1 tablespoon lumpfish or
Beluga caviar (or anything in between). Scatter 5
paper-thin slices of garlic on top of the caviar, and
garnish with a small dill sprig and a lemon wedge.
Add a sprig of parsley to the plate to freshen the
breath after eating the garlic.

NOTE: For a more substantial dish, serve the potato
with sliced smoked salmon or thinly sliced rare roast
beef or tenderloin.

Ouisie's, billed as "a little café
out of the way," is in a residential section of Houston,
near Rice University and the
Texas Medical Center, and its
patrons tend to be the aca-
demic and professional people
who have offices in the neighborhood or live nearby. The
café is open from eleven in the
morning until ten-thirty or
eleven-thirty at night, with
Little Bites served between
lunch and dinner. Ouisie's
Spud is offered all day long, as
a light lunch, a midafternoon
snack, or an appetizer.

OUISIE'S
—
HOUSTON

The staff at the Union Square Café is friendly, unusually accommodating, and young — not so very long ago owner Danny Meyer himself was a political science major at Trinity College. He grew up in St. Louis, where his father was in the travel business, and was lucky enough to live in Rome for a year and a half. He studied cooking there and subsequently in Bordeaux.

MEZZO DITALE WITH EGGPLANT

Serves 2

½ cup diced unpeeled eggplant
2 shallots, minced
1 clove garlic, minced
Crushed red pepper flakes to taste
2 tablespoons diced pancetta (Italian bacon)
3 tablespoons extra virgin olive oil
2 tablespoons Cognac or brandy
¼ cup dry white wine
¾ cup heavy cream
2 tablespoons grated Pecorino Romano cheese
10 basil leaves, chopped
2 quarts water
6 tablespoons salt
½ cup dry mezzo ditale or ditalini pasta
Chopped parsley for garnish

In a very hot sauté pan, stir-fry the eggplant, shallots, garlic, and red pepper flakes for 2 minutes. Add the pancetta and olive oil and cook for an additional 2 minutes. Remove the pan from the heat and add the Cognac. Return the pan to the heat, tip it so that the Cognac runs to one side, and let the liquid flame. When the flames subside, add the wine and reduce the mixture until there is very little liquid left. Pour in the cream, bring to a boil, and reduce, stirring occasionally, until the sauce has thickened. Add 2 tablespoons of the grated cheese and the basil, check the seasonings, and set aside.

Salt the water and bring it to a boil. Add the pasta and stir constantly at first, to avoid sticking. Cook until *al dente,* about 10 minutes. Drain, add to the sauce, and heat through. Serve in soup plates, garnished with the remaining grated cheese and chopped parsley.

desert cafe

SPAGHETTI SQUASH PANCAKES WITH CHIPOTLE PEPPER SAUCE

Serves 8

⅓ cup finely diced onion
1 cup finely diced sweet red pepper
6½ tablespoons corn oil
1 tablespoon ground pasilla pepper
1 teaspoon ground cumin
1 teaspoon minced garlic
Salt to taste
1 cup baked and chopped spaghetti squash
  (see Note)
¾ cup blue cornmeal
¾ cup flour
2 teaspoons baking powder
3 eggs
¾ cup milk

In a city becoming noted for fine cooking, the Desert Café offers a refreshing alternative — modern American cuisine, with nearly half of the menu devoted to original gourmet vegetarian dishes. The café is the brainchild of Richard Baker, a Zen master who also started the well-known Greens in San Francisco. In discussing the food, chef and co-owner Lawrence Vito stresses that ''no one but vegetarians and health-oriented patrons even notice the number of meatless dishes because of the unusual combinations, techniques, and ingredients used.'' Great attention is paid to fresh American ingredients, both regional southwestern and exotic.

DESERT CAFÉ

—

SANTA FE

½ chipotle pepper, chopped
1 cup sour cream
¼ teaspoon salt

Combine the ingredients for the sauce, mix well, and refrigerate.

Sauté the onion and red pepper in 5½ tablespoons of the oil until tender but not brown. Add the pasilla pepper, cumin, garlic, salt, and squash, and sauté for 1 more minute. Let cool. Sift together the cornmeal, flour, and baking powder and place in a bowl. Combine the eggs and the milk and add to the dry ingredients. Stir until there are no lumps. Add the vegetable mixture.

Heat a cast-iron skillet until a bead of water dances on the surface. Add the remaining 1 tablespoon corn oil to coat the bottom of the pan and add the pancake batter in large spoonfuls. Cook until the pancakes are evenly brown on both sides. Serve immediately, topped with a generous dollop of chipotle pepper sauce.

NOTE: To prepare the spaghetti squash, first pierce the skin several times with a fork to allow steam to escape as the squash bakes. Place in a baking pan with 2 inches of water in the bottom and bake for 1 hour at 350°. Split the squash and let it cool. Scoop out 1 cup of the strands and chop into 1-inch pieces.

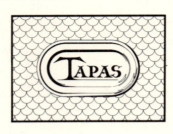

VEGETABLE STRUDEL

Serves 8

RATATOUILLE MIX

1 small eggplant, diced (do not peel)
1 medium onion, chopped
4 tablespoons olive oil
1 green pepper, diced
1 sweet red pepper, diced
1 medium zucchini, diced
1 summer squash, diced
½ head cauliflower, flowerets only, roughly
   chopped
1 head broccoli, flowerets only, roughly chopped
3 tomatoes, peeled, seeded, and chopped
2 cloves garlic, chopped
2 teaspoons chopped fresh basil
1 teaspoon chopped fresh thyme
1 bay leaf
2 tablespoons chopped fresh parsley
Salt and pepper to taste

Sprinkle the eggplant with salt, place in a colander, and let drain for 30 minutes. Rinse and dry thoroughly on paper towels. Sauté the onion in the olive oil until soft. Add the eggplant and peppers and sauté, stirring until soft. Add the remaining ingredients. Cover and cook over low heat for 15 minutes. Drain well and discard the bay leaf.

Robert B. Parker, author of the Spenser mysteries, is a regular patron of Tapas and chose to have the publication party for Taming a Sea Horse *at the restaurant in the spring of 1986. The owners were delighted to help with the party, especially since Tapas is called ''the class act of Porter Square'' on page 224 of the novel. The menu for the evening came right out of Parker's books, Spenser being the gourmand that he is.*

TAPAS

—

CAMBRIDGE,
MASSACHUSETTS

SPINACH MIX

1 10-ounce package frozen chopped spinach,
   thawed and drained
1 pound ricotta cheese
½ bunch green onions, chopped (use both white
   and green parts)
¼ cup grated Parmesan cheese
¼ teaspoon nutmeg
Salt and pepper to taste

Squeeze the spinach dry and combine with the remaining ingredients.

STRUDEL

12 leaves phyllo dough (approximately ½ package)
1 cup butter, melted
1 cup fresh breadcrumbs
½ cup grated Parmesan cheese

To assemble the strudel, lay out 2 sheets of phyllo dough; brush the top sheet with melted butter and sprinkle it with a mixture of the breadcrumbs and Parmesan cheese. Repeat five times with the remaining 10 sheets of phyllo, reserving some melted butter and crumbs for the top of the finished strudel. Spread the spinach mix along one long end of the stack of phyllo sheets. Cover the spinach with the well-drained ratatouille and roll up like a jelly roll. Brush the top of the strudel with butter and sprinkle with the remaining crumb and cheese mixture. Bake at 350° for 30 minutes, until the top is brown. Slice to serve.

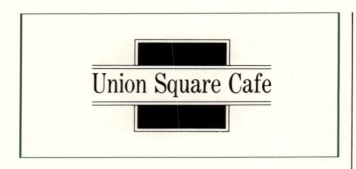

Union Square Cafe

Once a mecca for labor organizers and artists, the Union Square area is now a popular address for business and professional people seeking respite from exorbitant uptown rents. Union Square Café attracts a sizable clientele from the growing publishing, advertising, and design community surrounding the square.

RISOTTO WITH CELERY AND SWEET FENNEL SAUSAGE

Serves 4

1 shallot, minced
2 cloves garlic, minced
2 tablespoons extra virgin olive oil
1 cup arborio rice
½ cup dry white wine
2½ cups chicken stock or bouillon
¼ pound lean Italian sweet sausage, cooked in 2
   tablespoons olive oil and drained
2 celery stalks, sliced horizontally and parboiled in
   salted water for 3 minutes
¼ cup heavy cream
2 tablespoons grated Parmigiano Reggiano cheese
2 tablespoons grated Pecorino Romano cheese
2 tablespoons chopped parsley
Additional grated Parmigiano Reggiano for garnish

In a large skillet or sauté pan, sweat the shallots and garlic in the olive oil over a medium flame (do not brown). Add the rice and stir until it is coated with the oil, shallots, and garlic. Add the wine and continue to stir until it has evaporated. Increase the heat slightly and add 1 cup of the chicken stock to the rice. Stir constantly until the stock is almost completely absorbed. Continuing to stir, keep adding the stock, a cup at a time, until the rice has a creamy texture and is just barely resistant to the bite. The

UNION SQUARE
CAFÉ
—
NEW YORK CITY

process will take approximately ½ hour from the time the wine is added.

Lower the heat and stir in the sausage and celery; add the cream and the cheeses. Continue stirring over moderate heat until the cream is hot and the cheeses melted. At the last moment, add the parsley. Serve steaming hot in shallow soup bowls, garnished with the Parmesan cheese.

MYKONOS PLATE

Serves 2

½ pound baby shrimp, shelled and deveined
Olive oil
5 ounces Kasseri cheese, sliced (it will crumble), *or*
    Romano or Asiago cheese, grated
1 teaspoon oregano
2 teaspoons ouzo
2 lemon wedges for garnish

Place the shrimp in an 8-inch skillet or enameled gratin dish rubbed with olive oil and run under the broiler for 1 or 2 minutes. Top with the cheese and return to the broiler until the cheese melts. Remove from the oven, sprinkle with the oregano, and drizzle the ouzo over the top. Return to the broiler to ignite the ouzo and remove immediately. Garnish with the lemon wedges and serve from the pan, accompanied by French bread.

At the Harvard Book Store Café, where the motto is "Eat, drink, and be literary," the kitchen is open continuously from eight in the morning until eleven at night. The menu devised by executive chef Penelope Dincauze contains a number of international dishes and lots of fish. Many of the daily specials derive from Britisher Dincauze's previous cooking jobs in Cyprus and the Caribbean.

HARVARD
BOOK STORE
CAFÉ
—
BOSTON

Cafe Med

GRILLED PRAWNS WITH BLACK BEANS, CHILI, AND GARLIC

Serves 6

24 short-shelled prawns or other large prawns or
    shrimp
6 scallions and 6 sprigs cilantro for garnish
    (optional)

BLACK BEANS

1½ cups dried black beans
3 tablespoons olive oil
1 large onion, chopped
2 tablespoons minced garlic
6 dried Chinese red chili peppers
4 cups chicken stock
3 tablespoons tarragon vinegar
Salt and cayenne pepper to taste

MARINADE

1 cup sweet sherry
1 cup plum wine
1 tablespoon ground coriander
2 tablespoons dark soy sauce
2 cloves garlic, sliced
1 tablespoon lime juice
1 tablespoon grated fresh ginger

Shell and devein the prawns and set aside.
    Wash the black beans in a colander, picking them
over well and discarding any stones or broken beans.
Place the beans in a pot with water to cover, bring

In the heart of Georgetown,
Café Med attracts a diverse
crowd of "diners, dancers,
drinkers, strollers, shoppers,
and hangers-out." Originally
opened as a nightclub in 1983,
Café Med added the restaurant
in 1985 and has since been acclaimed as one of the most interesting in town. Chef Joe
Printz oversees a menu that is
advertised as New California-
American Cuisine.

CAFÉ MED
—
WASHINGTON, D.C.

to a boil, turn off the heat, and let sit, covered, for 1 hour (or soak in water to cover overnight).

Heat the oil in a skillet and sauté the onion and garlic over medium heat for 5 minutes or until the onions are opaque. Place the vegetables in a saucepan with the drained beans, chili peppers, chicken stock, vinegar, and salt and pepper. Simmer for 1½ hours, until the beans are cooked through but still firm.

Combine the ingredients for the marinade and marinate the prawns for 15 to 30 minutes *only*. Grill or broil the prawns for 2 minutes on each side.

To serve, place ¾ cup of the beans on each of six serving plates and top with four prawns per person. Garnish the dish with a scallion fan and a sprig of cilantro.

NOTE: The beans may be prepared a day or so in advance and reheated.

Washington Square Bar & Grill.

PRAWNS IN BRANDY SAUCE

Serves 6

18 prawns or jumbo shrimp
2 tablespoons flour
3 eggs
Corn oil for frying
Splash of white port
Splash of brandy

LEMON SAUCE

2 teaspoons unsalted butter
2 teaspoons flour
⅔ cup rich chicken stock, heated
⅔ cup white port
3 tablespoons fresh lemon juice, reduced to 1
   tablespoon over high heat
3 tablespoons softened butter

First, prepare the lemon sauce. In the top half of a double boiler, set over direct heat, melt the 2 teaspoons of butter. Stir in the flour to make a roux. Cook for 3 to 5 minutes. Add ⅓ cup of the hot stock and bring to a boil, stirring constantly. When the mixture is smooth, stir in the remaining stock. Add the port and lemon juice and whisk until smooth. Bring the sauce to a boil, whisking. As soon as bubbles appear, set the pan over boiling water and simmer gently, stirring occasionally, for 30 minutes or until the sauce coats a spoon lightly. Taste for tartness (it should be very tart) and add salt and lemon juice if necessary. Remove the pan from the heat and

A visit to San Francisco is incomplete without a stop at the Washington Square Bar & Grill, one of the country's most popular saloons. Its regulars include local and visiting politicians, media personalities, sports aficionados, and writers. Located in the Italian North Beach section of the city, it has traditional local fare at the heart of its menu. This recipe is a legacy from Aldo Persich, the original chef at WSB&G.

WASHINGTON
SQUARE
BAR & GRILL
—
SAN FRANCISCO

whisk in the 3 tablespoons softened butter until smooth. Hold the sauce over hot water until it is needed.

Clean and shell the shrimp, leaving the tails on for effect. Combine the flour and eggs and blend well. Place the shrimp in the batter and toss to coat each one. Bring approximately 3 inches of oil to frying temperature and deep-fry the shrimp, no more than four at a time, in a wire basket. Fry just long enough to set and color the coating, less than 1 minute. Drain the shrimp on a cloth towel.

Heat two sauté pans and put half the lemon sauce in each one. Bring the sauce to a simmer and add half the shrimp to each pan. Cook for 2 minutes, add a splash of port and brandy to each pan, and cook down, briskly, until the sauce is reduced enough to coat each prawn. Serve three prawns per person, pouring over any sauce left in the pan.

BAKED SMOKED MUSSELS WITH SPINACH

Serves 4

2 pounds large mussels
2 cups heavy cream
1 pound spinach leaves, thoroughly washed
4 tablespoons chopped shallots
2 tablespoons unsalted butter
Freshly grated nutmeg, freshly ground pepper,
    coarse (kosher) salt to taste
4 tablespoons freshly grated Parmesan cheese

Scrub the mussels, discarding any that are open. Place grapevine trimmings, herb wood trimmings (such as rosemary or thyme), or packaged wood chips in a home smoker or a kettle type of outdoor grill. Light the fire and allow it to burn until the flames die down. Lay the mussels on the wire rack and cover. Smoke for approximately 10 minutes or until the shells open fully. (You can smoke the mussels and refrigerate them for one or two days before continuing with the recipe.)

To prepare the filling, first reduce the cream by two thirds, until it is thickened and begins to separate, in a heavy saucepan. In a large sauté pan, wilt the spinach leaves (the water clinging to the leaves will be adequate moisture). Drain the spinach, cool

The White Dog Café occupies a row house across from the University of Pennsylvania Law School, but its homey interior resembles an eclectically decorated country inn more than an urban restaurant. Oak tables, chairs, and sideboards, exposed brick walls, and blue and white French bistro tablecloths are all softly lighted by hanging lamps with fringed silk shades, à la the twenties. Not surprisingly, each of the many family photographs on the walls includes at least one dog.

WHITE DOG
CAFÉ
—
PHILADELPHIA

slightly, squeeze in a clean towel to remove the excess moisture, and chop roughly. In a clean sauté pan, sauté the shallots in the butter until they are lightly browned and add the spinach. Stir until the spinach absorbs the butter, then add the reduced cream. Season generously, stir well to combine the flavors, and remove from the fire. Use immediately or refrigerate until the following day.

When ready to serve, remove the top shell of each mussel and discard. Mound a generous spoonful of the spinach filling over each mussel, fully covering the meat. Sprinkle with the Parmesan cheese and bake at 450° until the cheese is browned and the filling is hot. Divide among four plates and serve immediately.

SEA SCALLOPS WITH MINT, MONTRACHET & CAPPELINI

Serves 6

1½ cups heavy cream
6 ounces Montrachet cheese, cut in several pieces
1½ teaspoons cracked black pepper
18 large sea scallops, halved horizontally if too large
1½ tablespoons chopped parsley
1½ tablespoons chopped fresh mint
1 pound cappelini pasta
4 tablespoons unsalted butter
Salt and pepper to taste

In a large saucepan, gently heat the cream and Montrachet until the cheese has melted, being careful not to let the mixture boil. Add the pepper and the scallops, cover the pan, turn off the heat, and let the scallops poach in the hot cream for about 2 minutes. Combine the parsley and the mint, and when the scallops are still firm and not quite cooked through, add two thirds of the mixture to the sauce. Remove the scallops and set aside in a warm place.

Cook the pasta in boiling salted water and drain well. Melt the butter in a saucepan, add the pasta and the remaining herbs, and toss well. Bring the sauce just to a boil, season with the salt and pepper, and thin with more cream if necessary. Return the scallops to the sauce to heat. Divide the pasta among six plates and top with the scallops and sauce.

The Star Top Café, named for the shape of the burners on professional gas stoves, combines a funky ambience with ultra-sophisticated cooking. Bill Ammons calls the menu "omnidirectional," and Michael Short, co-owner and chef, describes his style of cooking as "frivolous and enjoyable. What I do is build intense flavor without all of the fuss." Much of the flavor is Oriental, requiring awesome lists of ingredients, but this relatively simple scallop dish shows Short's imagination at work.

STAR TOP CAFÉ

—

CHICAGO

Café Sport is so named because it shares a building with the Seattle Club, an athletic facility. Although the café was originally intended to augment the club's services, by now only a small percentage of its patrons carry squash rackets. The café has a nationwide reputation for its innovative menus, with Pacific Rim cuisine a special feature.

HOT AND SPICY SCALLOPS

Serves 4

2 cups chicken stock
1 whole dried red chili
2 cloves garlic, chopped
2 stars anise
1 teaspoon rinsed Chinese black bean
1 teaspoon chopped fresh ginger
1 pound scallops
2 tablespoons olive oil
1 teaspoon rice vinegar
1 clove garlic, chopped
1 dried red chili, chopped
Pinch of cilantro
1 tablespoon butter

Combine the chicken stock, whole chili, 2 cloves garlic, star anise, black bean, and ginger and cook until the mixture is reduced to a syrup (about ⅔ cup). Strain and set aside. (The syrup can be kept in the refrigerator for up to a month.)

Sauté the scallops in the olive oil along with the rice vinegar, 1 clove garlic, chopped chili, and cilantro. Remove the scallops when they are half done. Add 2 tablespoons of the reserved syrup to the pan drippings and reduce slightly. Whisk the butter into the sauce, return the scallops to the pan, toss, and serve immediately.

CAFÉ SPORT

—

SEATTLE

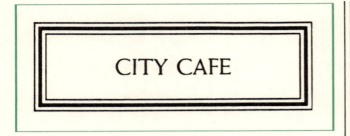

CITY CAFE

GRILLED OYSTERS WITH CREOLE MUSTARD VINAIGRETTE

Serves 6

36 oysters

CREOLE MUSTARD VINAIGRETTE

1 teaspoon salt
2 tablespoons Creole mustard (available in
   supermarkets or specialty food shops)
2 tablespoons wine vinegar (tarragon, if possible)
½ teaspoon chopped garlic
½ teaspoon pepper
½ teaspoon sugar
½ teaspoon dry mustard
½ teaspoon lemon juice
10 tablespoons vegetable oil
1 egg

Clean the oysters, checking to be sure that none of
the shells is open, and set aside. To make the vinaigrette, combine the remaining ingredients, except
the oil and egg, in a food processor. Blend until just
mixed, then add the oil and egg and process until
they are incorporated.

Grill the oysters until the shells open. Break off
and discard the top shells and place six oysters on
each plate with a small dish of the vinaigrette.

NOTE: Large clams may be substituted for the oysters.

*Mardi Schma likes to have her
patrons feel as if they are a
guest in someone's home. This
means having a staff that is
willing to go that extra mile to
provide something new and ex-
citing for each meal — just as
one would for a successful
party. An open kitchen lends a
feeling of informality, and the
grill is never idle.*

CITY CAFÉ
—
DALLAS

Frank Stone and Paul Larson have created something new to Atlanta — a sophisticated wine bar/restaurant with a grazing menu that changes every day. Most of the food comes in "small plate" portions, whether appetizer, entrée, salad, or dessert. Dishes are ordered in stages, so diners can opt for more or quit while they're ahead at any time. Chef Richard Mendoza's fare is subtle and imaginative without being trendy, and the presentation is exquisite.

ORIENTAL OYSTERS

Serves 4

16 large oysters
Rock salt
1 large red pepper
1 large yellow pepper
4 ounces snow peas
3 bunches green onions, tops only
6 tablespoons butter
1 tablespoon Oriental sesame oil
1½ teaspoons soy sauce
6 tablespoons flour
1 tablespoon curry powder

Shuck the oysters and place on a paper towel to dry. Reserve 16 of the best shells and wash thoroughly. Cover four plates with a layer of rock salt and place four shells on each one, positioned at 12, 3, 6, and 9 o'clock. Put the plates in a low oven to warm the shells while you prepare the rest of the dish.

Julienne-cut the vegetables into strips about 3 inches long. In a sauté pan, lightly cook the vegetables in 1 tablespoon of the butter and the sesame oil. Add the soy sauce, toss, and transfer the vegetables to another pan to keep warm. Wipe out the pan and heat the remaining butter.

Combine the flour and curry powder. Dip the oysters into the flour mixture, shaking to remove the

56 EAST

—

ATLANTA

excess, and sauté in the butter for just 1 minute. Divide the vegetables among the 16 shells, letting them extend over the edge a bit, and place an oyster on each bed of vegetables. Serve immediately.

OYSTER AND CORN FRITTERS WITH RÉMOULADE

Serves 4 to 6

1 cup milk
½ cup heavy cream
1 egg, plus 1 yolk
2 tablespoons flat beer
1 cup flour
1 teaspoon nutmeg
Pinch of cayenne pepper
1 cup fresh corn kernels
1 small sweet red pepper, roasted and diced fine
Unsalted butter for cooking
15 oysters, shucked, drained, and chopped

Whisk together the milk, cream, eggs, and beer. Combine the flour and spices and sift over the liquid mixture. Stir in the corn and pepper.

Heat the butter in a skillet until hot. Pour in ¼ cup batter for each fritter; cook three to four fritters at a time. Cook for 2 to 3 minutes, until bubbles begin to form. Sprinkle 1 tablespoon chopped oyster on each

Pacific Heights Bar & Grill has become known for its extensive selection of fresh oysters, with daily specials numbering as many as fifteen different varieties from all over the country. Raw oysters are served from a small tiled bar at the front of the restaurant, and chef Lonnie Williams has become adept at cooking them in imaginative ways. This dish is one of the most popular on the menu.

PACIFIC
HEIGHTS
BAR & GRILL
—
SAN FRANCISCO

fritter, turn, and cook for 2 to 3 more minutes. Place the fritters in a warm oven until all are cooked. Serve with the Rémoulade.

Rémoulade

Makes about 1½ cups

2 tablespoons light fish stock (see page 333)
1 tablespoon chopped sour pickle
1 tablespoon capers, chopped
1 tablespoon minced parsley
1 teaspoon mashed anchovy
1 teaspoon Dijon mustard
½ teaspoon minced fresh chervil
½ teaspoon minced fresh tarragon
¼ teaspoon white pepper
¼ teaspoon Tabasco
⅛ teaspoon salt
¼ teaspoon cayenne pepper (optional)
1 cup mayonnaise, preferably homemade (see page 334)
2 garlic cloves, minced
2 tablespoons chopped green onion tops

Combine all the ingredients except the mayonnaise, garlic, and onion tops. Beat the mixture into the mayonnaise. Stir in the garlic and onion tops. Refrigerate until ready to serve.

SMOKED TROUT FRITTERS

Makes about 50

2 cups flour
1½ teaspoons baking powder
1½ teaspoons salt
5 eggs
1 to 1½ cups (8 to 12 ounces) beer
½ teaspoon ground white pepper
¼ teaspoon nutmeg
1 tablespoon grated lemon zest
½ cup minced green onions
¼ cup diced red pepper (small dice)
1 tablespoon chopped fresh thyme
2½ pounds smoked trout, skinned and chopped
Vegetable oil for frying

Combine and sift the flour, baking powder, and salt. Make a well in the flour and drop in the eggs. Blend until the eggs are absorbed. Add the beer until a smooth, thick batter results. Add the white pepper, nutmeg, lemon zest, green onions, red pepper, and thyme and mix. Fold in the trout. Form the dough into 1-inch balls. Fry in a deep-fat fryer set at 375° until the fritters are golden brown on the outside and cooked through. Drain on paper towels. Serve with a cold horseradish–sour cream sauce.

West End Café, a sophisticated spot on the lower level of the One Washington Circle Hotel, serves breakfast, lunch, dinner, and Sunday brunch to hotel guests, doctors from the nearby George Washington University Medical Center, and numerous celebrities performing at the nearby Kennedy Center. Its reputation for offering carefully prepared American cuisine at reasonable prices attracts a sizable suburban clientele on weekends.

WEST END CAFÉ
—
WASHINGTON, D.C.

SOUPS

SOUPS

Cream of Pea Soup with Snow Peas
Tomato Pesto Soup
Spicy Tomato Soup with Cumin
Dilled Bean Soup
Carrot Ginger Soup
Curried Carrot Soup
Garlic Soup
Onion Soup
Jalapeño Cheese Soup
Black Bean Soup
Autumn Bean Soup
Chili Corn Chowder
Smoked Fish Chowder
Down East Seafood Chowder
Fish Soup with Saffron, Fennel, and Tomatoes
Chicken Barley Soup
Gumbo Ya Ya
Sopa de Lima
Seafood Gazpacho
Snow Pea Soup with Pickled Ginger, Sake, and
    Maguro
Summer Vegetable Soup
Vichyssoise with Sorrel
Chilled Leek Soup

PIRET M
BISTRO
GALLERY

CREAM OF PEA SOUP WITH SNOW PEAS

Serves 6

1 medium onion, minced
1 large leek, white and light green part only,
   washed and minced
½ cup unsalted butter
4 tablespoons flour
1 bay leaf
Pinch of nutmeg
5 cups chicken broth
Salt, pepper, and sugar to taste
1 16-ounce package frozen peas *or* 1 pound fresh
   shelled peas
1 to 1½ cups snow peas (4 ounces)
1½ teaspoons butter
2 egg yolks
1 cup heavy cream

In a large saucepan, cook the onion and leek in the ½ cup butter over medium heat until the onion is translucent but not brown (3 to 5 minutes). Add the flour and cook for 2 to 3 more minutes, stirring constantly. Add the bay leaf, nutmeg, chicken broth, salt, pepper, and sugar and simmer the mixture for 15 minutes. Add the peas and cook for 5 minutes.

Let the soup cool, then purée it in batches in a blender or food processor. Strain the mixture back into the pot and bring to a simmer.

String the snow peas and sauté them in the 1½ teaspoons butter for 2 minutes. Add to the soup.

Piret and George Munger have been in the food business in Southern California since 1975, when they opened a cookware store, the Perfect Pan, in San Diego. The shop grew to include a cooking school and a restaurant, and eventually Piret's bistro/charcuterie/patisserie combinations appeared in several locations. The Mungers' latest venture is Piret$_M$, a bistro-cum-gallery. This soup is the creation of Patty McDonald, a teacher at the cooking school for many years.

PIRET$_M$
—
SAN DIEGO

Whisk together the egg yolks and cream, pour in a little of the hot soup, and whisk the mixture into the pan of soup. Heat the soup gently, but do not let it boil. Adjust the seasonings and serve immediately.

Opening her own café was a dream Monique Hooker had been working toward for more than twenty years. Raised in Brittany, as a young girl she worked in restaurant kitchens near her home and in the South of France before immigrating to the United States in 1965. After more restaurant work and some teaching and catering in New York, she moved to Chicago in 1970 and began making a name for herself as a cooking instructor, food stylist, and caterer. By the time her two sons were old enough, in 1983, it was time for the dream to become a reality.

TOMATO PESTO SOUP

Serves 6 to 8

2 tablespoons chopped shallots
5 cups peeled, seeded, and diced tomatoes (fresh, if possible)
1 tablespoon olive oil
1 tablespoon chopped garlic
1 cup tomato juice
¼ cup Pesto (recipe follows)
Salt and white pepper to taste
1 cup heavy cream
Sour cream and chopped fresh basil for garnish

Sauté the shallots and tomatoes in the olive oil. Add the garlic and tomato juice and cook for about 20 minutes. Let the mixture cool, purée it in a food processor, and then pass it through a fine sieve. Return the soup to the pan, place over medium heat, and add the Pesto. Season to taste and stir in the cream. To serve it hot, bring to just below a boil. If you prefer it cold, refrigerate the soup after adding

MONIQUE'S
CAFÉ

—

CHICAGO

the cream. Garnish each serving with a dollop of the sour cream and a sprinkling of the basil.

Pesto

2 cups fresh basil leaves
2 tablespoons pine nuts or walnuts
4 medium cloves garlic
⅓ cup olive oil
½ cup freshly grated Parmesan cheese

In a food processor, combine all the ingredients except the cheese. Process until smooth, stopping several times to scrape down the sides of the bowl. Transfer the mixture to a bowl and stir in the cheese.

desert cafe

SPICY TOMATO SOUP WITH CUMIN

Serves 4 to 6

1 tablespoon butter
3 medium onions, chopped
4 sweet red peppers, chopped
2 cloves garlic, minced
3 tablespoons chili powder
4 cups vegetable stock
1 ounce miso
8 tomatoes, peeled, seeded, and chopped
1½ teaspoons cumin seed

The Desert Café occupies part of the former Sanbusco lumber warehouses on the edge of downtown Santa Fe. The interior has been transformed with the help of a Japanese master carpenter and several local artisans, with cyprus and cherry woods and soft desert colors predominating. Hanging paper lanterns, each one different, were designed by Isamu Noguchi. A large redwood burl carved into a free-form seat stands just inside the main entrance.

DESERT CAFÉ
—
SANTA FE

½ cup white wine
Salt to taste
¾ cup fresh or frozen corn kernels
Sour cream for garnish
Cilantro leaves for garnish

VEGETABLE STOCK

3 medium onions, sliced
1 carrot, sliced
1 stalk celery, sliced
4 cloves garlic, crushed
1 bay leaf
½ teaspoon chopped fresh thyme
10 parsley stems
2 quarts water

To prepare the stock, combine all the ingredients in a large pot, bring to a boil, and simmer for 1½ hours. Strain, discarding the vegetables.

Melt the butter in a heavy-bottomed 4-quart saucepan, add the onion, and sauté until transparent. Add the peppers and continue to sauté over low heat; add the garlic and chili powder and continue sautéing until there is no liquid left in the pan. In a separate pan, warm the vegetable stock and whisk in the miso, dissolving any lumps. Add the tomatoes and stock to the vegetables and simmer for about 40 minutes.

While the soup is simmering, toast the cumin seeds in a dry frying pan, to bring out their aroma and flavor. Grind the seeds in a spice grinder, use a mortar and pestle, or chop with a knife. Add the seeds, wine, and salt to the soup and purée in a blender or food processor. If necessary, thin the soup with additional stock. Add the corn, reheat, and serve, garnishing each serving with a dollop of sour cream and a cilantro leaf.

The Clark Café

DILLED BEAN SOUP

Serves 6 to 8

2 green onions, chopped
2 shallots, chopped
2 tablespoons butter or margarine
2 cups snipped fresh dill, lightly packed
1 tablespoon lemon juice
2 pounds green beans, ends removed
4 cups chicken broth
½ cup heavy cream
Dill sprigs for garnish

Sauté the green onions and shallots in the butter for about 5 minutes (do not brown). Add the dill and cook for another minute or so. Add the lemon juice and green beans and sauté for 5 minutes, stirring constantly. Add the chicken broth and simmer for 10 minutes, or until the beans are quite tender. Purée the mixture in batches in a food processor until smooth. Add the cream and mix well. Serve hot or cold, garnished with a sprig of dill.

The moving spirit behind the Clark Café is Jytte Brooks, whose husband is the museum's associate director. For a long time she had felt that visitors needed refreshment after feasting their eyes on the collection within. The café began in a small way, serving only lemonade and pastries. By now, up to 150 people a day are served lunch or tea Tuesday through Friday in July and August, weather permitting. Jytte Brooks is still in charge of the cooking, working with a small staff and many volunteers.

CLARK CAFÉ

—

WILLIAMSTOWN,
MASSACHUSETTS

The Brasserie menu offers superb soups, omelettes, sandwiches, bistro-style entrées, and delectable desserts from late morning through evening. Sheela Harden, who took over the restaurant in the early seventies after her student days at Bennington College, knows that just as she must keep prices modest and steer clear of the exotic, she must also satisfy her own passion for appealing and beautiful food.

brasserie

CARROT GINGER SOUP

Serves 6 to 8

1 large Spanish onion, sliced
3 cloves garlic, minced
10 to 12 slices fresh ginger, the size and thickness
    of a quarter
2 tablespoons butter
1 pound carrots, sliced
6 cups chicken stock
Salt and pepper to taste
Cold butter for garnish

In a large saucepan with a heavy bottom, cook the onions, garlic, and ginger in the butter until the onions are soft (do not brown). Add the carrots and the chicken stock. Bring to a boil and simmer until the carrots are quite soft. Drain the vegetables, reserving the stock. Purée the vegetables in a blender or food processor, with just enough stock to cover. Return the puréed vegetables to the reserved stock, mix well, and reheat the soup. Season and garnish each serving with a curl of cold butter.

THE BRASSERIE

—

BENNINGTON,
VERMONT

CURRIED CARROT SOUP

Serves 4 to 6

1 small yellow onion, chopped
1 stalk celery, chopped
2 cloves garlic, crushed
2 tablespoons butter
1½ tablespoons curry powder
6 carrots, peeled and chopped
1 large boiling potato, peeled and cut in 1-inch
  cubes
2 bay leaves
½ teaspoon thyme
6 cups chicken stock
Salt and white pepper to taste
¾ cup heavy cream
1 cup plain yogurt for garnish
2 tablespoons chopped fresh chives for garnish

Sauté the onion, celery, and garlic in the butter until soft (do not brown). Stir in the curry powder and cook for 2 or 3 minutes. Add the carrots, potato, bay leaves, thyme, chicken stock, and salt and pepper. Simmer for 45 minutes. Remove the bay leaves and purée the mixture in a food processor until smooth. Add the heavy cream and adjust the seasoning. Garnish each serving with a dollop of yogurt and a sprinkling of chives.

Rebecca Caras has become a fixture of the Boston restaurant and catering business.. Her retail endeavors began with a take-out shop in Cambridge, and she has since expanded to three locations offering a variety of services. Rebecca's, Rebecca's Café, and St. Cloud all represent café cuisine and ambience at its best.

REBECCA'S
—
BOSTON

Maison de Ville, one of the oldest hotels in the French Quarter, was built as a town house for A. Peychaud, a pharmacist, in the mid-eighteenth century. Peychaud is said to be the founder of the cocktail, specifically the bourbon and bitters Sazerac, still a New Orleans specialty. The front of the small hotel is distinguished by carved wood balconies that predate the wrought iron one expects in the French Quarter.

GARLIC SOUP

Serves 6 to 8

2 pounds onions, roughly chopped
1 cup chopped garlic
2 tablespoons butter
2 tablespoons olive oil
6 cups chicken stock
½ loaf stale French bread, in chunks
1 bouquet garni made from 10 3-inch sprigs parsley, 5 sprigs fresh thyme, and 1 bay leaf, tied together with cotton string
2 cups half-and-half or light cream
Salt and pepper to taste

Sauté the onions and garlic in the butter and olive oil over low heat, stirring frequently, until the vegetables are a deep gold (about 30 minutes). Add the chicken stock, bread chunks, and bouquet garni and simmer for 15 to 20 minutes. Remove the bouquet garni and purée the mixture in a blender or food processor. Heat the half-and-half and add it to the soup, along with the salt and pepper. Serve immediately or keep for a day to let the flavors mellow.

THE BISTRO AT
MAISON DE
VILLE

—

NEW ORLEANS

Napoleon House

Since 1797

NEW ORLEANS, LA.

ONION SOUP

Serves 10 to 12

1½ cups butter
4 cups sliced white onions
1½ cups flour
12 cups beef stock
1½ tablespoons salt
½ teaspoon cayenne pepper or to taste
1 egg yolk
2 tablespoons half-and-half
Croutons (optional)
Grated Parmesan cheese (optional)

In a large soup pot, melt the butter, add the onions, and cook slowly, until the onions are very soft but not brown. Add the flour, mix well, and cook for 5 to 10 minutes, stirring occasionally. Blend in the stock, salt, and cayenne pepper and bring to a boil. Reduce the heat and simmer for 15 minutes. Remove the pot from the heat.

Beat the egg yolk and cream together. Add a little of the soup and blend quickly. Pour the mixture back into the soup pot and blend well. Serve immediately or reheat later, being careful not to let the soup boil. Top with croutons and grated Parmesan cheese if you wish.

Among New Orleanians, the first choice for a drink and a bite to eat in the French Quarter is Napoleon House, a local institution that has remained unsullied despite a growing international reputation. Occupying the first floor of a house that was begun in 1797 and became the home of Mayor Nicholas Girod in the early 1800s, it takes its name from the fact that a group of Bonapartists planned to use the house as a haven for Napoleon after rescuing him from exile on the island of St. Helena. Napoleon died before the plan could be carried out, but the claim to fame lives on.

NAPOLEON
HOUSE
BAR & CAFÉ
—
NEW ORLEANS

Isabelle Moya opened Guadalupe Café in 1975 in an area that was then on the outskirts of downtown Santa Fe. Today the region is being restored, and more and more residents and tourists are discovering the good food and comfortable ambience of this simple restaurant. The menu includes both classic and innovative New Mexican fare, and fresh, natural ingredients are the rule (the only tins in the kitchen contain tomato products). An exception is the Velveeta used in this recipe — no other cheese has produced the proper consistency.

JALAPEÑO CHEESE SOUP

Serves 6

6 cups chicken broth
8 stalks celery, including leaves, diced
2 cups diced onion
¾ teaspoon garlic salt
¼ teaspoon white pepper
2 pounds Velveeta cheese, cubed
1 cup diced canned or fresh jalapeño peppers (if fresh, seed and parboil for about 3 minutes)
Sour cream for garnish

Place the first five ingredients in a large saucepan and cook over high heat until the stock is somewhat reduced and thick. In batches, purée the stock and portions of the cubed cheese in a blender or food processor until smooth. Return the soup to the pan and simmer for 5 minutes over very low heat. Add the diced peppers, mix well, and serve. Garnish with a spoonful of sour cream if you wish.

NOTE: Since the cheese is salty, do not substitute salted bouillon for the chicken broth.

GUADALUPE
CAFÉ
—
SANTA FE

BLACK BEAN SOUP

Serves 6 to 8

1 pound black beans
2 quarts chicken stock
1 cup canned tomatoes, drained
3 cloves garlic, chopped
1 or 2 dried red chilies, to taste
1 bay leaf
1 small ham hock
2 or 3 stalks celery, diced
1 large onion, chopped fine
2 or 3 carrots, chopped fine
3 tablespoons chopped parsley
Juice of 1 lemon
Salt, pepper, and cayenne pepper to taste
Sour cream, lime slices, and salsa (see page 202) for
    garnish

Soak the beans overnight in water to cover (or cover
with water, bring to a boil, and let sit, covered, for 1
hour); drain. Cook the beans for 1½ hours with the
chicken stock, tomatoes, garlic, chilies, bay leaf, and
ham hock. Add the celery, onions, carrots, parsley,
and lemon juice and cook for one more hour. Remove the ham hock, purée to a coarse consistency
in a food processor, and season to taste.

Garnish each serving with 1 tablespoon sour
cream, 1 tablespoon salsa, and a slice of lime. Corn-
sticks or cornbread makes the perfect accompaniment.

The décor at Café Sport is a familiar re-creation of Art Deco, with a mauve, turquoise, and black color scheme. The space is light and airy, and the beautifully prepared and presented food at reasonable prices keeps people coming back. Though the menu changes every day, this soup is almost always available and is invariably mentioned in reviews.

CAFÉ SPORT

—

SEATTLE

Nick and Sully are Ann Nick-lason and Jeannette Sullivan, who opened a gourmet deli in the Eastlake section of Seattle in 1983. Ann is now carrying on the business, which has a strong reputation for creative cooking using the best of Northwest ingredients. In addition to take-out and catering, café tables are available both indoors and out.

AUTUMN BEAN SOUP

Serves 8

1 cup dried pinto beans
1 cup dried lima beans
1 medium onion, chopped
2 ham shanks
2 bay leaves
5 cloves garlic, chopped
2 pounds fresh tomatoes, peeled, seeded, and chopped (reserve the juice)
1 tablespoon chopped fresh oregano
½ cup chopped parsley
4 cups cold water
Salt and pepper to taste

Soak the beans overnight in water to cover. Drain well.

Sauté the chopped onion with the ham shanks; add the drained beans, bay leaves, garlic, tomatoes and juice, oregano, and parsley. Add the cold water and bring to a boil. Reduce the heat to low, cover, and simmer for 1½ hours or until the beans are tender.

Remove the ham bones from the soup. Clean the bones thoroughly, dice the meat, and return the meat to the soup. Season to taste and reheat before serving.

NICK & SULLY
—
SEATTLE

CITY CAFE

City Café is a bright, cheerful spot for lunch, and in the evening it turns into the most romantic of cafés — thanks to well-designed lighting and flickering candles and fresh flowers on every table. Lace half-curtains at the windows add a European touch to the decor.

CHILI CORN CHOWDER

Serves 8

3 Serrano chili peppers, seeded and julienne-cut
1 tablespoon vegetable oil
1 tablespoon ground cumin
1 tablespoon ground coriander
2 large tomatoes, peeled and seeded
4 cups corn kernels (fresh or frozen)
1 medium onion, coarsely chopped
1 large tomato, peeled, seeded, and diced
2 cups milk
1½ cups chicken stock
4 new potatoes, diced and cooked
2 carrots, shredded
2 teaspoons salt
1 teaspoon white pepper
¼ to ½ teaspoon cayenne pepper

In a heavy saucepan or Dutch oven, sauté the peppers in the vegetable oil for 2 minutes. Add the cumin and coriander. Purée the 2 seeded tomatoes, 3 cups of the corn, and the onion in a blender or food processor. Add this mixture to the peppers and cook for 5 minutes. Add the rest of the ingredients, including the remaining cup of corn, and bring just to a boil. Serve immediately.

NOTE: You can add cooked clams, shrimp, or chopped chicken for a heartier soup.

CITY CAFÉ

—

DALLAS

This delightful café is a joint venture of Suzanne's, a carry-out and catering business on Connecticut Avenue, and the Phillips Collection, one of Washington's fine small museums. The café is on the lower level of the brownstone building at 21st and Q streets that was the home of Duncan Phillips, who opened it to the public in 1921 as the country's first museum of modern art.

Suzanne's

SMOKED FISH CHOWDER

Serves 6

4 tablespoons butter
½ cup minced onion
½ cup minced leeks, white part only
⅓ cup finely diced celery
⅓ cup finely diced carrot
2 medium potatoes, peeled and finely diced
3 tablespoons flour
¼ teaspoon thyme leaves
3 cups fish stock
3 cups heavy cream or part half-and-half
½ cup (fresh, frozen, or canned) corn kernels
¾ pound mixed smoked fish, boned, skinned, and
  flaked (such as salmon, bluefish, scallops, oysters,
  mussels)
2 tablespoons Cognac
Freshly ground black pepper to taste

In a large pot, melt the butter and sauté the onions and leeks until tender, about 15 minutes. Add the celery, carrot, and potatoes and cook for 10 minutes. Add the flour and stir constantly for 2 minutes. Add the thyme, stock, and cream and bring to a boil. Reduce the heat and simmer for 15 minutes. Add the corn and the fish and return to a boil. Remove from the heat immediately and add the Cognac and pepper. Serve immediately.

SUZANNE'S CAFÉ
AT THE PHILLIPS
COLLECTION
—
WASHINGTON, D.C.

DOWN EAST SEAFOOD CHOWDER

Serves 6 to 8

8 to 12 fresh mussels (1 for each bowl)
½ cup dry white wine
¾ cup water
½ pint freshly shucked oysters and their liquor
¼ pound salt pork (discard rind), cut in ¼-inch dice
¼ pound bacon, cut in ¼-inch pieces
2 tablespoons flour
2 medium leeks (white part only), cleaned and sliced
1 large onion, chopped
1½ pounds potatoes, peeled and cut in ½-inch dice
2 cups milk
2 pounds firm white fish (cod, halibut, cobia, bass)
¼ pound minced clams with liquor
2 cups half-and-half
Paprika to taste
Freshly ground pepper to taste
2 tablespoons sliced tops of green onions or snipped chives
2 tablespoons unsalted butter

In a covered Dutch oven, steam the mussels in the wine and water over high heat until the shells open (4 to 5 minutes). Remove the mussels and set aside. Strain the broth into a bowl and reserve. Strain the oyster liquor into the same bowl.

In a skillet, render the salt pork until it is crisp and

Alix Kenagy Carson grew up on the daily catch brought in by her father, a Nova Scotia fisherman, and she has created this chowder recipe to taste just like her mother's. The secret is to use only the freshest fish, whole milk, and real butter. At Indigo the chowder is served with hardtack, for an authentic New England experience.

INDIGO COASTAL
GRILL
—
ATLANTA

drain on paper towels. Fry the bacon in the Dutch oven until it is light brown. Add the flour, leeks, and onion and cook for 3 to 5 minutes (do not brown). Add the potatoes, milk, and combined seafood liquors and simmer for 15 to 20 minutes. Add the fish, clams, and half-and-half and simmer until the potatoes are cooked and the fish flakes easily. Add the seasonings and green onions or chives. Simmer for a few minutes, taste, and adjust the seasonings.

Just before serving, add the mussels and oysters. Ladle the chowder into heated bowls and garnish with the salt pork and a small pat of butter.

NOTE: For a bit of color, use ¼ pound salmon with 1¾ pounds white fish. The chowder is better if allowed to sit for an hour or two, or even overnight, before serving.

C A M P A G N E

FISH SOUP WITH SAFFRON, FENNEL, AND TOMATOES

Serves 4

Large pinch of saffron
3 tablespoons olive oil
½ small onion, chopped
4 cloves garlic, minced
1 small fennel bulb, trimmed of stalks and thinly
    sliced
1 carrot, julienne-cut
¼ teaspoon anise seed (optional)
Pinch of crushed red chili pepper
1 anchovy fillet
2 tablespoons minced parsley
1 pound fish (any kind), cut into 1-inch chunks
5 peeled tomatoes (fresh or canned, drained)
3 cups fish stock (see page 333)
4 strips orange rind, removed with a vegetable
    peeler
Salt and freshly ground pepper to taste

Pour about 1 teaspoon of hot water over the saffron
and let it steep while you proceed with the recipe.

Heat the oil in a heavy-bottomed pan until a haze
forms over it, then add the onion, garlic, fennel, carrot, anise seed, chili pepper, and anchovy. Stir a few
times and reduce the heat to low. In about 10 minutes, the vegetables should be fairly soft but still retain a slight crunch. Add the parsley, fish, and
tomatoes, crushing the tomatoes in your hands as
you add them. Raise the heat to high and let a little
of the liquid from the tomatoes evaporate; then add
the fish stock, the saffron and its liquid, the orange

The owners of Campagne, Ted
Furst and Peter Lewis, share
the role of restaurateur. Ted
does the cooking and Peter
manages "the front of the
house," including overseeing
an imaginative and sophisticated wine list. The food is
meant to reflect the spirit of
southern France with the best
of local ingredients — as Ted
Furst says, it's what happens
when an American living in
Seattle uses French techniques.

CAMPAGNE
—
SEATTLE

rind, and salt and pepper. Bring the soup to a boil as quickly as possible. Serve immediately with hot French bread or slices of French bread sautéed in olive oil.

NOTE: Any kind of fish will work well in this recipe. If you are using an oily fish, such as mackerel or tuna, a few drops of red wine vinegar added at the last moment will nicely set off the richness of the fish.

CHICKEN BARLEY SOUP

Serves 6

6 cups water
1 3- to 3½-pound chicken, body fat reserved
1 bouquet garni (6 peppercorns, 1 bay leaf, 3 sprigs parsley, 1 stalk celery with leaves, diced, in a cheesecloth bag)
2 large carrots, diced
1 large onion, diced
4 stalks celery, diced
Pinch of thyme
1 bay leaf
Freshly ground pepper to taste
1½ quarts good chicken stock or broth
½ pound medium barley, cooked until tender in 2 quarts boiling water and drained
½ cup dry sherry
Salt and pepper to taste

In a large kettle, bring the water to a boil. Add the chicken and bouquet garni and return to the boil.

The Empire is owned by Richard Ruskay, Jack Doenias, and Carl Laanes, who call themselves Nothing Heavy Inc. In the spirit of the corporate name, the bottom of their menu bears these words to the wise: ''Be nice,'' ''Sit up straight,'' ''Don't play with your food,'' ''Don't let your chauffeur drink,'' ''Don't be a stranger,'' ''Murray, call your mother.''

EMPIRE DINER

—

NEW YORK CITY

Boil the chicken for 10 minutes. Reduce the heat, cover, and simmer very slowly for 20 minutes. Turn off the heat and let the chicken cool in the liquid until it is cool enough to handle. Discard the chicken skin and remove the meat from the bones. Dice the meat.

Clean out the chicken kettle and slowly render the reserved chicken fat, discarding any browned particles. Sauté the diced vegetables in the fat for 4 to 5 minutes. Add the thyme, bay leaf, pepper, and chicken stock. Bring slowly to a simmer and cook, partly covered, until the carrots are tender. Add the diced chicken and accumulated juices, the barley, and the sherry. Simmer for 10 more minutes. Season with salt and pepper.

Brennan is part of the galaxy of famous names in the New Orleans restaurant world, and Mr. B's is owned by the branch of the family that operates the renowned Commander's Palace. The team in charge at Mr. B's is from the third generation, sister and brother Cindy and Ralph Brennan. Their goal is to refine old Creole cooking to reflect the modern preference for lighter eating without sacrificing the intense flavors that have made New Orleans cooking famous.

GUMBO YA YA

Serves 6 to 8

⅔ cup salad oil
1 cup flour
½ cup chopped green pepper
½ cup chopped white onion
¼ cup chopped celery
12 cups rich chicken stock
1 teaspoon minced garlic
2 bay leaves
1 teaspoon thyme
½ pound cooked chicken, shredded
½ pound andouille sausage, sliced
1 tablespoon Louisiana hot sauce
½ tablespoon filé
¼ cup chopped green onions
Salt and pepper to taste
3 cups boiled rice

In a large, heavy saucepan, heat the oil until it is almost smoking, then add the flour and cook until the mixture is medium brown, about 5 minutes.

Add the pepper, onion, and celery and continue cooking for 5 minutes. Add the chicken stock, garlic, bay leaves, and thyme and simmer for an additional 15 to 20 minutes. Add the chicken and sausage and simmer for 20 minutes more. Add the hot sauce, filé, green onions, and salt and pepper. Place a mound of rice in each soup plate and ladle over the gumbo.

NOTE: "Ya ya" means "rice" in an African dialect.

MR. B'S

—

NEW ORLEANS

SOPA DE LIMA

Serves 6

1 small sweet red pepper, seeded and chopped
1 small green pepper, seeded and chopped
1 onion, finely diced
1 large clove garlic, minced
5 tablespoons vegetable oil
1 pound ripe tomatoes, peeled, seeded, and
   chopped
3 3-inch fresh hot green Anaheim chilies, seeded
   and minced
6 cups chicken stock
Juice and rind of 1 Key lime or 1 regular lime
6 corn tortillas, cut into ½-inch strips
2 pounds chicken breasts, cooked, boned, and
   skinned, with the meat shredded
2 tablespoons chopped green onions
Lime slices for garnish

In a large saucepan, cook the peppers, onion, and garlic in 2 tablespoons of the oil over medium-low heat, stirring, until the peppers have softened (do not brown). Add the tomatoes and chilies and continue stirring. Add the stock and the juice and rind of the lime. Simmer for 2 minutes and then bring to a boil. Remove from the heat momentarily, then simmer for 5 minutes. Discard the lime rind and set aside.

   In a large, heavy skillet, heat the remaining 3 tablespoons oil until hot but not smoking and cook the tortilla strips in batches until they are crisp and golden (30 to 45 seconds). Transfer to a paper towel to drain and keep warm in a 250° oven.

A kitschy storefront operation on the border of the Morningside and Virginia Highlands neighborhoods in Atlanta, Indigo has the look of an authentic island getaway. Forties' vintage metal lawn chairs line the sidewalk out front, and weatherbeaten shutters frame the flashy setting-sun sign overhead.

INDIGO COASTAL
GRILL
—
ATLANTA

Add the shredded chicken to the soup and simmer until the chicken is hot. Season with salt and pepper or more lime juice. Top individual servings with the tortilla strips and green onions. Slip a slice of lime into each bowl.

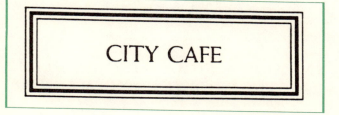

CITY CAFE

Mardi Schma's dream of owning her own restaurant came true in January 1986 when City Café opened. Her previous experiences in the food business were years of entertaining at home in Monterey, California (where seafood and produce of all kinds were in abundance), and owning a fish market in Dallas, which gradually began selling prepared foods. This recipe is a natural outgrowth of her earlier days.

SEAFOOD GAZPACHO

Serves 8

½ pound monkfish
½ pound clams
¼ cup dry white wine
10 ripe tomatoes, peeled and seeded
2 cucumbers, peeled
2 green peppers
6 stalks celery
2 cloves garlic
4 green onions
1 onion, grated
4 tablespoons vegetable oil
2 tablespoons wine vinegar
1 tablespoon Worcestershire sauce
4 shakes Tabasco
2 to 3 cups tomato juice

Cut the monkfish and clams into small pieces and poach quickly in the white wine. Drain and let cool. Chop the vegetables (you may use a food processor, but do not purée). Mix the seafood with the chopped vegetables and add the remaining ingredients, except the tomato juice. Add the tomato juice until the desired consistency is reached. Serve ice cold.

CITY CAFÉ
—
DALLAS

Backyard dining is an option at Star Top during warm weather. The barbecue/smoker is always busy, with oysters, grilled giant squid, lobsters, and even whole pigs and goats likely subjects. The pool table gets plenty of use, and guests are also urged to contribute to the graffiti mural covering one wall.

SNOW PEA SOUP WITH PICKLED GINGER, SAKE, AND MAGURO

Serves 6

3 cups white shellfish stock, clam juice, or chicken stock
1 cup sake
1 tablespoon Oriental sesame oil
1½ tablespoons aji mirin (sweet rice wine)
1 pound snow peas, trimmed
6 green onions, cut in 1-inch pieces
½ cup loosely packed pickled ginger (sushi ginger)
¼ teaspoon cayenne pepper
1 tablespoon blond miso
1 cup heavy cream

GARNISH

8 ounces maguro (sushi-quality red tuna), cut into ½-inch batons
Juice of ½ lemon
1 teaspoon wasabi powder
1 tablespoon mixed black and toasted sesame seeds
¼ cup pickled ginger
¼ cup thinly sliced (on the diagonal) green onions
Lemon slices

In a nonreactive pan, combine the stock, sake, sesame oil, and aji mirin. Bring to a boil and blanch the

STAR TOP CAFÉ
—
CHICAGO

snow peas for 2 or 3 minutes, until just tender. Remove with a slotted spoon and immediately immerse in ice water to arrest the cooking and stabilize the color. Set aside. Chill the stock over an ice bath.

When the stock is cold, add the snow peas, green onions, pickled ginger, cayenne, and miso to half of the stock and purée in a food processor. Pass the mixture through a fine sieve and add the remaining stock and the cream.

Just before serving, lay the maguro batons on a plate and squeeze lemon juice over them. Sprinkle with the wasabi powder and sesame seeds. Fill chilled bowls with the soup and add the tuna batons to each bowl. Top with the pickled ginger and green onions and a slice of lemon.

HARVARD BOOK STORE CAFE

SUMMER VEGETABLE SOUP

Serves 6

1 pound baby shrimp, cooked, peeled, and chilled
2 stalks celery, diced small
2 ripe tomatoes, peeled, seeded, and diced
1 green pepper, diced
1 cucumber, peeled, seeded, and diced
3 green onions, thinly sliced
1 large sprig dill, chopped
2 cloves garlic, crushed
Juice of 1 lemon
1 cup sour cream
1 cup yogurt
3 cups light cream
Salt and pepper to taste
Chopped parsley for garnish

Place the shrimp, celery, tomatoes, green pepper, cucumber, green onions, dill, garlic, and lemon juice in a large bowl. Add the sour cream, yogurt, and light cream and mix well. Add the salt and pepper. Chill the soup, covered, for up to 24 hours. Stir well before serving, adding additional cream if it seems too thick. Garnish each serving with chopped parsley.

NOTE: The flavor of this soup is improved if it is made the day before you serve it.

Good food and good books are a winning combination at the Harvard Book Store Café. Started by Frank Kramer in the spring of 1980, it is a favorite spot to see and be seen on elegant Newbury Street in Boston's Back Bay. Though on a given day one may see such well-known writers as Robert B. Parker, Justin Kaplan, and James Carroll, the café is also a comfortable neighborhood restaurant, where books are carried from shelf to table and a cup of coffee can be made to last all afternoon. In warm weather, tables line the sidewalk in front of the store.

HARVARD
BOOK STORE
CAFÉ

—

BOSTON

Campagne is a country-style French café in the middle of the Capitol Hill neighborhood of Seattle. With a minimum of fuss and expense, a two-room apartment has been transformed into an unpretentious yet elegant place for a memorable dinner. French provincial fabrics for tablecloths and banquette covers, bleached pine antiques, and a few well-chosen enamel French signs (Chat Lunatique, Attention Chien Bizarre) set the tone.

C A M P A G N E

VICHYSSOISE WITH SORREL

Serves 12

3 tablespoons butter
3 leeks (white part only), thoroughly washed and sliced
½ white Bermuda onion, sliced
4 or 5 new potatoes, peeled and sliced
6 cups chicken stock
1 teaspoon coarse (kosher) salt
1 bay leaf
10 ounces sorrel, washed and ribs removed
2 cups heavy cream
Salt and white pepper to taste

Melt 2 tablespoons of the butter in a soup pot and add the leeks and onion. Cook over low heat, covered, until the vegetables are soft but not brown. Add the potatoes, stock, and salt and bring to a simmer. Add the bay leaf and cook until the potatoes can be crushed against the side of the pot with a wooden spoon. Run the soup through a medium sieve or the medium plate of a food mill (a food processor will produce the wrong texture). Set aside.

Melt the remaining tablespoon of butter in a pan and add the sorrel and a pinch of salt. Cook the sorrel over medium heat, stirring, until it "melts" into a soft green mush (it will turn a drab color). Turn it out onto a board and chop finely with a knife. Add the sorrel and the cream to the soup and season with the white pepper and more salt, if necessary. Serve hot or cold. (If you serve the soup cold,

CAMPAGNE
—
SEATTLE

it will need more salt and may need to be thinned with milk.)

NOTE: Spinach (1½ pounds) may be substituted for the sorrel. If you use spinach, add a touch of lemon juice to the soup and garnish with a slice of lemon.

The kitchen at Trio Café is tiny, with many electrical restrictions, so its soups are always served cold — year-round. This one is simple to make and delicious.

CHILLED LEEK SOUP

Serves 8

3 large leeks
6 cups chicken broth
8 ounces cream cheese
chopped parsley or chives for garnish

Thoroughly clean the leeks and slice the white part and some of the green. Simmer the leeks in the chicken broth. When tender, remove from the heat and purée the mixture in a food processor. Return the soup to the pan and bring to a simmer. Add the cream cheese in small chunks, stirring until it is completely incorporated. Chill and garnish with the parsley or chives before serving.

TRIO CAFÉ

—

SAN FRANCISCO

SANDWICHES, PIZZAS, AND SAVORY TARTS

SANDWICHES, PIZZAS, AND SAVORY TARTS

Grilled Flank Steak with Green Peppercorn
   Mayonnaise
Grilled Chicken Breast Sandwich
Pimiento Cheese Sandwiches
Grilled Smoked Cheddar, Tomato, and Barbecued
   Onion Sandwich
The Master Potter's Lunch
Muffuletta
Mexican B.L.T.
Grilled Eggplant Sandwich
Roasted Pork Tenderloin Sandwich
A Snack from Provence
Syrian Sausage in Pita
Sausage Hoagie with Peperonata
Café Sandwich
Pizza Primavera
Pizza al Quatro Formaggi
Garlic Pizza
Pizza with Goat Cheese, Sun-Dried Tomatoes, and
   Black Olives
Fig Pizza
Montrachet Calzone
Calzone di Verdura
Calzone all Petitto
Roquefort Tart
Tomato-Pesto Tarts with Oregon Blue Cheese
Salmon Dill Tourte

BAY WOLF
RESTAURANT & CAFE

GRILLED FLANK STEAK WITH GREEN PEPPERCORN MAYONNAISE

Serves 6

1 flank steak (about 1¾ pounds)
½ cup red wine
½ cup olive oil
1 clove garlic, chopped
1 onion, chopped
1 cup sliced shallots
French bread

GREEN PEPPERCORN MAYONNAISE

1 egg
1 tablespoon green peppercorns
½ teaspoon salt
1 to 2 tablespoons lemon juice
1 cup olive oil

Trim the flank steak and marinate it in a mixture of the wine, olive oil, garlic, and onion for 2 to 4 hours.

Prepare the mayonnaise by beating the egg, peppercorns, salt, and lemon juice with an electric mixer or in a blender and slowly whipping in the olive oil, starting drop by drop. Refrigerate.

Sauté the shallots in the remaining ¼ cup olive oil over high heat for 2 to 3 minutes. Grill the flank steak over hot coals for 4 minutes on each side. The coals should be hot enough to sear and brown the outside of the meat while leaving the inside rare (this cut toughens if overcooked).

Slice the bread and heat it on the grill. Slice the

Michael Wild, executive chef at Bay Wolf, came late in life to sandwich-making, since he was raised in Europe, where the sandwich was found only in railway stations. Wild's cooking experience started when he was ten years old and was left on his own to prepare lunch — in France, that meant a proper meal.

BAY WOLF
—
OAKLAND,
CALIFORNIA

steak and assemble the sandwiches, spreading the bread liberally with the mayonnaise and piling on the shallots and sliced steak.

The mostly Italian menu at Marabella's stays the same all day and makes the café a perfect choice for a quick meal before or after concerts at the Academy of Music next door, home of the Philadelphia Orchestra.

GRILLED CHICKEN BREAST SANDWICH

Serves 6

6 8-ounce chicken breast halves, boned and skin removed
Vegetable oil
¾ cup sautéed sliced mushrooms, seasoned with salt, pepper, and garlic
6 sun-dried tomatoes
6 ounces thinly sliced provolone cheese
6 soft poppyseed or sesame seed rolls

Tenderize the chicken breasts with a mallet. Coat them with the oil and grill for 2 to 4 minutes per side. Remove from the grill and top each breast with 8 to 12 mushroom slices. Cut the tomatoes open, lay them flat, and place one over each layer of mushrooms. Top with a slice of cheese and run under the broiler until the cheese melts. Place each breast between the halves of a soft roll and serve immediately.

MARABELLA'S
—
PHILADELPHIA

PIMIENTO CHEESE SANDWICHES

Makes 3 cups cheese spread

1 pound white Cheddar cheese, grated
1 small red onion, chopped
2 4½-ounce jars pimiento, drained and chopped
1 bunch green onions, chopped
3 cloves garlic, minced
1 cup mayonnaise
White pepper to taste
Sliced whole-wheat bread

Combine the cheese, red onion, and pimiento. Mix the green onions and garlic with the mayonnaise, add to the cheese mixture, and blend thoroughly. Add the white pepper and mix again. Serve on whole-wheat bread. The spread will keep for several days in the refrigerator.

Elouise Cooper calls this her World War II special — and it never leaves the luncheon menu. Bearing little resemblance to the pimiento cheese we used to get in little glass jars, it is just one of the many family recipes she regularly re-creates or adapts.

OUISIE'S
—
HOUSTON

Attention to detail is evident in every aspect of the Desert Café — the design, workmanship, and selection of colors and materials for the décor; the imagination and quality of the cooking and presentation of the food, with diligent searches for seasonings and raw materials clearly worth the effort; and the helpfulness of a gracious and well-trained young staff, dressed in crisp khaki pants and handsome shirts, each a different primary color.

desert cafe

GRILLED SMOKED CHEDDAR, TOMATO, AND BARBECUED ONION SANDWICH

Makes 2

1 red onion
Olive or corn oil
Salt and pepper to taste
2 tablespoons sour cream
2 teaspoons horseradish
8 slices smoked cheddar cheese
1 large tomato, sliced
½ cucumber, peeled and sliced
4 slices sour rye bread

Slice the red onion ⅛ inch thick. Toss the slices in olive or corn oil, season lightly with salt and pepper, place on a cookie sheet, and broil until they are browned and slightly charred.

Mix the sour cream, horseradish, and salt and pepper and spread on all four slices of bread. Layer the cheese, tomato, cucumber, and red onion on two slices of the bread and top with the other two slices. Butter the outside of each slice and sauté the sandwiches over low heat in a covered frying pan. When one side is nicely brown, turn and brown the other side. Serve immediately.

NOTE: As in most sandwiches, there can be a good deal of flexibility in the quantities of ingredients. Use more or less according to the number of people you wish to serve and how thick they like their sandwiches.

DESERT CAFÉ

—

SANTA FE

brasserie

The Brasserie is part of a complex of shops at Bennington
Potters, a large pottery that
has been making stoneware
since 1948, carrying on a long
tradition of pottery-making in
Bennington. This sandwich
evolved as the workers enter-
tained themselves by kibbitzing
with the restaurant staff and
inventing their own lunch. It
has since become a Brasserie
classic.

THE MASTER POTTER'S LUNCH

Serves 1

1 French roll, about 6 inches long, sliced in half
   lengthwise
Approximately 1 cup Caponata (recipe follows)
2 or 3 slices Gruyère cheese
3 or 4 thin slices raw onion
2 tablespoons melted butter
3 thin slices ripe tomato
3 tablespoons grated Parmesan cheese

Place the bottom half of the roll on a baking sheet
and build the sandwich in layers: Caponata, slices of
cheese, slices of onion, and a drizzle of butter. Brush
butter on the top half of the roll and place it on the
baking sheet, cut side down.

Bake the sandwich for 20 minutes in a 400° oven,
until the Caponata is hot, the cheese is nicely melted,
and the onions are brown. Remove the top half of
the sandwich to a plate. Add the tomato slices and
grated Parmesan cheese to the bottom half and
brown under the broiler.

Caponata

Makes about 1 quart

2 medium eggplants, cut in 1-inch cubes
1½ teaspoons salt
¾ cup olive oil
1 Spanish onion, cut in 1-inch cubes

THE BRASSERIE
—
BENNINGTON,
VERMONT

2 stalks celery, cut in ¼-inch slices crosswise
6 tablespoons tomato paste
¼ cup red wine vinegar
2½ tablespoons sugar
¼ teaspoon pepper
¼ cup drained capers
10 pitted green olives, sliced

Spread the eggplant cubes on trays lined with paper towels and sprinkle with salt. Let stand for at least 2 hours, to release some of the moisture and tighten the flesh so that less oil will be absorbed when it is sautéed. Just before cooking the eggplant, wipe off the salty juices with paper towels.

Sauté the eggplant in batches in just enough olive oil to keep it from sticking, until golden brown and soft. Remove each batch to a heavy pot that will hold at least 2 quarts. Sauté the onion until transparent and add it to the eggplant. Sauté the celery until it is just soft and add it to the eggplant and onion.

Place the remaining ingredients in the sauté pan and gently bring to a simmer. Add the sauce to the vegetables and carefully fold everything together. Cover the pot and let the mixture simmer over low heat for about 20 minutes, stirring three or four times. Let the caponata cool and then refrigerate. It will keep well for over a week.

Since 1791
NEW ORLEANS, LA.

MUFFULETTA

Serves 2

1 muffuletta bun or equivalent
4 slices ham
5 slices Genoa salami
4 slices pastrami
1 cup Italian Olive Salad (recipe below)
3 slices provolone cheese
3 slices Swiss cheese

Cut the bun open and layer one side with all the ingredients in the order given. Cut the sandwich in quarters and warm in a microwave oven or, wrapped in foil, in a conventional oven until heated through.

NOTE: Muffuletta buns are about 5 inches in diameter. If you are using smaller rolls, you may want to adjust the quantities of meat, cheese, and olive salad accordingly.

There is some dispute about where this New Orleans specialty originated, but the sandwich has been a mainstay of the menu at Napoleon House since Sal Impastato's uncle, Joe Impastato, operated a grocery store and then a barroom on the premises, beginning in 1918. The olive salad turns a basic cold cut and cheese sandwich into something different, and at Napoleon House the sandwich is heated to let the cheese soften and the flavors blend. Muffuletta buns are large individual rounds of Italian bread topped with sesame seeds.

NAPOLEON
HOUSE
BAR & CAFÉ

—

NEW ORLEANS

Italian Olive Salad

Makes about 2 quarts

4 cups salad olives with pimientos, drained
1 cup drained canned mixed vegetables
1 cup chopped canned artichoke hearts
1 cup drained chick-peas
1 cup drained cocktail onions
4 tablespoons drained capers
⅔ cup drained pickled vegetables, chopped
1½ green peppers, chopped
3 bunches celery, chopped
2 cloves garlic, minced
1½ tablespoons oregano
1 cup olive oil
½ cup red wine vinegar
Salt and pepper to taste

Combine all the ingredients and chill for about 24 hours before using.

MEXICAN B.L.T.

Makes 6

12 slices bacon, preferably peppered bacon
12 slices sourdough bread
6 leaves leaf lettuce
1 tomato, sliced
1 red onion, sliced
¾ pound sliced baked turkey

GUACAMOLE

2 small avocadoes, peeled and pitted
¼ pound onion, chopped
1 tablespoon chopped cilantro
Juice of 1 lime
Salt and pepper to taste

PICANTE MAYONNAISE

1 cup mayonnaise, preferably homemade (see
    page 334)
¼ cup picante sauce

First, prepare the guacamole by mashing the avocadoes, adding the remaining ingredients, and mixing well. Place an avocado pit in the guacamole and set aside. Next, prepare the picante mayonnaise by combining the mayonnaise and picante sauce. Set aside.

Fry the bacon until crisp and drain on paper tow-

City Market is on the mezzanine of the LTV Center, one of the most handsome of Dallas's many modern skyscrapers. The building, designed by Skidmore, Owings and Merrill, is the world headquarters for the developer Trammel Crow; other occupants include law firms, accountants, an oil company, and of course LTV. All these tenants find City Market a perfect place for a quick lunch of surprisingly high quality.

CITY MARKET

—

DALLAS

els. To assemble the sandwiches, spread the guacamole on 6 slices of the bread and the picante
mayonnaise on the other 6 slices. Place layers of
lettuce, tomato, red onion, bacon, and turkey on the
pieces of bread spread with the guacamole, and top
with the bread spread with mayonnaise.

NOTE: It is important that the picante sauce, available at most supermarkets, be thick in order to main-
tain the proper consistency of the mayonnaise.
Cattlebaron's is a good brand, available chiefly in the
Southwest.

GRILLED EGGPLANT SANDWICH

Makes 4 to 6

2 large eggplants, cut in ½-inch slices
Olive oil
Salt and freshly ground pepper to taste
4 to 6 large sweet red peppers
4 to 6 cloves garlic, finely chopped
1 small bunch parsley, stems removed and chopped
1 loaf homemade whole-wheat bread
12 ounces Monterey Jack cheese with hot pepper,
    thinly sliced (or substitute plain Monterey Jack
    and add crushed red pepper to taste to the sweet
    red pepper mixture)

Brush each eggplant slice with olive oil. If possible, grill the eggplant over a hot mesquite or hardwood charcoal grill. Or lay the eggplant slices on a baking sheet in one layer and broil until browned on one side, then turn to broil a few minutes more. Be sure the slices are well browned, to accentuate the smoky flavor. Season with salt and pepper.

Roast the red peppers until the skins are charred. Peel and seed and cut into 1-inch strips. Combine the peppers, garlic, parsley, and enough olive oil to moisten the mixture.

To assemble the sandwiches, slice the bread in ¼- to ½-inch slices, cutting two pieces for each sandwich. Brush half the slices with olive oil and on the other half place a layer of eggplant, a layer of the

Owners Shimon and Koby Bokovza were born in Tunisia and raised in Israel, so it is not surprising that the menu overseen by their executive chef, Derek Davis, is a mix of ''sunshine'' cuisines. At the time this collection was compiled, Aliza Green (now at Philadelphia's White Dog Café) was executive chef, and she suggests that the eggplant for this sandwich can be cooked when your grill is being used for another purpose.

APROPOS
—
PHILADELPHIA

pepper mix, and a layer of cheese. Put both halves of each sandwich on a baking sheet and place in a 425° oven long enough to melt the cheese. Join the two halves and serve immediately.

ROASTED PORK TENDERLOIN SANDWICH

Serves 6

1 2-pound boneless pork tenderloin
1 cup orange marmalade
⅓ cup Dijon mustard
½ cup sherry
¼ cup soy sauce
1 clove garlic, minced
1 tablespoon grated fresh ginger
2 tablespoons sesame oil
6 small baguettes
Garlic butter

Marinate the pork in a mixture of the next seven ingredients for an hour at room temperature or overnight in the refrigerator. Roast the pork in a 350° oven for 45 minutes, turning once during that time. Let it sit for 15 minutes after it comes out of the oven, then slice thinly. Slice the baguettes horizontally, spread with garlic butter, and toast. Place the slices of pork on half of the toasted bread and drizzle over some of the baking juices.

KRAMERBOOKS
& AFTERWORDS
CAFÉ

———

WASHINGTON, D.C.

brasserie

A SNACK FROM PROVENCE

Serves 2

2 Spanish onions, thinly sliced
½ cup olive oil
Scrap of bay leaf
Salt and pepper to taste
1 7-inch length crusty French bread, halved
    lengthwise
4 anchovy fillets, patted dry and cut in half
    lengthwise
4 calamata olives, each cut off the pit into 4 or 5
    crescents

Cook the onions in the olive oil with the scrap of bay leaf until they are very soft and sweet (do not brown). This may take as long as a half hour. Add the salt and pepper.

Place the bread on a baking sheet, cut sides up. (If necessary, trim the bottom crust to ensure stability.) Spread half the onion mixture on each half, being sure to go all the way to the edges. Use all of the olive oil, letting it soak into the bread. Lay the anchovy strips and olive pieces in a design on top of the onions.

Bake for 20 to 25 minutes in a 400° oven, until the edges are brown and the onions are sizzling.

You just don't ask a Vermonter to request a dish with the name pissaladière, *at least not without a chuckle, so at the Brasserie the traditional* niçoise *open-face sandwich has been given a euphemistic name.*

THE BRASSERIE

—

BENNINGTON,
VERMONT

Charlie Abdo and Peter Kelly operate an establishment familiar to long-time residents of the old Brewerytown section of Philadelphia — a neighborhood taproom. Charlie discovered the site after working as a general contractor in the area. He oversees the food part of the operation and Peter manages the bar. The clientele ranges from old-timers to young professionals, and the idea is to make everyone feel at home. This sausage recipe comes from Charlie's Aunt Samie, who used to cook for Arab dignitaries visiting the UN.

casual drinking & dining

SYRIAN SAUSAGE IN PITA

Serves 6

2 pounds leg of lamb, ground once
2 tablespoons chopped fresh tarragon
2 teaspoons ground coriander seed
1 teaspoon allspice
2 tablespoons red wine
¼ cup pine nuts
1 tablespoon salt
½ teaspoon pepper
5 feet narrow sausage casing (see Note)
Butter and olive oil
6 individual pita rounds
1 bunch coriander, chopped

To make the sausage meat, combine the first eight ingredients in a large bowl. Mix well with your hands. Using a sausage stuffer or a pastry bag, stuff the casings, twisting every 3 inches.

Sauté the sausage in a mixture of half butter and half olive oil until brown, turning occasionally. Serve in pita rounds, sprinkled with plenty of chopped coriander.

NOTE: If you wish to skip the casing step, form the sausage meat into patties and sauté until brown.

NORTH STAR
BAR

—

PHILADELPHIA

SAUSAGE HOAGIE WITH PEPERONATA

Serves 6

12 links hot Italian sausage

PEPERONATA

3 tablespoons olive oil
2 cloves garlic
2 medium red onions, cut in ¼-inch slices
3 green peppers, cut lengthwise in ¼-inch strips
4 tablespoons unsalted butter
½ teaspoon celery seed
½ teaspoon thyme
½ teaspoon oregano
½ teaspoon basil
½ teaspoon salt
½ teaspoon white pepper
½ cup dry white wine
4 medium tomatoes, peeled and cut in ¼-inch strips

6 Italian hoagie rolls, halved

Place the sausage links on a baking pan and bake at 400° for 30 minutes.

Heat a large skillet. Add the olive oil and garlic and sauté until the garlic is brown. Remove the garlic and add the onions and green pepper. Sauté until they soften, stirring frequently. Add the butter,

THE CAFÉ PETITTO
—
WASHINGTON, D.C.

seasonings, wine, and tomatoes; cook for 7 minutes.

Drain the sausage and cut each link in half lengthwise. Place four halves on one side of each hoagie roll and top with the peperonata.

CAFÉ SANDWICH

Serves 6

3 5-inch French baguettes or hoagie rolls
2 tablespoons Dijon mustard
6 ounces prosciutto, sliced paper thin
12 slices Swiss cheese
12 slices fresh tomato
2 cups julienne-cut vegetables (carrots and zucchini are recommended)
1 cup sliced mushrooms
1 medium red onion, sliced thin
¼ cup mayonnaise
½ cup vinaigrette dressing

Slice the rolls horizontally, spread with the mustard, and layer each half with the prosciutto, cheese, tomato, another piece of cheese, the vegetables, mushrooms, and onion. Mix the mayonnaise with the vinaigrette and pour over the top of each open-face sandwich. Place the sandwiches on a cookie sheet and bake for 8 to 10 minutes in a 375° oven, until the tops are brown and the dressing has set. Serve with sweet gherkin pickles.

Petaluma

Petaluma has an open kitchen and a large white tile pizza oven visible to diners in half of the L-shaped dining room. At least five different pizzas are available at both lunch and dinner.

PIZZA PRIMAVERA

Makes 2 9-inch pizzas

8 ounces pizza dough (see page 337)

TOMATO SAUCE

1 14-ounce can whole tomatoes, drained
¾ teaspoon salt
¾ teaspoon oregano
¾ teaspoon basil

Purée the tomatoes in a food processor or blender and add the remaining ingredients. Set aside.

TOPPING AND ASSEMBLY

½ pound mozzarella cheese, cubed
½ medium zucchini, julienne-cut
½ medium yellow squash, julienne-cut
½ carrot, julienne-cut
⅓ cup sliced mushrooms
1 cup broccoli flowerets
2 tablespoons olive oil

Sprinkle flour on a pastry board and press the dough into 9-inch rounds. Place the rounds on baking sheets or pizza tiles sprinkled with cornmeal. Spread the tomato sauce over each round, leaving an inch free around the edges. Quickly blanch the zucchini,

PETALUMA

—

NEW YORK CITY

yellow squash, carrot, and broccoli and refresh in cold water. Divide the cubes of cheese among the pizzas and place them evenly over the tomato sauce.

Arrange the vegetables and mushrooms on top of the cheese and drizzle over the olive oil. Place in a 400° oven and bake until the crust is crisp and brown and the cheese melted, about 15 minutes.

PIZZA AL QUATTRO FORMAGGI

Makes 1 10-inch pizza

8 ounces pizza dough (see page 337)
2 ounces grated mozzarella cheese
3 ounces grated provolone cheese
1 ounce gorgonzola cheese, crumbled
1 tablespoon grated Romano cheese
1½ teaspoons olive oil
1 tablespoon sun-dried tomato, minced

Pat the dough into a 10-inch round and trim to a perfect circle. Sprinkle the cheeses over the dough and drizzle the olive oil over the cheese. Bake the pizza in a 500° oven (preheated for an hour) on a stone or baking sheet for 5 to 8 minutes. Cut into six pieces and sprinkle with the sun-dried tomatoes.

Café Spiaggia has caught on as an elegant place for a casual meal, for shoppers and businesspeople alike, and the wait can be as long as two hours. Antipasti, pasta, and pizza (baked in special wood-burning ovens) are central to the menu — traditional categories with interesting combinations of fresh ingredients making the difference. The pizzas have crisp thin crusts and not a sign of tomato sauce.

CAFÉ SPIAGGIA

—

CHICAGO

desert cafe

Larry Vito and Richard Baker
are attempting to create a true
vegetarian cuisine, and Vito
finds the endeavor a challenge
after several years of working
for New York establishments
featuring nouvelle cuisine
— Le Plaisir, Chez Odéon,
and Green Street, where he
was executive chef.

GARLIC PIZZA

Makes 4 9-inch pizzas

1 pound pizza dough (recipe follows)
½ cup Garlic Paste (recipe follows)
1 cup Pizza Sauce (recipe follows)
6 ounces Fontina cheese, grated
24 baked garlic cloves
4 teaspoons basil pesto (see page 68)

DOUGH

2½ teaspoons active dry yeast
1⅓ cups warm water
2 teaspoons malt syrup
1 tablespoon olive oil
1 cup flour
2¼ cups semolina flour

Combine the yeast, water, and malt syrup and allow
to proof in a large bowl for 5 minutes. Add the remaining ingredients and blend well. Knead with a
dough hook or by hand for 7 minutes. Divide the
dough into 4-ounce pieces and roll into balls. Cover
each ball with plastic wrap and let rest at room temperature for 15 or 20 minutes. Roll each ball into a
9-inch circle, brush lightly with olive oil, cover with
plastic wrap, and allow to rise in a warm place for
30 minutes.

GARLIC PASTE

9 heads garlic
¼ cup olive oil
½ cup water

DESERT CAFÉ
—
SANTA FE

Slice off the pointed ends of the garlic heads and toss the heads of garlic in a bowl with the olive oil. Wrap the cloves tightly in an aluminum foil envelope along with the water and bake in a 350° oven for about 1 hour, until the garlic cloves become soft enough to squirt out of their skins. Reserve 24 cloves and mash the rest into a paste.

PIZZA SAUCE

¾ cup diced onions
2 tablespoons olive oil
2 teaspoons minced garlic
½ teaspoon chopped fresh oregano
½ teaspoon chopped fresh thyme
½ teaspoon chopped fresh basil
¼ teaspoon chopped fresh rosemary
1 16-ounce can peeled tomatoes, drained and
    chopped
5 tablespoons tomato paste
Salt and freshly ground black pepper to taste

In a heavy saucepan, sauté the onion in the olive oil over low heat until translucent. Add the garlic and sauté for about 10 seconds. Add the herbs and sauté for another 10 seconds. Add the tomatoes, simmer for 20 minutes, and stir in the tomato paste. Simmer for about 10 minutes more, until the sauce is thick and smooth, and season with the salt and pepper.

ASSEMBLY

Spread a ⅛-inch layer of garlic paste over each crust (more or less, according to taste). Then spread on a layer of sauce, top with the grated cheese, and bake on a pizza stone or baking sheet in a 400° oven until the crust begins to brown. Garnish each pizza with six of the reserved baked garlic cloves and continue to bake until the crust is well browned. Remove from the oven and brush with the basil pesto. Cut into quarters or sixths and serve immediately.

PIZZA WITH GOAT CHEESE, SUN-DRIED TOMATOES, AND BLACK OLIVES

Makes 1 8-inch pizza

6 ounces pizza dough (see page 337)
Flour
¾ cup tomato sauce
1½ teaspoons oregano
1 4-ounce package grated mozzarella cheese
3 sun-dried tomatoes, cut in ¼-inch strips (8 per tomato)
3 large pitted black olives, halved lengthwise
4 ounces Montrachet cheese

Coat the ball of dough with flour and shape into an 8-inch round. Spread with the tomato sauce and sprinkle with oregano. Top with the mozzarella. Bake in a 400° oven for 8 to 10 minutes. Remove from the oven and arrange the pieces of sun-dried tomatoes and olives over the cheese, making sure that each slice will have 2 strips of tomato and 1 olive half. Crumble the goat cheese evenly over the top.

Return the pizza to the oven and bake for 15 more minutes, until the crust turns light brown on the underside. Remove from the oven and cut into four or six slices.

Gabriel Marabella and his partner, Neil Stein, are dedicated to giving their patrons good food and good value, and sophisticated management techniques allow them to accomplish their goal profitably. At this writing, very few of the menu items, including entrées, cost more than $9, and those that do are listed in the "Over Nine Section."

MARABELLA'S
—
PHILADELPHIA

The mood and décor at Apropos make it a popular gathering place for a mix of fashionable Philadelphians, including artists, politicians, athletes, models, and business executives. Readers of both W *and* Rolling Stone *feel at home here. Black granite tables and contemporary Italian chairs with mauve upholstery fill a spacious multilevel setting that also includes a dance floor and a baby grand piano. A din of cheerful conversation competes with the varied musical offerings — everything from swing to a Brazilian band.*

FIG PIZZA

Serves 6

1 12- to 14-inch round pizza dough (or 2 8-inch rounds) (see page 337)
Extra virgin olive oil
4 ounces thinly sliced prosciutto
8 ounces very ripe figs (Mission or Kadota or a combination), sliced ¼ to ½ inch thick
1 8-ounce container Mascarpone cheese
¼ pound chopped walnuts
Fresh mint leaves for garnish

Brush the pizza round with the olive oil, leaving a 1-inch border free of oil. Lay the prosciutto all over the dough, then arrange the figs over the prosciutto. Brush the figs with a little of the olive oil. Place dollops of the Mascarpone between the fig slices and scatter the walnuts over the top. Bake the pizza in a 500° oven (using a preheated pizza tile if you have one) until the dough is bubbled and brown and the figs are caramelized along the edges. Garnish with the mint leaves and serve immediately.

NOTE: This pizza makes an excellent appetizer, cut in small wedges and served with a glass of champagne.

In addition to café service for breakfast, lunch, and dinner, Nick & Sully is a popular take-out shop and caterer. One foresighted customer has followed Calvin Trillin's advice and taken a selection of its goodies along on an airplane trip — a welcome alternative to airline fare.

MONTRACHET CALZONE

Makes 6

DOUGH

1 ¼-ounce package dry yeast
½ cup plus 2 tablespoons warm water
Pinch of sugar
1½ to 2 cups flour
½ teaspoon salt
1 tablespoon olive oil

FILLING

1½ leeks, white part only, cleaned and sliced
1 tablespoon butter
4 ounces Montrachet cheese
6 ounces ricotta cheese
¼ cup sour cream
½ cup grated mozzarella cheese
1 tablespoon chopped parsley
1 tablespoon minced garlic
1 tablespoon minced sweet red pepper
Salt and pepper to taste

1 egg beaten with 1 tablespoon water, for egg wash
Chopped herbs for garnish

To make the dough, dissolve the yeast in the water; add the sugar and ¾ cup flour. Let rise until doubled in bulk (about 45 minutes). Beat down the dough

NICK & SULLY
—
SEATTLE

and add the remaining ingredients, adding the flour gradually. Knead the dough well for 6 to 8 minutes. Divide the dough into 6 balls and set aside.

To prepare the filling, first sauté the leeks in the butter until they are soft but not brown. Cream the soft cheeses and sour cream together and add the remaining filling ingredients, including the leeks.

Roll the balls of dough into circles approximately 7 inches in diameter. Place ¼ cup filling in the center of each circle, fold over the dough, and pinch the edges closed tight. Brush with the egg wash and sprinkle with fresh herbs. Bake in a 425° oven for 20 minutes.

CALZONE DI VERDURA

Serves 6

DOUGH

1 .6-ounce cake yeast
2 cups lukewarm water
Pinch of sugar
4½ cups flour
1½ teaspoons salt
2 tablespoons olive oil

FILLING

2 tablespoons olive oil
3 medium zucchini, cut in large dice
2 medium eggplant, peeled and cut in large dice
½ pound mushrooms, sliced
1 tablespoon finely chopped garlic
3 red peppers, julienne-cut
Salt and pepper to taste

Olive oil
8 ounces goat cheese
¼ cup chopped fresh basil

To make the dough, mix the yeast with the water and sugar in a large bowl and let stand for 5 minutes. Add the rest of the ingredients and mix for 8 minutes, preferably with a dough hook. Place the dough in a bowl oiled with olive oil and let rise until doubled in bulk (about an hour).

After her student days, Michela Larson spent three years in Europe and came home wanting to open an Italian deli. She got her start in the food business peeling carrots in the kitchen at Another Season in Boston. Subsequently she ran a catering business and then started a restaurant at the Harvard School of Public Health. Those lucky enough to know about Salon Rouge considered it one of the best places in town for lunch.

MICHELA'S

—

CAMBRIDGE,
MASSACHUSETTS

To prepare the filling, heat the olive oil in a skillet and add the zucchini, eggplant, mushrooms, and garlic; cover and cook for 2 or 3 minutes. Stir the vegetables and add the red pepper. Cook for 6 to 8 minutes, until the vegetables are soft. Remove from the heat, drain off the juices, add the salt and pepper, and let cool.

Place the pizza dough on a floured board or counter and press or roll to approximately 12 inches in diameter, making sure the dough is an even thickness. Sprinkle cornmeal on a pizza paddle or cookie sheet and place the dough on top. Rub olive oil on the dough with your fingers. Place the vegetable mixture on one half of the circle of dough. Crumble the cheese over the vegetables and sprinkle with the basil.

Fold the plain side of the circle over the filling and press the two sides of the dough together to seal. Slide the calzone onto the baking paddle or sheet and bake for 15 minutes at 450°, or until golden brown. Cut the calzone into six slices, crosswise, and serve immediately.

CALZONE ALL PETITTO

Serves 6

DOUGH

1¼ cups water
1 tablespoon olive oil
1 teaspoon soft butter
1 teaspoon salt
½ beaten egg
3 cups flour
½ cup durum flour

FILLING

4 ounces hot Italian sausage meat
2 medium eggs
1 10-ounce package frozen chopped spinach,
    thawed, drained, and squeezed dry
1½ cups unseasoned breadcrumbs
1½ cups grated Parmesan cheese
½ cup chopped roasted red pepper
¾ cup finely chopped onions
½ teaspoon dried oregano
½ teaspoon white pepper

To make the dough, place the water in a large bowl
and add the olive oil, butter, salt, and beaten egg.
Add both flours gradually, until the dough becomes

After closing their previous restaurant, Petitto's, Byron and
Roger Petitto spent six months
in Calabria, rekindling their
interest in family and native
foods. One of the most popular
dishes that came out of this
trip is their Calabrian pizza
— a deep-dish pie with a fried
crust, served with thirty different toppings. That recipe remains a family secret, alas,
but their calzone is a close
cousin.

THE CAFÉ
PETITTO
—
WASHINGTON, D.C.

too stiff to stir. Remove to a floured board and knead until the dough is smooth and elastic. Let it stand while you prepare the filling (since there is no yeast in the dough, it will not rise).

To make the filling, sauté the sausage and drain off the grease. Reserve 1 egg. Place all the other ingredients in a large bowl and mix well (if the mixture seems dry, add another egg).

Divide the dough into six portions and roll each one into a circle ¼ inch thick. Divide the filling among the six circles, placing it on only one half of the circle. Fold the other half over the filling and firmly press the edges together. Beat the remaining egg and, using a pastry brush, paint the tops of the calzones. Place on a greased baking sheet and bake at 400° until brown, about 55 minutes. Serve warm.

ROQUEFORT TART

Serves 6 to 8

CRUST

2 cups flour
⅔ cup butter
1 tablespoon sugar
Dash of salt

FILLING

4 ounces Roquefort cheese, at room temperature
8 ounces cream cheese, at room temperature
2 eggs
2 tablespoons milk
2 tablespoons butter
2 teaspoons dried chives
Dash of cayenne pepper

To make the crust, combine all the ingredients in a bowl with a pastry blender until the mixture is crumbly. Refrigerate for at least 1 hour and press into a 10-inch quiche pan. Bake the empty shell at 450° for 10 minutes.

To make the filling, blend the cheeses until they are smooth. Add the remaining ingredients and mix until smooth. Pour into the baked shell and dot with butter. Bake at 350° for 30 minutes, until brown and set. Serve hot or at room temperature in wedges or, as an hors d'oeuvre, cut in small pieces.

Trio Café is in what used to be called the Western Addition section of San Francisco. An old neighborhood that managed to survive the 1906 earthquake, it has seen a good deal of gentrification in the last fifteen years. Patrons of the café originally came from the immediate area, but the word is out, and people now come from all over the city and beyond.

TRIO CAFÉ

—

SAN FRANCISCO

NOTE: The crust dough may be prepared several days in advance and refrigerated. Also, it may be baked a day before filling.

Enoteca *means "wine library" in Italian and the term perfectly describes the combination retail wine shop and restaurant operated by Malinda Pryde and her partner, Tom Darden, in the basement of the historic Times Square Building in downtown Seattle. Patrons may browse, library style, among the shelves of wine bottles in the front of the store and then take their choice to one of the café tables in the attractive eating area.*

TOMATO-PESTO TARTS WITH OREGON BLUE CHEESE

Serves 4

½ 17¼-ounce package frozen puff pastry sheets
4 ounces Oregon blue cheese (or another blue cheese)
8 ounces cream cheese, at room temperature
2 ripe tomatoes (about ½ pound), thinly sliced
½ cup pesto, preferably homemade (see page 68)

Cut the puff pastry sheets in 5-inch circles, or other shapes approximately the same size, and bake according to package instructions. Let cool completely, preferably overnight, or leave in the oven for an hour after turning off the heat. Slice the pastries horizontally and lay, cut side up, on a baking sheet.

Blend the blue and cream cheeses in a food processor until fluffy. Spread ¼ cup of the cheese mixture over each puff pastry round, making sure to go all the way to the edge. Cover the cheese with the tomato and top with the pesto. Broil 4 inches from the flame for 4 to 5 minutes, until hot and bubbly. Serve immediately.

CHARCUTERIE
PATISSERIE

SALMON DILL TOURTE

Serves 6 to 8

1 sheet frozen puff pastry
2 tablespoons chopped shallots
1 10-ounce package frozen chopped spinach,
   thawed, drained, and squeezed dry
2 tablespoons butter
¼ pound Gruyère cheese (or Swiss), grated
10 ounces fresh salmon fillet, skin removed, cut in
   1-inch pieces
3 eggs
1½ cups half-and-half
4 tablespoons chopped fresh dill
Salt and pepper to taste

Line a 9-by-2-inch round cake pan with the puff pastry. Cover with foil and fill it with beans or rice to weight down the dough. Bake in a 375° oven for 15 minutes. Remove the beans or rice and the foil and let the crust cool.

Sauté the shallots and spinach in the butter for 2 minutes, without letting them brown. Sprinkle 2 tablespoons of the grated cheese over the pastry, then add a layer of the spinach and a layer of the salmon. Repeat the procedure, reserving some of the cheese.

Beat the eggs with the half-and-half until well blended. Add the dill and salt and pepper. Pour over the salmon and sprinkle with the rest of the cheese. Bake at 375° for 30 minutes. Serve in wedges.

Monique Hooker finds the creativity of the artists, photographers, architects, and interior designers who work near the café an inspiration for her own creativity. She devised this tourte, which is easier to make than a quiche, for a picnic before an outdoor concert.

MONIQUE'S
CAFÉ
—
CHICAGO

ENTRÉES AND ACCOMPANIMENTS

Meat and Poultry

Seafood

Pasta

MEAT AND POULTRY

Grilled Flank Steak with Coriander Pesto
Ouisie's Chicken-Fried Steak with Cream Gravy
North Star Chili
Roast Pork with Prunes
Pork Loin Chops Stuffed with Sausage
Lamb and Spinach in Phyllo
Lamb and Fig Kebabs with Cucumber Salad
Lamb Chops with Port Wine and Tarragon
Veal Steak with Sweet Potato, Red Pepper, and
    Marsala
Veal Savoyard
Sweetbreads with Capers and Lemon
Braised Rabbit with Porcini and Polenta
Chicken à la Gallega
Free-Range Chicken with Peperonata
Jerked Chicken with Salsa
Pollo Limonese
Breast of Chicken Relleno
Breast of Chicken with Oranges and Cucumber
Saltimbocca di Pollo
Chicken with Cabbage
Chicken Shortcake with Herb Biscuits
Chicken Pot Pie
Tuscan Chicken
Chicken Fricassee with Smoked Mussels
Great White Bean Pot
Poussin with Cabernet Sauce and Curried Corn
    Fritters
Smoked Duck Breast with Pears and Persimmons
Grilled Duck Breasts with Endive, Radicchio, and
    Mushrooms

To keep everyone, including the kitchen staff, from getting bored, the menu at USA Café changes every week. Although dishes from all parts of the country are likely to appear, the Southwest is especially well represented. Pesto made with coriander and pumpkin seeds instead of basil and pine nuts is a welcome change.

GRILLED FLANK STEAK WITH CORIANDER PESTO

Serves 6 to 8

2½ pounds flank steak

MARINADE

½ cup olive oil
¼ cup wine vinegar
½ teaspoon salt
½ teaspoon pepper
1 teaspoon minced garlic
2 teaspoons chili powder
1 teaspoon sugar
½ cup minced onion

CORIANDER PESTO

¾ cup toasted and ground pumpkin seeds
1 cup chopped mild green chilies
¾ cup grated Parmesan cheese
¼ cup chopped parsley
⅓ cup chopped fresh coriander (cilantro)
1½ teaspoons minced garlic
½ teaspoon salt
2 tablespoons corn oil

Place the flank steak in a shallow baking dish. Combine the marinade ingredients and pour over the steak. Cover with plastic wrap, making sure it is flush against the meat, and refrigerate overnight.

USA CAFÉ
—
PHILADELPHIA

To prepare the pesto, blend all the ingredients in a food processor until smooth.

Grill or broil the flank steak and serve with the pesto.

NOTE: The pesto will keep in the refrigerator for a few days but should be brought to room temperature before serving.

OUISIE'S CHICKEN-FRIED STEAK WITH CREAM GRAVY

Serves 6

1 cup flour
1 teaspoon salt
1 teaspoon freshly ground black pepper
3 eggs
2 cups milk
½ cup heavy cream
6 7-ounce sirloin cutlets, no more than ½ inch thick
Vegetable oil for frying

Combine the flour and salt and pepper in a shallow dish or baking pan. In a separate shallow dish, beat the eggs and add the milk and cream. Pound each sirloin cutlet flat with a tenderizing mallet or the edge of a plate.

Dip each cutlet in the egg mixture, then in the seasoned flour, then in the egg, then in the flour again. Slip the cutlets into a skillet containing about an inch of oil heated to 350°. Cook until the cutlets

Tuesday is chicken-fried steak day at Ouisie's, at both lunch and dinner. The steak comes with gravy and mashed pota-toes or **the works** *— mashed new potatoes, corn pudding, black-eyed peas with bacon, and turnip greens. To look truck-stop authentic, the steak drapes over the side of the plate. But Ouisie doesn't run a truck stop and her version of this southern classic starts with top-grade sirloin.*

OUISIE'S
—
HOUSTON

are a rich golden brown. Drain the meat on a double thickness of paper towels and serve immediately with Cream Gravy (recipe below).

CREAM GRAVY

3 tablespoons bacon grease
3 tablespoons flour
1½ cups milk
1½ cups beef stock (see page 331)
1 tablespoon Worcestershire sauce
Tabasco to taste
1 teaspoon puréed garlic
Cayenne and freshly ground black pepper to taste

Combine the bacon grease with the flour in a cast-iron skillet and cook until the mixture colors slightly. Heat the milk until hot but not boiling. Remove the skillet from the heat and add the hot milk to the roux, whisking to combine. Add the stock, return the skillet to the heat, and continue stirring and scraping the bottom and sides of the pan. Add the remaining ingredients. Allow the gravy to simmer, stirring frequently, for 20 to 30 minutes. If it becomes too thick, add a little more milk or stock.

When the North Star Bar first opened, a neighborhood patron insisted that chili be added to the menu. Charlie Abdo invited him to submit a recipe, and two days later the recipe and a four-page thesis on the history of chili arrived. The dish has become a favorite with North Star regulars and has even won a local contest.

North Star Bar

casual drinking & dining

NORTH STAR CHILI

Serves 8

Olive oil
2 medium onions, roughly chopped
4 pounds top round of beef, cut in ¾-inch cubes
2 cloves garlic, minced
6 ounces beer
3 bay leaves
2 28-ounce cans Italian plum tomatoes, drained
1 cup tomato purée
1 tablespoon salt
1 tablespoon pepper
1 tablespoon oregano
1 tablespoon basil
1 tablespoon ground cumin
2 teaspoons chili powder
1 teaspoon Mombassa chili powder (substitute cayenne pepper to taste if unavailable)
4 stalks celery, cut in ½-inch pieces
3 cups cooked kidney beans, drained
½ cup molasses

Coat the bottom of a stockpot with the oil and wilt the onions. Add the beef and garlic and brown with the onions. Add the beer and bay leaves and simmer over low heat for 10 minutes.

Crush the tomatoes, drain, and add to the beef

NORTH STAR
BAR
—
PHILADELPHIA

mixture. Add the purée and simmer for 5 minutes. Add the spices, celery, kidney beans, and molasses and simmer for a final 10 minutes.

NOTE: At North Star the chili is served in an edible bread bowl — made by hollowing out a 5-inch round loaf — topped with grated Monterey Jack cheese, and run under the broiler.

ROAST PORK WITH PRUNES

Serves 6 to 8

2 cloves garlic
1 3-pound boneless pork roast
2 tablespoons butter
3 carrots, sliced
2 medium onions, sliced
4 shallots, chopped
½ teaspoon ground thyme
20 pitted prunes
1 cup brown stock or dry white wine
Salt and pepper to taste

Cut each garlic clove into 4 strips and make 8 incisions in the roast; insert a piece of garlic in each slit. Bring the butter to sizzling hot in a Dutch oven (with cover) and sauté the roast until it is brown. Cover the pot, turn the heat to low, and let the roast sim-

One of the appealing aspects of the food at this café is that many of the recipes have been in Monique Hooker's family for generations. Raised on a farm in Brittany, Monique was the eighth of ten children, and "everything came out of the back yard or off the farm." Pork is the staple meat in the region, and this was the dish always served to friends visiting for the first time.

MONIQUE'S
CAFÉ
—
CHICAGO

mer for 25 minutes, turning it from time to time.

Place the vegetables around the roast and sprinkle them with the thyme. Cover and cook over very low heat for another 25 minutes. Place the prunes on top of the pork and continue cooking for 10 minutes.

Place the roast on a carving board. Using a slotted spoon, remove the vegetables and prunes to a serving platter and keep warm. Place the Dutch oven over high heat and add the stock or wine to deglaze the pan. Let the liquid simmer for a minute or so.

Carve the roast, arrange it with the vegetables and prunes on the serving platter, and pour over a little of the sauce. Pass the remaining sauce separately.

CITY CAFE

PORK LOIN CHOPS STUFFED WITH SAUSAGE

Serves 6

6 1½- to 2-inch boneless pork loin chops
1 pound sausage meat (preferably veal), sautéed and cooled
1 cup sliced mushrooms, sautéed in butter until soft
2 tablespoons chopped fresh sage
2 tablespoons chopped parsley
Salt and pepper to taste

Cut a pocket in each pork chop and stuff with a mixture of the remaining ingredients. Grill over hot coals or under a broiler for 15 to 20 minutes, turning once. Be careful not to overcook.

*City Café was an immediate success and was picked by **D** magazine as one of the twelve best restaurants in the city in 1986, its first year of operation. Much of the clientele comes from the Highland Park neighborhood, and in spite of the somewhat elegant atmosphere, a "come as you are" dress code prevails.*

CITY CAFÉ

—

DALLAS

EMPIRE

LAMB AND SPINACH IN PHYLLO

Serves 6

4 tablespoons olive oil
1 clove garlic, lightly crushed
1 large onion, chopped
1½ pounds ground lamb shoulder
1 tablespoon beef extract, Bovril or equivalent
2 10-ounce packages frozen chopped spinach,
    thawed, drained, and squeezed dry
1 tablespoon Chinese oyster sauce
1 teaspoon Oriental sesame oil
¼ teaspoon ground coriander
⅛ teaspoon ground cumin
⅛ teaspoon ground nutmeg, preferably fresh
¼ teaspoon ground cinnamon
1 pound phyllo dough
1 pound unsalted butter, melted
½ cup plain dry breadcrumbs

YOGURT SAUCE

1 pint plain yogurt
Juice and grated rind of 2 large lemons
¼ cup finely minced parsley, squeezed dry

Heat the olive oil in a large sauté pan until it beads. Add the crushed garlic, sauté until brown, and discard. Add the onion and sauté until brown. Add the lamb, crumbling it with a fork, and sauté until all traces of pink are gone. Pour off the excess oil.

Stir the beef extract into the lamb mixture until it is evenly distributed. Add the spinach and cook over

In true diner fashion, the Empire is open twenty-four hours a day. It attracts a varied crowd — businesspeople at lunch and neighborhood loft dwellers at any time of day or night. Bridge and tunnel commuters often stop for a bite, since they can usually find a place to park on Tenth Avenue. Throughout the day, Bea Lyons holds forth at the piano.

EMPIRE DINER
—
NEW YORK CITY

high heat until all the liquid has evaporated. Stir in the oyster sauce, sesame oil, and spices. Remove from the heat and set aside.

Butter the bottom and sides of an 11½-by-8-by-6-inch baking pan (preferably one that can go to the table). Lay one sheet of the phyllo in the bottom of the pan and gently pat out any air bubbles. Using a pastry brush, lightly and evenly brush the phyllo with melted butter. Top the buttered sheet with another sheet of phyllo and repeat the process until about one third of the sheets have been used.

Gently spread half the meat mixture over the stack of phyllo sheets, making sure to reach the corners. Top with half of the breadcrumbs. Add another layer of buttered phyllo sheets, spread the remaining meat mixture on top, and sprinkle with the rest of the breadcrumbs. Top with the remaining phyllo sheets, buttering each one as before. Score the top lightly into six squares with a very sharp paring knife, being careful not to cut through to the meat. Bake in the upper third of a 400° oven for approximately 20 minutes, until the top is golden brown.

While the lamb is baking, prepare the sauce by combining all the ingredients. Remove the lamb from the oven, let sit for 10 minutes, and cut into six squares. Serve at the table from the baking dish, passing the sauce separately.

North Star Bar

casual drinking & dining

North Star advertises itself as a place for "casual drinking and dining," and the dining is enhanced by the most eclectic of menus — from Cuban black bean soup to fajitas to imported-cheese burgers to wild mushroom lasagna.

LAMB AND FIG KEBABS WITH CUCUMBER SALAD

Serves 6

2½ pounds leg of lamb, cut in 1-inch cubes
1 medium eggplant, peeled and cut in 1-inch cubes
1 1-pound package dried figs

MARINADE

1¾ cups olive oil
½ cup red wine
3 tablespoons soy sauce
2 cloves garlic, crushed
1 tablespoon dried rosemary
1 teaspoon pepper

Combine the ingredients for the marinade and marinate the lamb cubes in the refrigerator overnight. One hour before grilling the kebabs, add the eggplant and figs to the marinade.

Alternate pieces of the lamb, eggplant, and figs on skewers and grill over mesquite, charcoal, or in an oven broiler, turning frequently, for approximately 8 to 10 minutes. Serve with Cucumber Salad.

Cucumber Salad

¼ cup finely chopped red onion
1 clove garlic, minced

NORTH STAR
BAR
—
PHILADELPHIA

½ cup plain yogurt
½ cup sour cream
2 tablespoons chopped fresh parsley
3 cucumbers, peeled

Combine all the ingredients except the cucumbers. Halve the cucumbers lengthwise and remove the seeds. Slice into ¼-inch pieces. Add to the dressing just before serving.

LAMB CHOPS WITH PORT WINE AND TARRAGON

Serves 4

8 loin lamb chops, ¾ to 1 inch thick and well trimmed
2 cloves garlic, halved
½ cup unsalted butter
⅔ cup finely chopped onion
1 cup finely chopped carrot
⅔ cup finely chopped celery
½ cup Port wine
1 cup lamb, beef, or veal stock (see page 331)
1 tablespoon chopped fresh tarragon
Salt and freshly ground pepper to taste

About 30 minutes before serving, rub the lamb chops with the garlic and let them stand for 10 minutes. Sear the chops in a little of the butter in a cast-

A special feature of the cooking school at Piret$_M$, and earlier at Piret's, is the number of well-known guest chefs who give classes and demonstrations. Over the years, Jacques Pépin, Paula Wolfert, Diana Kennedy, Giuliano Bugialli, and many others have made frequent trips to San Diego. This is a Paula Wolfert recipe, with Munger adaptations.

PIRET$_M$

—

SAN DIEGO

iron skillet over high heat. Remove the chops and set aside.

In the same pan, over low heat, cook the onion, carrot, and celery, covered, adding butter as needed to keep the vegetables from sticking. After 5 minutes, raise the heat to high, add the Port, and stir to deglaze the pan. Add the stock and half of the tarragon and reduce the mixture by half, continuing to cook over high heat. Strain the sauce into a bowl, pressing the vegetables to release their juices. Add the salt and pepper.

Wipe out the skillet and cook the chops in a little butter until they are done to your taste (no more than medium rare is advised). Arrange on a heated serving platter. Reheat the sauce, whisking in a little butter, and pour it over the chops. Sprinkle on the remaining tarragon and serve immediately.

VEAL STEAK WITH SWEET POTATO, RED PEPPER, AND MARSALA

Serves 6

¼ cup blended olive oil
6 4-ounce veal steaks, cut from the loin
4 sweet potatoes or yams, boiled, peeled, and
    quartered

Michela Larson's hope for her smart new restaurant was that it be ''moderately unpretentious and playful.'' Part of the playfulness can be found in the oversized silverware, plates, and wineglasses, which impart a delightful Alice-in-Wonderland effect.

MICHELA'S
—
CAMBRIDGE,
MASSACHUSETTS

¼ pound pancetta, sliced thin, with each slice
    halved
5 or 6 medium red peppers, each cut in 8 slices
    lengthwise
10 scallions, white part only, halved lengthwise

SAUCE

¼ cup chopped fresh ginger
2 cups Marsala
4 cups dark veal stock (see page 332)
2 tablespoons butter
Salt and pepper to taste

In a large saucepan, combine the ginger, Marsala, and veal stock and reduce to 1½ cups over high heat.

In a large sauté pan, heat the olive oil and lightly brown the veal steaks. Remove the steaks to a shallow baking casserole large enough to hold them in one layer. Distribute the sweet potatoes, pancetta, and red peppers around the steaks and bake in a 375° oven for 20 minutes. Add the scallions and continue baking for 4 more minutes.

Bring the sauce to a boil and add the butter and salt and pepper. Serve the veal and vegetables from the baking dish. Pour a little of the sauce over the veal and pass the rest separately.

EMPIRE

VEAL SAVOYARD

Serves 6

2 large shallots, finely minced
2 tablespoons plus ½ cup unsalted butter
Pinch of thyme leaves
6 ounces dry sherry
½ cup veal stock (see page 332) *or* 1 teaspoon beef
   concentrate
2 cups heavy cream
1½ pounds veal cutlets, pounded ⅓ inch thick and
   cut in 12 pieces of equal size
6 tablespoons flour
½ teaspoon salt
½ teaspoon white pepper
½ pound mushrooms, sliced ¼ inch thick

To prepare the sauce, sauté the shallots in the 2 tablespoons butter in a heavy saucepan until translucent but not brown. Add the thyme and sherry and bring the mixture to a boil. Add the stock or concentrate and stir to melt thoroughly. Reduce the mixture over high heat until it is the consistency of honey, being careful not to burn it. Stirring constantly, add the cream and bring the mixture to a full simmer (do not boil). Cook, uncovered, whisking from time to time and scraping down the sides, until the liquid is reduced by one half. Remove the sauce from the heat and set aside.

Dredge the veal in a mixture of the flour and salt and pepper and sauté it, a few pieces at a time, in the ½ cup butter over high heat until it is moderately

The menu at the Empire Diner offers everything from old-fashioned diner fare like steak and eggs, chili, and strawberry shortcake to ethnic favorites: hummus, Chinese chicken wings, fried wontons, and nachos. The Blue Plate Special gives chef Mitchell Woo a chance to show off his haute cuisine training under the tutelage of a Belgian chef. A far cry from hot roast beef sandwiches on soft white bread, this veal dish is a typical Special.

EMPIRE DINER

—

NEW YORK CITY

brown on both sides. Remove to a warm platter. Sauté the mushrooms until they start to release their juices. With a slotted spoon, transfer the mushrooms to the veal plate and pour the excess butter out of the pan. Drain the juices from the veal plate into the sauté pan and add the veal and mushrooms. Pour over the sauce and toss the mixture over moderate heat for a few seconds to combine the flavors and allow the sauce to coat the meat. Arrange the veal on a platter and top with the mushrooms and sauce. Serve with steamed rice and buttered peas.

SWEETBREADS WITH CAPERS AND LEMON

Serves 6

3 pounds veal sweetbreads
1 onion, chopped
2 stalks celery, chopped
2 medium carrots, chopped
2 tablespoons peanut oil or butter
1 bouquet garni made from 10 3-inch sprigs
    parsley, 5 sprigs fresh thyme, and 1 bay leaf, tied
    together with cotton string
4 tablespoons white wine *or* 1 tablespoon white
    wine vinegar
1 cup flour
3 eggs, beaten with 3 tablespoons water
2 cups plain breadcrumbs
2 tablespoons butter
2 tablespoons peanut oil

SAUCE

1 cup white wine
4 tablespoons drained capers
2 tablespoons lemon juice
1 cup butter, in pieces

Soak the sweetbreads in cold water to cover overnight, changing the water once or twice. The next day, sweat the onion, celery, and carrots in the oil or butter in a pan large enough to hold all the sweet-

This dish is one of the most popular on the Bistro's menu and Susan Spicer has been preparing it for years. On one occasion Walter Cronkite made a special trip to the kitchen to offer his compliments. Preparation of the sweetbreads must be started the day before cooking, but following these simple instructions will make the job simpler than you might have guessed.

breads for 10 minutes. Add the sweetbreads and pour in cold water just to cover. Add the bouquet garni and the white wine or vinegar. Bring to a boil, lower the heat, and simmer for about 15 minutes, until the sweetbreads are firm but not hard. Remove the sweetbreads and place in a bowl of ice water to stop the cooking.

Place the sweetbreads on a tray or two large plates. Cover with a clean damp cloth and another tray or plate to weight them down. Refrigerate for about 2 hours. Later, remove any fat or tough membrane and butterfly or slice the sweetbreads in half. Dredge in the flour, dip in the beaten egg, then dip in the breadcrumbs.

Heat the butter and oil and sauté the sweetbreads on both sides until golden brown. Remove from the pan and keep warm in a low oven.

To prepare the sauce, first remove any excess crumbs from the sauté pan. Off the heat, pour in the wine, capers, and lemon juice. Over high heat, reduce the mixture by half. Whisk in the butter, piece by piece, until the sauce has emulsified (it will be creamy and white). Immediately remove the sauce from the heat; divide the sweetbreads among six plates, and spoon the sauce over each portion.

Cafe Med

BRAISED RABBIT WITH PORCINI AND POLENTA

Serves 6

3 2½-pound rabbits
¼ cup olive oil
3 onions, chopped
3 cloves garlic, minced
2 tablespoons chopped fresh thyme *or* 1½ teaspoons dried thyme
1½ cups sliced fresh porcini mushrooms (see Note)
2 cups game, rabbit, or chicken stock
1 bottle rich red wine, such as a Cabernet or Vino Noble
Salt and freshly ground black pepper to taste
Thyme sprigs for garnish

POLENTA

2 cups stoneground yellow cornmeal
6½ cups cold water
1 tablespoon salt

To prepare the polenta, whisk the cornmeal into the water and add the salt. Bring the mixture to a boil over medium heat, whisking as it heats to remove all lumps, then turn the heat to low. Cook, stirring frequently, for 15 to 20 minutes, or until it is a thick paste that leaves the sides of the pan. Pour onto a greased baking sheet and smooth with a rubber spatula to an even thickness. When the polenta is cool, cut six 6-inch squares from one side, saving the rest for another use.

The menu at *Café Med* changes every Tuesday and is kept small to allow Joe Printz to prepare everything from scratch, using only fresh ingredients. There are usually four entrées, three desserts, and one or two appetizer, salad, pizza, and pasta choices.

Cut each rabbit into six pieces, removing the loin from the backbone. Heat the oil in a Dutch oven and sauté all the pieces until brown. Remove the rabbit with a slotted spoon and add the onions and garlic. Sauté over medium heat until the onions are brown, about 10 minutes. Add the thyme and porcini and sauté an additional 4 minutes. Add the stock and wine, bring to a boil, and reduce over high heat for 5 minutes. Return the rabbit pieces, except the loins, to the Dutch oven and place it, covered, in a 350° oven for 1½ hours.

Remove the pan from the oven and add the loins, allowing them to warm over low heat. Place the polenta squares on a hot grill or sauté them in a little butter or olive oil until lightly browned.

To serve, place a polenta square in the center of each serving plate and top with three pieces of rabbit and some sauce. Garnish the plates with sprigs of thyme.

NOTE: Two ounces of dried porcini may be substituted for the fresh. Soak them in 1 cup boiling water for 30 minutes, then wash under running water to remove any grit. Strain the soaking liquid and add it to the stock.

el farol

CHICKEN À LA GALLEGA

Serves 4 to 6

3½ to 3¾ pounds whole chicken breasts with bone
   in (3 or 4 whole breasts)
2 tablespoons Achiote Oil (recipe follows)
2 teaspoons coarse (kosher) salt
4 tablespoons olive oil
8 whole cloves garlic, peeled
4 bay leaves
1 tablespoon paprika, preferably Spanish
½ teaspoon cayenne pepper
2 tablespoons flour
2 cups chicken stock
Black olives and a bouquet of Italian parsley or
   fresh thyme for garnish

Place the chicken breasts skin side up on a work
surface and, using the palms of both hands, press
down to crack the breastbone and flatten the breasts
as much as possible. Brush the skin with the 2 tablespoons of Achiote Oil and sprinkle with 1 teaspoon
of the salt. Transfer the chicken to a rack and bake it
in a 450° oven for 30 to 45 minutes, until the
chicken is cooked but still moist and the skin is crisp
and golden.

    While the chicken is baking, heat the olive oil in a
skillet and add the garlic cloves and bay leaves. Once
the garlic has turned golden, add the paprika, cay-

El Farol occupies a one-story adobe building on Santa Fe's Canyon Road, once an Indian trail winding along the Santa Fe River and now the site of many artists' studios, galleries, and shops. Called a ''cowboy bar'' by residents, the outside resembles the sheriff's office in every Western you've ever seen, and the barroom could well be the scene of a good fight. Off the bar is a rabbit warren of small rooms with whitewashed walls and dusty floors, cheered up by frescoes and paintings and faded turquoise blue woodwork — a delight for preservationists as well as gourmands.

enne, and flour, stirring with a wire whisk. Add the chicken stock and continue whisking while the mixture comes to a gentle boil over medium-high heat. Add the remaining teaspoon of salt and cook over low heat for about 10 minutes, stirring occasionally. When the sauce has thickened and there is no flour taste, remove the garlic cloves and bay leaves, correct the seasonings, and set aside.

Let the chicken cool slightly. When cool enough to handle, carefully remove all the bones, leaving the skin intact. Halve each whole breast lengthwise, giving you 6 or 8 breast halves with reddish-gold crispy skin. Set aside. Gently heat the sauce, stirring occasionally, and pour onto a serving platter. Arrange the chicken breasts over the sauce, skin side up. Garnish the platter with black olives and fresh herbs.

Achiote Oil

⅓ cup annato seeds (available in Latin-American groceries)
1 cup vegetable oil

Combine the annato seeds and oil in a small saucepan and cook over medium-high heat for 2 minutes — no longer. Let the oil stand until it is cool, then strain through a sieve lined with cheesecloth.

NOTE: Achiote oil is used to add color and a slightly saffron taste to various dishes. It keeps well in a cool dark place or in the refrigerator for up to a year.

Petaluma

FREE-RANGE CHICKEN WITH PEPERONATA

No matter what the weather on New York's Upper East Side, a visit to Petaluma puts one in mind of the sunny Southwest. Peach walls and light blue ceilings, tan rawhide chairs, and cheerful paintings and prints by Frank Stella and David Hockney make the chaos of First Avenue seem a million miles away.

Serves 6

6 cloves garlic
3 sprigs rosemary
3 free-range chickens
Olive oil

PEPERONATA

1 medium eggplant, peeled in strips to give a
   striped effect
1 medium Spanish onion, thinly sliced
½ cup virgin olive oil
1 large yellow pepper, seeded and cut in 1½-inch
   cubes
1 large sweet red pepper, seeded and cut in 1½-
   inch cubes
1 large green pepper, seeded and cut in 1½-inch
   cubes
2 medium tomatoes, peeled, seeded, and cut in
   large dice
Salt and pepper to taste

Place 2 cloves of the garlic and 1 sprig rosemary in the cavity of each chicken and rub the outside with olive oil. Roast in a 350° oven for 40 minutes, until the skin is crisp and brown and the meat juicy.

To prepare the peperonata, first cut the eggplant into 1-inch cubes, sprinkle with salt, and let sit in a

PETALUMA

—

NEW YORK CITY

colander for about an hour. Cook the onion in the olive oil in a large sauté pan, until the onion is soft. Add the peppers, turn up the heat, and cook for 4 minutes, stirring constantly.

Drain the eggplant, pat dry, and add to the onions and peppers. Cook for 4 more minutes and add the tomatoes. Cook for 6 minutes, then add the salt and pepper.

To serve, split the chickens, discard the garlic and rosemary, and place a half chicken on each of six individual plates. Spoon the peperonata next to the chicken.

NOTE: For a more elegant dish — if you feel ambitious — bone the roasted chicken and serve it on a bed of the peperonata.

JERKED CHICKEN WITH SALSA

Serves 6

3 small broiler chickens, split
2 cups soy sauce
½ cup Tabasco
2 lemons, sliced
4 cloves garlic, sliced
3 small fresh jalapeño peppers, quartered
　　lengthwise and seeded
Salt and pepper to taste

SALSA

3 cups diced fresh tomatoes
½ cup minced onion
Juice of 1 lemon
1 tablespoon chopped cilantro
½ teaspoon oregano
1 tablespoon chopped parsley
2 cloves minced garlic

Marinate the chickens in a mixture of the next five
ingredients for at least 2 hours or as long as overnight. Salt and pepper the chickens and grill over
charcoal or bake in a 450° oven for 45 minutes.

　　Combine all the ingredients for the salsa. Serve the
chicken hot with rice pilaf and salsa or at room temperature with potato salad and sliced tomato and
avocado, letting the salsa serve as a dressing for the
salad as well as a sauce for the chicken.

*Ruth Adams Bronz, who was
called Miss Ruby by a child-
hood friend, opened her first
Miss Ruby's Café in the Berkshire Hills of Massachusetts in
1977. After four years, she
found she needed a more year-
round clientele and eventually
moved to New York's Chelsea
district in 1984. This recipe
comes from a Jamaican mem-
ber of the kitchen staff.
''Jerked'' is a corruption of
''jugged'' and refers to the
marinating process.*

MISS RUBY'S
CAFÉ
—
NEW YORK CITY

At Michela's, every detail of the design and accessories has been handled with great care, down to the handmade marbled paper used for menus and cards. In the dining room, soft variations on the red, green, and white of the Italian flag are a backdrop for handsome black lacquered chairs. The back wall bears an outsize pointillist rendering of a ten-thousand-lire note, a permanent copy of the note Michela Larson was given by a friend before the restaurant opened, à la the framed dollar bill that hangs on every deli wall.

POLLO LIMONESE

Serves 6

3 whole chicken breasts, boned and halved, with
   skin left on
1 cup flour
1 tablespoon coarse (kosher) salt
1½ tablespoons freshly ground black pepper
1 cup vegetable oil

MARINADE

Grated rind from 2 lemons
½ cup chopped fresh basil leaves
¼ teaspoon salt
¼ teaspoon pepper
2 cloves garlic, crushed
½ cup olive oil

Combine the ingredients for the marinade and marinate the chicken breasts, covered tightly, in the refrigerator for about 8 hours.

Combine the flour, salt, and pepper and dredge the chicken, coating it well. In a sauté pan, heat the oil to the smoking point. Place the chicken, skin side down, in the oil. Cook for 7 or 8 minutes, turn, and continue cooking for another 7 or 8 minutes. The chicken should be crispy and brown. Drain on paper towels and serve immediately with a sauté of vegetables, such as zucchini, sweet peppers, and mushrooms.

BREAST OF CHICKEN RELLENO

Serves 6

6 large chicken breasts, boned and skin removed
2 cups grated Monterey Jack cheese
3 eggs, lightly beaten
1 cup milk
2 cups flour
2 cups yellow cornmeal
Vegetable oil for frying
Green Chile Sauce (recipe follows)

Poach the chicken breasts in salted water until they are just cooked through, about 10 minutes. Drain and cool slightly. Make a horizontal incision in each breast and pack as much cheese as possible into the opening (reserving some extra cheese for the final baking).

Combine the eggs and milk. Coat the breasts with flour, dip in the egg batter, and roll in the cornmeal. Pour about 1 inch of vegetable oil into a cast-iron skillet or sauté pan, heat, and cook the breasts until golden brown on both sides. Place the breasts in a buttered shallow baking dish, cover with the Green Chile Sauce and the remaining grated cheese, and bake in a 450° oven until the cheese melts, approximately 5 minutes.

The basic ingredient of spicy northern New Mexican food is the chili pepper, and the sauce known simply as "chile" — whether it be green, red, or vegetarian — is a staple of every household. Isabelle Moya's chile recipe comes from her Spanish mother-in-law (who used lard instead of vegetable oil), and it makes a great accompaniment for tacos and enchiladas as well as this New Mexican variation on chicken Kiev.

GUADALUPE
CAFÉ

—

SANTA FE

Green Chile Sauce

5 7-ounce cans diced mild green chilies
2 7-ounce cans diced hot green chilies
1 clove garlic, minced
3 to 4 cups water
Salt to taste
½ cup vegetable oil
½ cup flour

Place the mild and hot chilies and their liquid in a saucepan with the garlic, 3 cups of water, and salt and bring to a boil. Remove from the heat. In a separate small pan heat the oil and slowly add the flour, stirring to make a paste. Reheat the chili mixture until it simmers and slowly add the flour paste, stirring constantly until it becomes a sauce. If it seems too thick, add more water.

CAMPAGNE

BREAST OF CHICKEN WITH ORANGES AND CUCUMBER

Serves 4

1 small cucumber
2 oranges
1 tablespoon vegetable oil
Salt and pepper to taste
2 large chicken breasts, bone and skin attached, split, *or* 4 whole small breasts, bone and skin attached
½ cup white wine
1 teaspoon whole coriander seeds
1 cup heavy cream
2 tablespoons unsalted butter
1 tablespoon chopped fresh dill

Peel the cucumber, split it lengthwise, and remove the seeds. Slice into batons about 2 inches long and ⅛ inch square. Set aside. Remove the peel and pith from one of the oranges and, using a sharp knife, cut the meats from between the membranes. Set aside. Juice the other orange.

Heat the oil in a large skillet, salt and pepper the chicken breasts, and place them in the skillet, skin side down. When the skin has browned nicely, turn the chicken and place the skillet in a 400° oven. When the breasts have cooked through, in about 12 to 15 minutes, remove them from the pan and keep warm.

Add the cucumber to the pan and sauté briefly in the fat. Leaving the cucumber in the pan, drain off most of the fat, then deglaze the pan with the wine.

Campagne has only fifteen tables — except in fair weather, when dining in the garden is possible. Ted Furst and Peter Lewis have purposely kept the restaurant small, in order to do all the cooking, managing, and greeting themselves. The result is exceptional quality in every aspect of the Campagne experience.

CAMPAGNE

—

SEATTLE

Add the orange juice and the coriander seeds and reduce the liquid by two thirds. Add the cream, reduce until slightly thickened, then whisk in the butter and the dill. Season with salt and pepper.

Slice the breast meat off the bone, arrange on individual plates, garnish with the orange sections, and pour the sauce over all.

NOTE: Although chicken is much tastier when cooked on the bone, if you want to save time, you may used boned chicken breasts. They will also take less time to cook.

SALTIMBOCCA DI POLLO

Serves 4

4 chicken breast halves, boned and skin removed
4 fresh sage leaves
4 small slices prosciutto
Flour
Olive oil
½ cup white wine
2 cups chicken stock
2 tablespoons chopped parsley

Pound the chicken breast halves with a mallet until they are even in size. Place 1 sage leaf and 1 slice prosciutto on each half, cover with plastic wrap, and pound until the sage and prosciutto lightly adhere to the breast. Lightly flour the chicken, dusting off the excess.

Heat the olive oil in a sauté pan and cook the chicken, prosciutto side down first, until it is golden brown on both sides and barely cooked through. Remove the chicken from the pan. Add the wine and reduce, then add the chicken stock and reduce until the stock thickens. Return the chicken to the pan and reheat. Add the parsley and serve immediately.

Anthony Mantuano, executive chef of Spiaggia and Café Spiaggia, was the only Chicago chef named to Food & Wine *magazine's 1986 honor roll of twenty-five ''hot, new super-star chefs.'' Before Spiaggia opened in 1984, Mantuano spent seven months in Italy working in restaurants in several regions, an experience that enables him to serve ''contemporary interpretations of traditional recipes, using modern methods to suit today's tastes.''*

CAFÉ SPIAGGIA

—

CHICAGO

The Munger bistros have always featured a generous selection of hearty French country dishes, and this one has been a favorite for many years. A great advantage to busy home cooks is that it can be prepared in advance, refrigerated, and baked just before serving. Add potatoes — baked, boiled, or roasted — and you have a meal.

CHICKEN WITH CABBAGE

Serves 4

4 slices bacon, coarsely chopped
3 whole chicken breasts, halved, boned, and
   skinned
1 cabbage, cut into 8 wedges
1 cup sliced mushrooms
2 cloves garlic, minced
1 onion, finely chopped
1 bay leaf
½ cup dry white wine
1 cup chicken stock
1 tablespoon thyme
½ cup minced fresh parsley
Salt and pepper to taste

In a large skillet, sauté the bacon until crisp. Drain on paper towels. Cut the chicken breasts across the grain into slices 1 inch thick and sauté in the bacon fat until nicely browned. Transfer the chicken to a casserole large enough to hold the pieces in one layer and arrange the cabbage wedges over it.

Lightly sauté the mushrooms, garlic, and onion. Sprinkle them over the cabbage, with the bay leaf, wine, stock, bacon, and seasonings. Bake, covered, in a 400° oven for 45 minutes. Using a slotted spoon, place the vegetables and chicken on a warmed platter; on top of the stove reduce the casserole liquids until thickened. (For a thicker sauce, whisk in a little flour and water mixed into a paste.) Pour the sauce over the chicken and serve immediately.

PIRET_M

—

SAN DIEGO

CHICKEN SHORTCAKE WITH HERB BISCUITS

Serves 6

1 large fowl, 6 to 7 pounds
2 carrots
4 stalks celery
1 large onion
½ bunch parsley
2 bay leaves
2 whole cloves
1 tablespoon peppercorns
Herb Biscuits (recipe follows)

SAUCE

½ cup butter
4 stalks celery, sliced
1 carrot, sliced
2 small leeks, cleaned and sliced, white part only
1 pound mushrooms, sliced
¼ cup flour
4 cups hot chicken stock
Salt and pepper to taste

Place the fowl in a large pot with water to cover. Roughly chop the carrots, celery, onion, and parsley and add to the pot with the bay leaves, cloves, and peppercorns. Bring the water to a boil and cook the fowl for 2 to 2½ hours, until tender. Let cool in the stock, then remove and pick all the meat from

American Eclectic Cooking is what Miss Ruby's advertises. The menu changes every two weeks, with a different regional or sectarian cuisine featured each time. Preceding each bill of fare is a ''say-so'' in which Ruth Bronz gives the historical and cultural background for the menu. This dish comes from one of the popular Shaker menus, and we learn that the Shakers were the first in this country to sell culinary herbs.

MISS RUBY'S
CAFÉ
—
NEW YORK CITY

the bones. Strain the stock, skim off the fat, and set aside.

To make the sauce, melt the butter in a Dutch oven. When the foam subsides, add the celery, carrot, and leeks and sauté until the leeks are translucent. Add the mushrooms and stir until the butter is absorbed. Add the flour and toss until the butter and vegetables absorb it and everything begins to brown lightly. Add the stock, stirring constantly, and salt and pepper. Add the pieces of picked chicken (do not cut or tear; they should be chunky) and stir gently. Leave over heat just long enough to warm the chicken through and serve between buttered Herb Biscuits.

Herb Biscuits

Makes 8 to 10

3 cups flour
1 teaspoon salt
1 tablespoon dried tarragon *or* 2 tablespoons
   chopped fresh tarragon
2 tablespoons baking powder
5 ounces shortening (a little over ½ cup Crisco or
   other solid vegetable shortening) *or* butter
2 cups milk, or less

Sift together the dry ingredients and work the shortening in with your fingers or a pastry cutter until the mixture is the consistency of rough cornmeal. Stir in the milk until a soft dough forms. Immediately turn the dough out onto a heavily floured board and pat or roll to a ½-inch thickness. Cut into 2- to 3-inch biscuits and set, touching, on a baking sheet. Bake at 425° for 12 to 15 minutes, until golden brown.

NOTE: Although the chicken and sauce may be reheated after preparing, the biscuits should be served just out of the oven.

CHICKEN POT PIE

Serves 6 to 8

6 pounds chicken legs (with thighs attached)
2 cups dry white wine
3 cups mixed diced vegetables, including in roughly equal quantities as many as possible of the following: green beans, carrot, celery, fennel, leek, onion, sugar snap peas, red pepper (roasted, peeled, seeded, and diced), winter squash, and sun-dried tomato (reserve the trimmings from the onion, carrot, celery, leek, and fennel for the stock)
1 bay leaf
½ cup mixed chopped fresh herbs, including: ¼ cup chopped parsley and a total of ¼ cup of a mixture of dill, lovage, marjoram, tarragon, or thyme (reserve the stems for the stock)
½ cup unsalted butter
½ to ¾ cup flour
Coarse (kosher) salt, freshly ground black pepper, and cayenne pepper
3 tablespoons butter
1 sheet frozen puff pastry (preferably an all-butter brand)
1 egg mixed with 2 tablespoons half-and-half

Roast the chicken legs in a baking pan in a 400° oven for 1 hour, until the drumstick moves freely in the

The chef and part owner of the White Dog Café is Aliza Green, who has a strong reputation in food-conscious Philadelphia, partly based on her previous jobs as executive chef at Apropos and Di Lullo. Since she joined Wendy Born and Judy Wicks as part of the management team at this café, the menu has become slightly more sophisticated, though with no loss of informality or commitment to American ingredients and traditions. The careful preparation, interesting vegetables, and fresh herbs central to this variation on a basic dish are a good example of Green's style.

WHITE DOG
CAFÉ
—
PHILADELPHIA

joint. Remove the chicken and deglaze the pan with the white wine. Remove the chicken meat from the bones and set aside. Discard the skin. Place the bones in a stockpot along with the white wine deglazing mixture. Add cold water to cover and bring to a boil. Skim off all the white albumen. Add the vegetable trimmings, bay leaf, and herb stems. Simmer for 3 to 4 hours, then strain. Reduce the stock to 5 cups over high heat.

In a separate pan, melt the ½ cup butter and stir in enough of the flour to make a thick paste. Cook the roux for 5 to 10 minutes, stirring constantly with a wooden spoon or whisk. Heat the chicken stock to a simmer and, little by little, whisk the roux into the stock, allowing it to come to the boil as the roux is added. The finished chicken velouté should be thick enough to coat a spoon. Season with the salt and black pepper and a pinch of the cayenne pepper. Set aside.

In a wide sauté pan, heat the 3 tablespoons butter and cook the diced vegetables for several minutes. Add the chicken meat, after carefully picking it over to remove the cartilage and tendons. Add the chicken velouté and bring the mixture to a boil. Immediately remove it from the heat and let cool to room temperature before adding the fresh herbs.

Roll out the puff pastry (using the scraps for decorations — dog bone shapes, of course, are the embellishment of choice at the White Dog Café). Spoon the chicken mixture into six individual deep oven-proof bowls or a 2-quart casserole. Brush the rims with the egg wash and place the puff pastry over the top, making sure to seal the edges well. Brush more egg wash on the pastry, put the decorations in place, and cut a few steam vents. Bake in a 400° oven for about 30 minutes, until the top is browned and the filling is bubbling.

KRAMERBOOKS
&afterwords
A café

Although in the early days the menu stuck fairly close to quiche, soup, and salad, today there is a definite international focus at Afterwords — Mexican, Italian, Oriental, and Cajun dishes are all popular. Many of the waiters and waitresses are from other countries and help to influence the menu.

TUSCAN CHICKEN

Serves 6

½ cup olive oil
3 potatoes (about 1½ pounds), peeled, boiled, and
    cooled and sliced ¼ inch thick
6 boneless chicken breast halves, with skin
6 fresh plum tomatoes
1 teaspoon salt
1 teaspoon cracked pepper
2 cloves garlic, minced
1 bunch parsley, chopped
1 tablespoon dried rosemary (or more, if fresh)

Using some of the olive oil, grease the bottom of a large shallow casserole. Layer the sliced potatoes in the casserole. Place the chicken breasts on top, leaving room around the sides and between the breasts. Quarter the tomatoes and arrange them around the breasts. Sprinkle the salt and pepper over all.

Combine the remaining olive oil, garlic, parsley, and rosemary and brush over the chicken and tomatoes. Bake in a 425° oven for 5 minutes; reduce the heat to 350° for 10 minutes, making sure that the potatoes are brown around the edges and the chicken is cooked through.

NOTE: This is a good dish to prepare ahead. Also, running the casserole under the broiler after baking gives the chicken skin a crisp finish.

KRAMERBOOKS
& AFTERWORDS
CAFÉ
—
WASHINGTON, D.C.

Under Sheela Harden's able hand, this restaurant has become highly regarded for its excellence and consistency: there are the regulars who return every week and the regulars who return every year. A favorite fair-weather activity for tourists and natives alike is a leisurely meal, small or large, on the terrace, where even the tabletops are made of local stone.

brasserie

CHICKEN FRICASSEE WITH SMOKED MUSSELS

Serves 4

6 cups rich homemade chicken stock (see
  page 330)
2 chicken breast halves, boned and skinned
2 chicken thighs, skinned
2 chicken legs, skinned
Salt and pepper to taste
¼ ounce dried cèpes mushrooms
½ cup butter
½ cup flour
1 cup heavy cream
2 ounces fresh smoked mussels (large)

Bring the stock to a bare simmer and poach the chicken pieces in the stock until their juices run clear (the boneless breasts will cook much faster). Remove the chicken, sprinkle with the salt and pepper, and set aside. Strain the stock through a layer of cheesecloth.

Gently simmer the cèpes in 2 cups of the stock until it is reduced by half. Melt the butter; when the foam subsides, whisk in the flour. Cook the roux over medium heat for about 5 minutes, but do not let it brown. Remove the pan from the heat and whisk in the 4 remaining cups of hot stock.

Return the sauce to the heat and simmer gently until the mixture is reduced by half (this could take as long as an hour). Skim off any fat and scum that accumulate on the surface.

Strain the cèpes reduction into the sauce and discard the cèpes. Whisk the heavy cream into the sauce and add salt and pepper. Simmer for a few minutes. Slice the breast meat into medallions and neatly cut the dark meat off the bones. Add the meat to the sauce, reheat, and add the mussels. Serve immediately, with rice.

GREAT WHITE BEAN POT

Serves 6

1 pound white beans
½ pound kielbasa, sliced
1 chicken, cut up as for frying
2 large stalks celery, with leaves, sliced
1 large white onion, chopped
1 teaspoon oregano
1½ teaspoons thyme
2 cloves garlic, minced
1 2-inch piece lemon rind
2½ cups water, or more
2½ cups white wine, or more
Salt and pepper to taste
Chopped parsley for garnish

Carefully pick over the beans and place them in a large pot. Cover with water to 2 inches above the beans and bring to a boil. Turn off the flame and let

Ruth Adams Bronz isn't interested in fancy imported ingredients and calls herself a ''supermarket cook.'' For her, beans are the quintessential American food, and this recipe for a lazy person's cassoulet is one of her favorites. It lends itself to endless variations — black, kidney, or pinto beans instead of white; chorizo or andouille sausage or chunks of ham or fresh pork instead of kielbasa; the addition of carrots, turnips, or other root vegetables.

MISS RUBY'S
CAFÉ
—
NEW YORK CITY

the beans sit for 45 minutes to an hour. Drain thoroughly.

Meanwhile, dry-sauté the kielbasa in a Dutch oven and remove. In the sausage oil left behind (add vegetable oil if there doesn't seem to be enough), sauté the chicken pieces until they are nicely browned. Add the celery, onion, herbs, garlic, and lemon rind. Continue cooking until the onion is translucent.

Return the sausage to the pot, top with the beans, and add the water and wine to cover two inches above the beans. Stir gently to distribute the meats and vegetables evenly. Cover and cook at a low simmer for 1½ to 2 hours, until the beans are tender but not broken. Season with the salt and pepper and serve in large soup bowls with a sprinkling of parsley. Accompany with garlic bread and a salad.

NOTE: If the chicken cooks with the beans the whole time, it will be falling off the bone (and the bones may be removed). If you want the chicken to be firmer and more moist, don't add it to the pot until 45 minutes before the end of the cooking process.

POUSSIN WITH CABERNET SAUCE AND CURRIED CORN FRITTERS

Serves 6

3 to 6 poussin or Cornish game hens, at room
temperature
⅔ cup Cabernet Sauvignon wine
1½ cups raspberry jam
Vegetable oil
Salt and pepper to taste

Split and flatten the hens and set aside.

Combine the wine and jam in a heavy saucepan
and simmer the mixture until the jam is fluid. Immediately strain the sauce through a fine sieve to get
rid of the seeds. Set aside and keep warm.

Oil both sides of the hens, season with salt and
pepper, and grill or broil for 4 to 6 minutes on each
side. Serve with the sauce and accompany with Curried Corn Fritters.

Curried Corn Fritters

1 tablespoon butter
1½ tablespoons curry powder
1½ cups flour
1½ teaspoons baking soda

The restaurant part of Enoteca
has expanded gradually and
now includes dinner service as
well as one of the longest
lunches in town — served any
time between eleven-thirty and
five o'clock. It's a popular spot
for meeting friends after work
for wine and a meal and for
the pre-theater crowd. The
regular dinner menu features
a great many grilled dishes
with innovative sauces.

ENOTECA
WINE SHOP &
RESTAURANT
—
SEATTLE

½ teaspoon salt
3 eggs
¾ cup half-and-half
10 ounces corn kernels, fresh or frozen (thawed)
Vegetable oil for frying

Melt the butter, add the curry powder, and cook for 2 minutes. Set aside. Sift the dry ingredients together. Beat the eggs and half-and-half. Combine the curry powder, the dry ingredients, and the egg mixture, being careful not to overmix. Stir in the corn.

Heat ½ inch vegetable oil in a frying pan. Flick a small bead of batter into the oil to make sure it sizzles, then drop the batter in by small spoonfuls and cook until golden brown on both sides. Drain the fritters on paper towels.

BAY WOLF

RESTAURANT & CAFE

SMOKED DUCK BREAST WITH PEARS AND PERSIMMONS

Serves 6

6 smoked duck breasts, skin removed
3 Bosc or Anjou pears, peeled, cored, and sliced
3 persimmons, preferably Japanese Fuyo, peeled
  and sliced
3 tablespoons lemon juice
6 tablespoons butter
3 tablespoons minced ginger

Thinly slice the duck breasts and arrange on individual serving plates. Toss the sliced fruit with the lemon juice to keep it from darkening and set aside. Melt the butter in a large frying pan. Add the ginger and simmer over medium heat for 1 minute. Add the fruit and any accumulated juices. Turn the heat to high and toss the fruit gently until it is just heated through. Spoon the fruit and juices next to the duck on the plates. Serve immediately.

The cooking at Bay Wolf was described in a Gourmet magazine review as having ''a French foundation, a California framework, and embellishments that are clearly the kitchen's own.'' And there's an herb garden in the back yard. This may sound like a brand-new, up-to-the-minute establishment, but in fact Bay Wolf was ahead of its time and has been open since 1975.

BAY WOLF

—

OAKLAND,
CALIFORNIA

Eating in the kitchen has proved very popular, and since opening day Cucina has been packed by longtime Chianti aficionados as well as new patrons. Only twelve tables and a small counter share space with a working kitchen — a roaring grill, racks hung with drying pasta, cases for cheese, produce, and sweets, and a wall of wine bins. The food is the décor, with white tile walls and a black and white marble floor forming a simple backdrop.

GRILLED DUCK BREASTS WITH ENDIVE, RADICCHIO, AND MUSHROOMS

Serves 4

½ cup blueberries
4 tablespoons fruit mustard
1 teaspoon Colman's dry mustard
4 duck breasts
Salt and pepper to taste
Olive oil
1 large head radicchio
2 large Belgian endives
8 slices pancetta (Italian bacon)
Juice of 2 lemons
8 large mushroom caps
Chopped garlic (optional)

In a food processor blend the blueberries, fruit mustard, and dry mustard until creamy.

Remove the fat from the duck breasts and pound until ¼ inch thick. Season with the salt, pepper, and olive oil.

Quarter the radicchio head and halve the endives. Wrap a slice of the pancetta around each piece of lettuce and season with the salt, pepper, olive oil, and lemon juice. Brush the mushrooms with the olive oil and lemon juice (and stuff with chopped garlic if you wish).

Place the lettuces and mushrooms on a grill or under a broiler and cook for 10 minutes, turning frequently. Grill or broil the duck breasts for 1½ minutes on each side. Serve the duck with the grilled lettuces and mushrooms, garnished with the fruit mustard purée.

SEAFOOD

Poached Salmon with Mustard-Lemon Sauce

Salmon with Basil, Peppers, and Champagne
  Mignonette

Grilled Salmon with Fresh Fruit Coulis

Marinated Filet Mignon of Tuna

Grilled Tuna with Rosemary Beurre Blanc

Red Snapper Baked in Corn Husks

Red Snapper with Melon Sauce

Redfish Nantua

Cayenne Redfish with Creamy Garlic Sauce

Mahi-Mahi with Tomato Sauce

Grilled Marinated Monkfish

Crabcakes

Softshell Crabs with Tomato Cream Sauce

Pan-Fried Oysters en Brochette

Shrimp and Andouille Sausage with Creole
  Mustard Sauce

Gulf Shrimp with Poblano Butter

Jambalaya

The Balboa Cafe

POACHED SALMON WITH MUSTARD-LEMON SAUCE

Serves 6

6 shallots, finely chopped
1 tablespoon olive oil
2 cups dry white wine
Parchment paper
6 6-to-7-ounce salmon fillets
3 tablespoons coarse-grain mustard
Juice of 3 lemons
½ pound unsalted butter, softened
Salt and pepper to taste
1 lemon, thinly sliced, for garnish

In a large sauté pan, cook the shallots in the olive oil (do not brown). Add the white wine and bring to a boil. Butter the parchment paper with unsalted butter. Add the salmon to the pan and cover with the paper, buttered side down. Gently poach the salmon until it is slightly underdone. Remove to a warm plate, cover, and keep warm.

Reduce the wine left in the pan to 1 tablespoon. Add the mustard and lemon juice and blend well with a whisk. Turn off the heat and add the butter, a little at a time, continuing to whisk. Add the salt and pepper. Place a salmon fillet on each plate, spoon over the sauce, and garnish with a slice of lemon.

Although the menu at Balboa always includes hamburgers, much of the fare reflects the influence of Jeremiah Tower, brought in by owners Doyle and Kathy Moon and Jack Slick to upgrade the food at the former neighborhood café. The current chef is Philippa Spickerman, a graduate of the California Culinary Academy.

BALBOA CAFÉ
—
SAN FRANCISCO

The recipes included from West End Café are those of Janet Terry, who preceded the current executive chef, Melissa Ballinger. A fine arts major in college and an accomplished calligrapher, Terry began her career in the culinary world by working with François Dionot at Washington's celebrated L'Académie Cuisine.

SALMON WITH BASIL, PEPPERS, AND CHAMPAGNE MIGNONETTE

Serves 4

35 shallots
1 tablespoon olive oil
2 tablespoons freshly ground black pepper
1 25-ounce bottle champagne vinegar
4 6-ounce salmon fillets
Salt and pepper
20 large fresh basil leaves
2 sweet red peppers, sliced horizontally
2 yellow peppers, sliced horizontally

To make the sauce, peel the shallots and slice horizontally into thin rings. Coat a stainless steel or enamel saucepan lightly with the olive oil, add the shallots and pepper, and heat over a low flame just until warm. Add the vinegar and again heat just until warm. Remove from the heat and let sit for 1 hour.

Season the salmon fillets with salt and pepper and bake in a 375° oven until just rare, from 6 to 10 minutes. Steam the basil leaves and sliced peppers for 2 minutes. Place on top of the salmon and ladle 2 tablespoons of the sauce over each portion.

NOTE: Since very little fat is used in this recipe, it is a good dish for people watching their diets. Roasted new potatoes and steamed baby squash with blossoms make attractive accompaniments.

WEST END CAFÉ
—
WASHINGTON, D.C.

GRILLED SALMON WITH FRESH FRUIT COULIS

Serves 6

6 6-ounce salmon fillets
Flour
Vegetable oil

FRESH FRUIT COULIS

6 peaches, apricots, or nectarines, blanched for 10
    seconds, peeled, and pitted, *or* 6 plums, unpeeled
1 tablespoon chopped fresh mint, thyme, cilantro,
    or other herb
1 tablespoon rice vinegar
1 tablespoon lemon juice
Salt and pepper to taste

To make the coulis, roughly chop the fruit and purée
it with the rest of the ingredients in a food processor.
    Dust the salmon with the flour, shaking off the
excess, and brush with the oil. Grill over mesquite or
hardwood coals until barely cooked through. Serve
with the coulis.

This popular Café Sport preparation can be varied in many ways. Any white fish can be substituted for the salmon, and in any quantity, and the choice of herb for the coulis is up to you. The coulis will keep well in the refrigerator for as long as a week.

CAFÉ SPORT

—

SEATTLE

There is a cozy, warm feeling about the Union Square Café. Meals are served in three different areas, including an oyster bar that makes the café a comfortable choice for single diners. Dark green wainscoting, creamy white walls, cherry floors, and simple bistro chairs create an atmosphere that encourages conversation among the diverse patrons — from artists in sweatshirts to professionals in pinstripes. Grilled tuna steak is far and away the menu's top seller.

MARINATED FILET MIGNON OF TUNA

Serves 2

2 8-ounce yellow-fin tuna steaks, 2 to 2½ inches thick
Shaved pickled ginger (sushi ginger) for garnish

MARINADE

1 cup soy sauce *or* teriyaki sauce
Juice of 1 lemon
¼ cup dry sherry
2 tablespoons finely chopped fresh ginger
¼ cup chopped green onions
1 clove garlic, minced
Dash of cayenne pepper
2 tablespoons freshly ground black pepper

Prepare the marinade by combining all of the ingredients. Place the tuna steaks in the marinade and refrigerate for 5 to 8 hours, turning them periodically.

Drain, reserving the marinade, and cook on a very hot grill for 1 to 2 minutes on all sides (top, bottom and sides), until the outside is charred brown and the center is just warm. Be careful to cook the tuna just until it is rare, to assure that it will be moist and tasty. Serve immediately, garnished with the pickled ginger. Spoon the remaining marinade over the top,

UNION SQUARE CAFÉ

—

NEW YORK CITY

to taste. Grilled vegetables, such as zucchini or baby eggplant, are an excellent accompaniment.

NOTE: The freshness and initial redness of the tuna are critical to the success of this recipe. For a less salty marinade, use less soy sauce and more lemon juice.

GRILLED TUNA WITH ROSEMARY BEURRE BLANC

Serves 6

½ cup fresh lemon juice
6 cloves garlic, smashed
1 teaspoon cracked black pepper
½ teaspoon salt
¼ cup olive oil
6 6-ounce pieces fresh albacore or yellow-fin tuna
6 sprigs fresh rosemary for garnish

Combine the first five ingredients to make a marinade and marinate the tuna for 1 hour (be sure it is only 1 hour). Remove the tuna from the marinade and grill the fish until it is medium rare to medium (a 1-inch piece should take about 8 minutes). Serve with Rosemary Beurre Blanc and add a small sprig of rosemary to each plate.

"PacBag," as it has come to be known by regular customers, is both a neighborhood gathering place and a restaurant attracting such celebrities as San Francisco's Mayor Dianne Feinstein, Shirley MacLaine, and Francis Ford Coppola. Grilled fish with reduction sauces and herb butters are mainstays of the entrée section of the menu.

PACIFIC
HEIGHTS
BAR & GRILL

—

SAN FRANCISCO

Rosemary Beurre Blanc

1½ tablespoons chopped shallots
¾ cup dry white wine
Dash of lemon juice
Pinch of white pepper
1 tablespoon heavy cream
2 tablespoons chopped fresh rosemary
1 cup butter

Combine all the ingredients except the butter in a heavy saucepan and reduce over medium heat until the liquid has almost disappeared. Turn off the heat and whisk in the butter 1 tablespoon at a time. Strain the sauce and adjust the seasoning.

RED SNAPPER BAKED IN CORN HUSKS

Serves 6

12 large corn husks
1 sweet red pepper, julienne-cut
1 yellow pepper, julienne-cut
1 green pepper, julienne-cut
1 red onion, julienne-cut
2 tomatoes, peeled, seeded, and julienne-cut
4 green onions, cut on the diagonal into small pieces
1 jalapeño pepper, seeded and diced
½ cup white wine
½ cup fish stock (see page 333)
1 small *jícama*
1 chayote squash
9 shrimp (about ½ pound)
½ cup unsalted butter
6 8-ounce snapper fillets
12 basil leaves
4 sprigs cilantro
Salt and pepper to taste
6 lemon wedges for garnish

Soak the corn husks in water for 1 hour, to keep them from burning during baking.

Combine the red, yellow, and green peppers, the red onion, the tomatoes, and the green onions and

Andrew Thomson, the executive chef at Café Pacific, was born in England and trained at hotels in England, France, and Italy. Though he no longer prepares the classic sauces of haute cuisine, he is grateful for the basic training he received. The menu he oversees is dominated by seafood dishes, always popular in landlocked Dallas.

CAFÉ PACIFIC

—

DALLAS

set aside. Add the jalapeño pepper to the wine and fish stock.

Julienne-cut the *jícama* and chayote squash and set aside. Clean the shrimp and cut each one, on the diagonal, into four pieces.

Lay 6 of the corn husks on a work surface and rub the inside of each with a little butter. Pour 1 tablespoon of the fish stock mixture into each husk and place a snapper fillet on top. Divide the pepper mixture among the six husks, spooning it on top of the fish. Top each fillet with 2 basil leaves, some cilantro, and 6 pieces of shrimp.

Transfer the husks to a baking pan and pour over the remaining fish stock mixture. Top with knobs of butter and sprinkle with the salt and pepper. Cover the fish with the remaining six corn husks and bake in a 375° oven for 20 minutes.

After making sure the fish is cooked through, place each fish package on a plate, remove the top husk, and randomly arrange the squash and *jícama* over the fish and around the plate. Pour over any remaining baking juices and serve with or without the top husk. Garnish each plate with a lemon wedge.

RED SNAPPER WITH MELON SAUCE

Serves 4

1 ripe honeydew melon, about 1½ pounds
12 tablespoons butter
4 6-ounce red snapper fillets
4 jumbo shrimp, peeled and deveined
½ cup flour seasoned with salt and pepper
Salt and pepper to taste

Cut the melon away from the rind and chop into 1-inch pieces. Sauté in 4 tablespoons of the butter for about 4 minutes, until tender. Purée in a blender or food processor and set aside in a saucepan.

Dip the red snapper and shrimp in the flour and shake to remove any excess. Sauté slowly in 6 tablespoons of the butter for about 6 minutes, turning once after 3 minutes. Remove from the pan and drain on paper towels.

Place the saucepan containing the melon over medium heat and add 2 tablespoons of the butter, stirring until it has melted and the sauce is hot. Place a snapper fillet in the center of each plate and top with a shrimp. Surround the fish with the melon sauce, covering the entire plate.

The menu at 56 East has a unique format. It changes every day, listing wines on one side and food on the other. When the menu is folded in a certain way, the foods line up with a selection of wines most appropriate for each dish. As many as forty different wines are available daily, by the taste (2 ounces), by the glass, or by the bottle.

56 EAST

—

ATLANTA

There is more to New Orleans than the French Quarter, and a ride on the famous streetcar line that runs down St. Charles Avenue will take you first through the lovely Garden District and then to the Uptown neighborhood, where Clancy's was one of the first "white tablecloth" restaurants. The bistro was opened in 1984 by a group of twelve businessmen who wanted a fine dining establishment with an unpretentious atmosphere and a casual dress code near their Uptown homes.

REDFISH NANTUA

Serves 4

12 tablespoons butter
2 tablespoons vegetable oil
4 6-ounce redfish fillets
Flour for dredging
Salt and pepper
½ pound crayfish or small shrimp
¼ teaspoon saffron threads
2 cloves garlic, minced
6 tablespoons brandy
1 cup heavy cream
Salt, white pepper, and cayenne to taste

Heat 4 tablespoons of the butter and the vegetable oil in a sauté pan. Dredge the redfish lightly with flour, knocking off the excess, and sprinkle with the salt and pepper. When the oil is hot, sauté the fish for 1 minute on each side. Move the fish to a baking pan and place in a 250° oven while you prepare the sauce in the same sauté pan.

Place the crayfish, saffron, and garlic in the sauté pan and cook for less than a minute. Add the brandy and cream and reduce by half. Whip in the remaining butter. Season with the salt, white pepper, and cayenne.

Place a redfish fillet on each plate and top with the sauce.

CLANCY'S

—

NEW ORLEANS

CAYENNE REDFISH WITH CREAMY GARLIC SAUCE

Serves 6

2 cups fresh breadcrumbs
1 teaspoon cayenne pepper
Salt to taste
6 7-ounce redfish fillets
1 cup butter, melted
Clarified butter for sautéing (see page 335)

Combine the breadcrumbs with the cayenne pepper and salt. Dip each fish fillet into the melted butter and then into the seasoned breadcrumbs. Pat the crumbs into the fish on both sides.

Heat the clarified butter in a large sauté pan. Cook the fish until the underside is brown; turn and brown the other side. (Do not let the fish brown too quickly or it will not be cooked through.)

Serve with Creamy Garlic Sauce and sautéed snow peas.

Creamy Garlic Sauce

Juice and grated zest of 4 medium (or 3 large)
  lemons
6 to 8 cloves garlic, minced, according to taste
1 cup sour cream
2 cups peanut oil
Salt and pepper to taste

Elouise Cooper (Ousie) has worked magic on a 1920s commercial building that once housed the Sunset Food Market. Part of the parking area in front has been made into a "verandah" sporting handsome chintz-covered rocking chairs and colorful window-boxes filled with flowers and herbs. On rainy days, the corrugated overhang has the effect of the proverbial tin roof.

OUISIE'S
—
HOUSTON

Place the lemon juice, zest, and garlic in the bowl of a food processor and blend well. Add the sour cream and incorporate. With the machine running, very slowly add the oil, as if you were making mayonnaise. The mixture should seem stiff. Season with salt and pepper.

MAHI-MAHI WITH TOMATO SAUCE

Serves 4

4 6-ounce mahi-mahi fillets
Salt and pepper to taste
2 tablespoons olive oil
Lemon wedges and chopped parsley for garnish

TOMATO SAUCE

2 tablespoons olive oil
2 cloves garlic, minced
8 fresh tomatoes, peeled, seeded, and diced
2 tablespoons tomato paste
2 teaspoons sherry wine vinegar
Salt and pepper to taste

CRUMB TOPPING

1 cup plain breadcrumbs
½ clove garlic, minced
3 tablespoons grated Manchego or Parmesan cheese
1 teaspoon oregano

To prepare the sauce, heat the olive oil in a sauté pan and add the garlic. When the garlic is aromatic

Part of the fun at Café Ba-Ba-Reeba! is the abundant décor. Humorous murals, one of them depicting Chicago politics past and present in the style of Picasso's Guernica, *and signs bearing witty Spanish proverbs cover the walls. Most of all, however, there is food everywhere — an open kitchen with mesquite grills, festoons of hanging hams, sausages, garlic, and peppers, and serving dishes on the bar filled with most of the nearly thirty different* tapas *offered every night.*

CAFÉ
BA-BA-REEBA!
—
CHICAGO

but not brown, add the tomatoes and tomato paste. Simmer, stirring, for about 5 minutes, until the mixture begins to get a little dry. Add the vinegar and salt and pepper and set aside.

Combine the ingredients for the crumb topping and set aside.

Salt and pepper the fish fillets. Brush a shallow baking pan large enough to hold the fillets in one layer with some of the olive oil, place the fish in the pan, and brush the top of the fish with the remaining oil. Sprinkle with the crumb topping and bake for 6 to 10 minutes in a 500° oven.

To serve, ladle some sauce onto each serving plate and place a fish fillet on top. Garnish with the lemon wedges and parsley and serve immediately.

Though evenings at the Balboa are bustling, lunchtime attracts neighborhood residents and businesspeople and allows for a more relaxed experience — a chance to enjoy the Old World décor, including a portrait of Balboa himself.

GRILLED MARINATED MONKFISH

Serves 6

1 bunch cilantro
2 cloves garlic
2 tablespoons lemon juice
¼ cup tahini (sesame seed paste)
½ cup peanut oil
6 6-ounce monkfish fillets
Salt and pepper to taste
12 Japanese eggplants, sliced lengthwise into 3
  slices each
¼ cup toasted sesame seeds

Place the cilantro, garlic, lemon juice, tahini, and peanut oil in the bowl of a food processor and blend for 2 to 3 minutes. Lay the fish fillets in a shallow glass or enamel pan, pour over the marinade, and marinate for roughly 1 hour. Grill the fish until done, adding salt and pepper during the cooking.

Salt and pepper the sliced eggplant and grill. Place the fish on individual serving plates and arrange the eggplant slices next to each fillet.

NOTE: Japanese eggplants are about 3 inches long and are available at many produce counters.

BALBOA CAFÉ

—

SAN FRANCISCO

CRABCAKES

Serves 6

1 loaf commercial white bread (not French bread),
  crusts removed
1 pound crabmeat
2 tablespoons chopped parsley
¼ teaspoon freshly ground pepper
½ small sweet red pepper, finely chopped
½ small green pepper, finely chopped
¼ cup finely chopped onion
Vegetable oil for frying
Coarse-grain mustard

MAYONNAISE

1 egg
1 tablespoon coarse-grain mustard
¾ cup oil (½ cup vegetable and ¼ cup olive)
2 teaspoons lemon juice
2 teaspoons red wine vinegar
3 shakes of Tabasco
Dash of Worcestershire sauce

First, make the mayonnaise. Put the egg and mustard in a blender or whisk by hand; gradually add the oil, blending continuously. Toward the end, slowly add the lemon juice, vinegar, Tabasco, and Worcestershire. Set aside.

    Using a food processor, make crumbs out of the bread. Place the crabmeat, mayonnaise, parsley, and

Tom Douglas, the executive chef and general manager, had worked at various Seattle restaurants before helping to open Café Sport in January 1984. Over the years, Douglas taught himself to cook by making a point of eating the best food available. A transplant from the East Coast, he once worked at the Hotel DuPont in Wilmington, Delaware, and was the first chef to offer crabcakes in Seattle.

CAFÉ SPORT

—

SEATTLE

pepper in a bowl. Mix in the red and green peppers and the onion. Add approximately half of the bread-crumbs, until the mixture feels pasty. Reserve the remaining crumbs.

Form the crab mixture into 12 patties and roll in the remaining breadcrumbs. Fry the cakes in a small amount of vegetable oil until they are golden on both sides. Drain on paper towels and serve with coarse-grain mustard.

SOFTSHELL CRABS WITH TOMATO CREAM SAUCE

Serves 6

6 eggs
2½ cups flour
2 teaspoons salt
2 teaspoons ground cumin
2 teaspoons pepper
2 teaspoons minced garlic
12 jumbo softshell crabs
3 cups cornmeal
1 cup clarified butter (see page 335)
Basil sprigs for garnish

TOMATO CREAM SAUCE

3 ripe tomatoes, peeled, seeded, and diced
½ cup fresh basil leaves, coarsely chopped
1 teaspoon minced garlic
2 tablespoons butter
2 cups heavy cream
1 teaspoon salt

Whisk the eggs for 1 minute, add ½ cup of the flour,
the salt, cumin, pepper, and garlic, and blend well.
Dredge the crabs in the remaining 2 cups flour and
toss lightly in the egg batter. Coat evenly with the
cornmeal and sauté in the clarified butter on both
sides until golden brown. Keep warm in a 300° oven
while you make the Tomato Cream Sauce.

USA CAFÉ
—
PHILADELPHIA

Sauté the tomatoes, basil, and garlic in the butter. Add the cream and salt and simmer until the sauce has thickened. Place two crabs on each of six individual serving plates and top with the sauce (or serve the sauce on the side). Garnish the plate with a sprig of basil or layer basil leaves on top of the crab.

CITY CAFE

City Café takes its name from the hundreds of like-named establishments in cities and towns all over the United States. Mardi Schma, its owner and chef, likes nothing better than taking driving trips around the country, picking up new recipe ideas wherever she goes. The resulting cuisine is all her own.

PAN-FRIED OYSTERS EN BROCHETTE

Serves 6

36 oysters
12 mushrooms
12 pieces thick bacon (about the size of the mushrooms)
1½ tablespoons each salt, garlic powder, paprika, and cayenne
1 teaspoon pepper
¾ teaspoon each white pepper, onion powder, oregano, and thyme
Flour for dusting
Bacon fat

Using six wooden skewers, alternately thread 6 oysters, 2 mushrooms, and 2 pieces of bacon on each one. Combine the spices and sprinkle the mixture on all sides of each skewer. Dust the skewers with flour and fry until brown in bacon fat. Drain on paper towels and serve immediately.

CITY CAFÉ

—

DALLAS

SHRIMP AND ANDOUILLE SAUSAGE WITH CREOLE MUSTARD SAUCE

Serves 4

16 jumbo shrimp, peeled with tail left on
1 pound andouille sausage, diagonally sliced in
    ½-inch slices
2 sweet red peppers, cut in 1-inch squares
2 green peppers, cut in 1-inch squares
Creole Seafood Seasoning (recipe follows)
1 pound butter, melted

Thread the shrimp, sausage, and red and green peppers on four skewers in an alternating pattern. Sprinkle with the seafood seasoning and brush with melted butter. Cook over a grill, turning and basting with the melted butter, until the shrimp are cooked through. Serve with Creole Mustard Sauce (recipe follows) and rice.

Creole Seafood Seasoning

Makes ¾ cup

8 tablespoons salt
2 tablespoons granulated garlic
½ tablespoon granulated onion
½ teaspoon cayenne pepper
2 tablespoons pepper

Though it's in the heart of the French Quarter, on the beaten path of thousands of tourists a year, Mr. B's focuses on its New Orleans clientele. A handsome brasserie décor of etched glass, polished oak, white linen, dark green leather, and yards of brass railing makes a relaxed setting for business or pleasure. The open hickory-stoked grill can be seen from almost every table.

MR. B'S
—
NEW ORLEANS

½ teaspoon thyme
½ teaspoon oregano
2 tablespoons paprika

Blend all the ingredients in a mixing bowl and store in a sealed container.

Creole Mustard Sauce

Makes ¾ cup

1 cup dry vermouth
1 teaspoon white wine vinegar
1 teaspoon chopped shallots
1 teaspoon chopped fresh tarragon
1 tablespoon diced peeled roasted sweet red pepper
½ cup heavy cream
1 teaspoon Dijon mustard
1 teaspoon Creole mustard
1 tablespoon unsalted butter
Salt and cayenne pepper to taste

Combine the vermouth, vinegar, and shallots in a sauté pan. Reduce over high heat to approximately 2 tablespoons. Add the tarragon, red pepper, and cream and cook for 1 to 2 minutes to reduce slightly. Swirl in both mustards and cook for less than a minute. Swirl in the butter and salt and cayenne pepper.

GULF SHRIMP WITH POBLANO BUTTER

Serves 4

16 Gulf shrimp (colossal size), peeled and deveined

POBLANO BUTTER

½ pound unsalted butter, softened
1½ poblano peppers, roasted, seeded, and finely
  diced
1 tablespoon minced cilantro
1 tablespoon minced garlic
Salt and pepper to taste

Prepare the shrimp and set aside in the refrigerator. Combine the ingredients for the poblano butter. Thread the shrimp on skewers and grill over hot coals or a gas grill, basting with the poblano butter. Serve with rice and dab the remaining butter on top.

NOTE: The poblano butter can be doubled, with any left over frozen for later use with grilled fish, chicken, omelettes, or rice.

The interior at Indigo is meant to look beat-up and weathered, so there are brown paper table coverings, unfinished hardwood floors, and rough plaster walls. A six-foot sailfish dangles from the center of a sky blue ceiling and rafters, and a fully stocked saltwater aquarium stands near the front door. All this spells success, and the wait is at least an hour on weekends. A 1956 jukebox entertains those standing in line.

INDIGO COASTAL
GRILL
—
ATLANTA

At Napoleon House the drinks are great, the small menu fills the bill, and the ambience is peerless. Wrought-iron lanterns with topaz glass hang from the ceilings, dimly illuminating the crumbling plaster walls hung with posters and paintings, many of them Napoleonic memorabilia. An eighteen-foot wooden bar lines the main room, and wide low arches lead to the back rooms and patio. In the background there is always classical music, including patrons' requests — a holdover from the early days, when Sal Impastato's uncle played Caruso recordings in his grocery store.

JAMBALAYA

Serves 8

1 pound smoked sausage, sliced
1 pound boneless chicken breasts or a combination
  of light and dark meat
½ cup vegetable oil
2 cups chopped onion
2 cups chopped green pepper
2 cups chopped celery
2 cups chopped green onion
4 cloves garlic, minced
2 16-ounce cans tomatoes, drained and chopped
1 teaspoon thyme
2 teaspoons black pepper
½ teaspoon cayenne pepper
2 teaspoons salt
2 cups long grain rice
½ teaspoon ground cumin
½ teaspoon allspice
3 cups beef bouillon
1 pound shrimp, peeled and deveined

In a Dutch oven, sauté the sausage and chicken in the oil until the chicken loses its pink color. Add the onion, green pepper, celery, green onion, and garlic and sauté until the vegetables are tender. Add the remaining ingredients, except the shrimp, let the mixture come to a boil, cover, and cook over low heat until the liquid is nearly absorbed. Add the shrimp and continue cooking until the rice is done (about 30 minutes in all).

NOTE: If you wish, you may add the shrimp after the heat has been turned off. They will cook through as you blend them into the hot jambalaya.

PASTA

Tagliolini with Smoked Chicken and Walnut Sauce
Fettuccine Roberto
Three-Dot Fettuccine
Farfalle Due Colore con Verdure
Red Chili Pasta with Salsa, Prawns, and Cilantro
Penne with Lobster and Green Tomato Sauce
Linguine with Spicy Mussel Sauce
Whole-Wheat Pennette with Olive Pesto and Bufala
   di Mozzarella

TAGLIOLINI WITH SMOKED CHICKEN AND WALNUT SAUCE

Serves 6

1 cup walnuts
2 cups heavy cream
3 medium zucchini, cut in half and sliced thinly
    lengthwise
1 pound fresh tagliolini pasta, cooked in boiling
    water for 1 to 2 minutes and drained
10 ounces smoked chicken breast meat, cut in strips
¾ cup grated Pecorino Romano cheese
¼ teaspoon nutmeg
1½ teaspoons salt
1½ teaspoons white pepper

Toast the walnuts in a 350° oven for about 15 minutes. Purée in a food processor until finely ground. Set aside. In a large saucepan, bring the cream to a simmer over medium heat. Add the zucchini and ground walnuts and return to a simmer. Add the pasta and chicken, bring the mixture to a simmer, and remove from the heat. Stir in the grated cheese, nutmeg, and salt and pepper. Serve immediately.

NOTE: If you are unable to find tagliolini — a pasta that is slightly narrower than fettuccine but broader than linguine — fresh white fettuccine may be substituted.

Michela's is a stylish restaurant in the renovated Carter Ink Building on the Charles River, next to MIT and a growing complex of high-tech establishments. Michela Larson and her chef, Todd English, offer inventive North Italian cooking in three settings — a sunny atrium café, a spacious formal dining room, and an abundantly stocked take-out counter.

MICHELA'S
—
CAMBRIDGE,
MASSACHUSETTS

Along with the usual categories, the menu at Afterwords has a section called House Rules, with no less than seventeen admonitions, provisos, and answers to frequently asked questions — everything from ''We will not accept personal checks'' to ''We no longer serve Coca-Cola products.''

FETTUCCINE ROBERTO

Serves 6

2 shallots, chopped
4 tablespoons butter
3 tablespoons flour
½ cup Scotch whisky
1 quart half-and-half
½ cup capers, rinsed and drained
6 ounces smoked salmon, cut in squares
1 teaspoon pepper
18 ounces fettuccine

Sauté the shallots in the butter until tender. Add the flour, stir to make a paste, and cook for 3 minutes. Add the Scotch and stir; add the half-and-half. Bring the sauce to a boil, stirring, and simmer until it is thick and smooth. Add the capers, salmon, and pepper, and adjust the seasoning if necessary.

Cook the fettuccine in a large pot of boiling water according to package instructions. Drain well and toss with the salmon-caper sauce. Serve immediately.

KRAMERBOOKS
& AFTERWORDS
CAFÉ

—

WASHINGTON, D.C.

Washington Square Bar & Grill.

THREE-DOT FETTUCCINE

Serves 2

8 tablespoons chicken stock
1 cup heavy cream
6 threads saffron
4 thin slices pancetta, cut in ¼-inch squares
2 cloves garlic, minced
1 teaspoon butter
10 ounces fettuccine
Salt and pepper to taste
Roasted red, yellow, and green peppers for garnish

Combine the stock and the cream and reduce by half over high heat. Rub the saffron threads between your fingers to crush them and fold into the hot liquid, to steep until the liquid cools. Cook the pancetta and garlic in the butter over low heat until the fat from the pancetta is rendered and the garlic is soft.

Cook the fettuccine in a large pot of boiling salted water until it is *al dente*. Drain.

Pour the cream mixture into a sauté pan, add the pancetta and garlic, and slowly heat the sauce. Season with the salt and pepper. Toss the pasta with the hot sauce. Serve in hot bowls, garnished with tiny dots of the three colors of pepper, cut with a #8 round pastry tip.

NOTE: This recipe can be expanded to serve up to 8 people by simply multiplying the quantities by two, three, or four.

WSB&G, as it is familiarly known, is the headquarters for local shenanigans of all kinds, including the annual dinner honoring the winner of the Herb Caen Write-Alike contest. Anyone who has ever read the San Francisco Chronicle knows Herb Caen's column, the inimitable source for "who's doing what when." Mary Etta Moose, the wife of partner Ed Moose, oversees the kitchen here and devised this dish for the 1986 dinner, naming it after Caen's three-dot writing style. For those who choose to forgo authenticity, the pepper garnish can be cut in strips instead of tiny dots.

WASHINGTON
SQUARE
BAR & GRILL
—
SAN FRANCISCO

Anthony Mantuano has had a lifelong attachment to Italian food. His grandparents ran an old-fashioned Italian grocery in Kenosha, Wisconsin, selling freshly butchered meats and sausages and vegetables from their own garden, and home-made pastas and regional specialties were common fare. Today the greatest relaxation for Mantuano and his wife, Cathy, head captain at Spiaggia, is a trip back to Kenosha, where their parents insist on doing the cooking.

FARFALLE DUE COLORE CON VERDURE

Serves 6

6 tablespoons butter
8 ounces broccoli flowerets
24 snow pea pods
3 cups heavy cream
½ teaspoon salt
1 teaspoon pepper
6 tablespoons grated Parmigiano Reggiano or Granna Padana cheese
1 pound farfalle (butterfly pasta), half tomato and half spinach

Melt the butter in a sauté pan. Add the broccoli and snow peas and sauté until golden brown. Add the cream, salt, pepper, and cheese and reduce until the sauce is the desired thickness. Cook the pasta *al dente* and drain well. Add the pasta to the cream mixture and toss to coat evenly. Serve immediately.

CAFÉ SPIAGGIA

CHICAGO

RED CHILI PASTA WITH SALSA, PRAWNS, AND CILANTRO

Serves 4

20 prawns
2 ounces peeled and trimmed fresh ginger,
  julienne-cut
Vegetable oil for sautéing
Salsa
4 tablespoons butter
1 tablespoon chopped cilantro
1 recipe Red Chili Pasta (about 1½ pounds)

RED CHILI PASTA

¼ cup ground red chili (New Mexico hot)
3 cups flour
2 teaspoons salt
1 teaspoon ground cumin
3 eggs
1 tablespoon vegetable oil

SALSA *(makes about 1 quart)*

10 ripe tomatoes, peeled, seeded, and diced
1 tablespoon lemon juice
1 tablespoon lime juice
1½ tablespoons red wine vinegar
5 green onions, chopped
1 jalapeño pepper, seeded and chopped
½ teaspoon salt
¼ teaspoon freshly ground pepper

Although a hamburger is always available at Café Sport, most of the menu reflects the popularity of both Oriental and American Southwest cuisines. If you don't want to go to the trouble of making your own pasta for this dish, fresh red chili pasta is sometimes available in specialty food shops.

CAFÉ SPORT
—
SEATTLE

3 tablespoons chopped parsley
¼ cup chopped cilantro

First, prepare the pasta. In the large bowl of an electric mixer, combine the dry ingredients, then add the eggs and the oil. Mix until the dough comes together, stopping occasionally to scrape the mixer blades. Place the dough in a plastic bag and let stand for at least an hour before rolling and cutting in thin strips (refrigerate overnight if possible).

Next, make the salsa by combining all the ingredients. Set aside.

Sauté the prawns and the ginger strips in the oil for 2 or 3 minutes. When the prawns are half done, toss in 8 tablespoons of salsa, the butter, and the cilantro. Continue cooking until the butter melts and the shrimp have turned red (be careful not to overcook). Keep the prawns warm.

Cook the pasta in boiling salted water for 1 to 2 minutes. Drain and toss immediately with the prawns and their drippings. Serve immediately.

PENNE WITH LOBSTER AND GREEN TOMATO SAUCE

Serves 6

3 1½-pound lobsters
1 large Spanish onion, chopped
2 tablespoons plus ½ cup olive oil
12 to 15 green tomatoes or tomatillos, blanched,
    peeled, seeded, and chopped
¼ cup chopped fresh oregano *or* 1½ tablespoons
    dried
1 tablespoon chopped garlic
2 cups chicken stock
½ cup white wine
16 ounces penne (quill-shaped pasta)
3 ounces prosciutto, julienne-cut
¾ cup grated Parmesan cheese
Sprigs of oregano for garnish

Plunge the lobsters into boiling water and boil for 10 to 12 minutes. Drain and let cool. Remove the tail meat and roughly chop it. Reserve the claws for garnish.

In a saucepan, sweat the onion in the 2 tablespoons olive oil for 2 minutes. Add the green tomatoes, oregano, and garlic and sweat for 5 minutes. Add the stock and wine and simmer for 12 to 15 minutes. Remove from the heat and purée half the

In preparation for launching her restaurant, Michela Larson spent several months in Italy to become familiar with various regional styles of cooking, and she saw to it that her chef, Todd English, did the same. As a result, Michela's offers a light, elegant cuisine that is inventive but still true to basic Italian precepts. Seasonal ingredients are a springboard for many of English's innovations.

MICHELA'S
—
CAMBRIDGE,
MASSACHUSETTS

mixture in a food processor. Combine both halves again and set aside.

Bring a large pot of water to a boil and cook the pasta according to package instructions. While the pasta is cooking, heat the ½ cup olive oil in a sauté pan and add the lobster and prosciutto. Cook for 3 minutes over medium heat. Add the tomato sauce and bring to a simmer. Drain the penne and add it to the sauce, stirring until thoroughly mixed. Add the Parmesan. Transfer to a serving platter and garnish with sprigs of oregano and the lobster claws.

LINGUINE WITH SPICY MUSSEL SAUCE

Serves 8

1½ pounds linguine, preferably fresh
1 cup dry white wine
½ cup butter
Juice of 1 lemon
4 pounds mussels, scrubbed and beards removed
½ cup chopped parsley
1 lemon, cut in wedges, for garnish

SAUCE

8 to 10 cloves garlic, sliced paper thin
1 ounce jalapeño peppers, seeded and thinly sliced
2 tablespoons olive oil
2 pounds tomatoes, peeled, seeded, and chopped
1 teaspoon basil
1 teaspoon thyme

First, prepare the sauce. Lightly sauté the garlic and peppers in the olive oil until the garlic softens but does not brown. Add the tomatoes, basil, and thyme and simmer gently for 5 to 10 minutes, stirring frequently.

In a Dutch oven, reduce the wine and butter by half, add the sauce and lemon juice, top with the mussels, and cover tightly. Steam over medium heat just until the mussel shells open.

In a large amount of boiling salted water, cook the

Wine tastings and winemaker dinners are regular features at Enoteca. In addition to traditional tastings, comparing similar wines from various vintners, some surprising combinations of wine and food have been tasted — including Cabernet and chocolate. One of the liveliest of the winemaker dinners was Flamenco Night, complete with dancers and an authentic Spanish menu.

ENOTECA
WINE SHOP &
RESTAURANT
—
SEATTLE

linguine until *al dente* and drain. Divide the linguine among eight dinner or soup plates, top with the mussels and sauce, and sprinkle with the parsley. Garnish each serving with a lemon wedge.

WHOLE-WHEAT PENNETTE WITH OLIVE PESTO AND BUFALA DI MOZZARELLA

Serves 4 to 6

½ cup extra virgin olive oil
1 clove garlic, minced
6 tomatoes, peeled, seeded, and diced
2 tablespoons chopped fresh basil
Salt and pepper to taste
3 ounces olive pesto (Olivada)
1 pound whole-wheat pasta, preferably with bran, cooked *al dente*
8 ounces smoked Bufala di Mozzarella

In a large casserole, heat the olive oil. Add the garlic, tomatoes, basil, and salt and pepper and cook for 10 to 15 minutes. Add the olive pesto. Add the pasta and mozzarella to the sauce, mix well, and serve.

NOTE: To make your own olive pesto, purée 3 ounces pitted black olives with 3 tablespoons olive oil.

SALADS

SALADS

Sorrel Chicken Salad
Chicken and Tortellini Salad
Marigold Mint Chicken Salad
Smoked Chicken and Ham Salad
Fisherman's Salad
Thai Seafood Salad
Warm Shrimp Salad
Oriental Shrimp and Pasta Salad
Italian Rice Salad
Shrimp and Whole-Wheat Fettuccine Salad
Mussel Salad with Mango Mustard Dressing
Lobster Margarita
Bay Scallop, Clementine, and Baby Banana Salad
Tuna and White Bean Salad
New Wave Niçoise
Bean and Beef Salad
Mediterranean Antipasto Salad
Chicken Liver and Spinach Salad
Spinach Salad with Duck Cracklings
Northwest Potato Salad
Texas Caviar

USACAFE

AT THE COMMISSARY

This is a popular summer choice at USA Café, with the slightly sour taste of the sorrel enhanced by the lemon juice in the mayonnaise. If you are tired of waiting for this green to show up at your produce market, grow it at home if the climate is fairly cool and damp.

SORREL CHICKEN SALAD

Serves 6

2 pounds boneless chicken breasts
1 cup water
Salt and pepper to taste
Assorted fresh greens dressed with vinaigrette
1 avocado, peeled and sliced
2 oranges, cut in sections between membranes

SORREL MAYONNAISE

3 egg yolks
1 teaspoon salt
½ teaspoon dry mustard
½ teaspoon freshly ground black pepper
Juice of 2 lemons
1 cup olive oil
¼ pound sorrel leaves

Place the chicken breasts on a jelly roll pan and cover with the water and salt and pepper. Cover the pan with foil and bake at 350° for 15 minutes or until just cooked through. Remove from the oven and let cool. Cut into bite-size pieces.

To make the mayonnaise, place the egg yolks, seasonings, and lemon juice in a bowl and whisk to combine. Add the olive oil drop by drop, whisking vigorously until the mixture thickens. Chop all but 1 handful of the sorrel and add to the mayonnaise.

Toss the chicken pieces with the mayonnaise.

USA CAFÉ
—
PHILADELPHIA

Place freshly dressed greens on each plate and top with the chicken. Garnish the plates with slices of avocado and orange sections and the remaining sorrel leaves rolled and cut in strips (a chiffonade).

ERASMUS CAFÉ

CHICKEN AND TORTELLINI SALAD

Serves 6 to 8

1 pound tortellini with meat
6 boneless chicken breast halves, poached and skin removed
1 green pepper, cut in ½-inch squares
1 sweet red pepper, cut in ½-inch squares
4 ounces pine nuts, sautéed in butter until golden
1 6½-ounce can pitted black olives
1 6½-ounce can Spanish olives
1 6½-ounce can chick-peas
½ pound mushrooms, sliced
1 cup vinaigrette (see page 334)
Chopped parsley for garnish

Prepare the tortellini according to package instructions, drain well, and set aside. Cut the chicken in ½-inch pieces and place in a large bowl with the tortellini and the remaining ingredients. Gradually add the vinaigrette to the salad until the mixture is adequately coated. Serve at room temperature or slightly chilled, garnished with the parsley.

MARIGOLD MINT CHICKEN SALAD

Serves 6

1 cup Basmati or wild rice
¾ cup blanched almonds
4 whole chicken breasts, boned and skinned
Salt and pepper
1 bunch watercress, stems removed
1 cup chopped celery

VINAIGRETTE

½ teaspoon Dijon mustard
3 tablespoons white vinegar
½ teaspoon salt
½ teaspoon pepper
1 tablespoon chopped marigold mint or fresh
    tarragon
½ cup vegetable oil
¼ cup olive oil

Cook the rice according to package instructions. Drain and rinse in cool water. Set aside. Toast the almonds in a 350° oven until they are golden brown. Cool the almonds and coarsely chop by hand or in a food processor.

Remove the fat from the chicken breasts. Sprinkle with the salt and pepper and bake in a 325° oven for

Unlike many speedy, cafeteria-style breakfast and lunch spots, City Market makes a point of using only fresh ingredients, and all mayonnaises and salad dressings are made in its own kitchen. The menu for the five days of the week is printed on Monday and is available at the cash desk for those who want to be sure to catch their favorite dish. The marigold mint called for in this popular salad is a Mexican herb available locally; tarragon may be substituted in other parts of the country.

CITY MARKET

—

DALLAS

15 to 18 minutes. Cool the chicken and dice the meat.

To make the vinaigrette, place the mustard, vinegar, salt, pepper, and marigold mint or tarragon in the bowl of a food processor. Process for 30 seconds, then slowly add the oils in a stream while the machine is running. Taste and adjust the seasonings.

Place the chicken, rice, watercress, celery, almonds, and vinaigrette in a large bowl and toss to mix well. Serve chilled.

NOTE: Basmati rice comes from Pakistan and is available at health food stores or specialty food shops. Its long, slender grains do not burst during cooking.

SUZANNE'S

SMOKED CHICKEN AND HAM SALAD

Serves 8 to 10

1½ pounds ham, julienne-cut
5 smoked chicken breasts, boned, skinned, and
   julienne-cut
1 pound red potatoes, preferably red bliss
1 pound green beans
½ pound small zucchini, sliced thin
1 cup thinly sliced carrots
¼ cup finely chopped parsley
Salt and pepper to taste

DRESSING

⅓ cup red wine vinegar
2 tablespoons Dijon mustard
1½ teaspoons dried basil
1 shallot, finely minced
1 cup olive oil

Make the dressing by combining the first four ingredients and slowly adding the olive oil. Mix well.

Cook the potatoes in boiling water until just tender. Drain, cool, and chill. When cold, peel and cut in thick slices. Blanch the green beans in boiling water for 4 minutes. Drain, refresh in cold water, drain again, and set aside. Follow the same procedure for the zucchini and carrots and set aside.

As one might expect, both the food and the décor at Suzanne's reflect the beauty and standards of its museum surroundings. The two rooms of the café are paneled in light oak, with cane-backed chairs and tables to match. Fresh flowers in museum-quality vases grace the tables, and paintings from the collection hang on the white walls. The effect is lovely and provides a soothing space for a quick meal or a leisurely visit with friends.

SUZANNE'S CAFÉ
AT THE PHILLIPS
COLLECTION
—
WASHINGTON, D.C.

In a large bowl, combine the ham, chicken, potatoes, vegetables, parsley, and dressing. Toss, taste, and add the salt and pepper.

NOTE: If smoked chicken breasts are not available, plain cooked breast meat may be used, though the salad will lack some zip. To compensate, substitute balsamic vinegar in the dressing and add more basil and shallots.

Washington Square Bar & Grill.

FISHERMAN'S SALAD

Serves 6

½ pound cleaned calamari (see Note below)
½ pound sea or bay scallops
Shredded greens

MARINADE

1 cup celery, sliced thin
¼ cup thinly sliced sweet onion
6 green onions, sliced into thin diagonals
2 tablespoons minced parsley
1 tablespoon oregano flowers *or* 1 tablespoon
   fresh marjoram
⅓ cup extra virgin olive oil
¼ teaspoon freshly ground pepper
Up to ¼ cup white wine vinegar (added a little at a
   time until the marinade is tart enough for your
   taste)

Cut the cleaned calamari into thin rings, cutting the tentacles in halves or quarters if they are large. Cut the scallops into strips of the same size (leave bay scallops whole). Holding the calamari rings in a strainer, colander, or towel, lower them into simmering water for a count of 15; lift them out the minute they whiten, before they become tough. Dip them into cold water and then towel dry. Combine with the raw scallops.

Combine the ingredients for the marinade, add the fish, and marinate in the refrigerator overnight or

Sam Deitsch and Ed and Mary Etta Moose opened the doors at the *Washington Square Bar & Grill* in 1973, taking over from an Italian bar that had operated in the building since 1935. Sam and Ed had known each other in St. Louis, where Sam owned a bar and Ed worked as a fund-raiser and alumni director for St. Louis University. Ed met Mary Etta through Sam, and by the mid-sixties all three had ended up in San Francisco. Mary Etta is a superb cook and has become an aficionado of life in North Beach. She is the co-author of **The Flavor of North Beach**, a guide to restaurants, coffeehouses, and bakeries in the area, where this recipe was originally printed.

WASHINGTON
SQUARE
BAR & GRILL
—
SAN FRANCISCO

longer. Bring the fish to room temperature before serving, well drained, on a bed of shredded greens.

NOTE: To clean calamari, pull out the heads and tentacles, cut the tentacles off above the eyes, and pop out the hard little round, bitter-tasting mouth, located in the center of the tentacles. Working under cold running water, loosen the strip of plastic spine and pull it out of the body, squeezing and washing away all the insides and rubbing off the skin.

THAI SEAFOOD SALAD

Serves 6

½ pound sea scallops
½ pound shrimp, peeled and deveined
1 cup lime juice (4 to 6 limes)
¼ teaspoon crushed red pepper flakes
2 cups broccoli flowerets
2 3¾-ounce packages cellophane noodles
1 head Boston lettuce
8 radishes, thinly sliced
½ cucumber, peeled and thinly sliced
Salt and pepper
Chive spears for garnish

DRESSING

1 clove garlic
3 tablespoons lime juice
1½ tablespoons tamari sauce
1 dried hot red pepper (or to taste)
2 tablespoons olive oil
2 teaspoons hot chili oil (or to taste)

Steam the scallops until half cooked, about 2 minutes. Steam the shrimp also until half cooked, about 1 minute. Place the scallops and shrimp in a nonreactive container and toss with the lime juice and red pepper flakes. Refrigerate, stirring occasionally, for about 3 hours.

Cook the broccoli flowerets in boiling salted water

The décor at West End Café is both restful and elegant, featuring a pleasant combination of green plants, imaginatively chosen fresh flowers, attractive fabrics, and interesting artwork. The walls of two of the rooms are hung with Erté prints and Karsh photographs of notables, including George Bernard Shaw, Muhammad Ali, Winston Churchill, and Norman Mailer. In the bar area is a collection of pictures of Monet's gardens at Giverny.

WEST END CAFÉ

—

WASHINGTON, D.C.

until tender but still crisp and refresh in cold water. Pour boiling water over the cellophane noodles and let sit for about 5 minutes, until they are tender but not mushy. Drain the noodles.

Combine the ingredients for the dressing and toss with the shrimp, scallops, and broccoli. Arrange the lettuce leaves, radishes, and cucumbers on individual salad plates. Place a handful of cellophane noodles on each plate, then mound the seafood salad on top. Garnish with 2 or 3 whole chive spears.

Clancy's

WARM SHRIMP SALAD

Serves 6

½ cup olive oil
24 large shrimp, shelled and deveined
4 tablespoons dry vermouth
Pesto
3 tablespoons red wine vinegar
6 tablespoons balsamic vinegar
½ teaspoon sugar
Salt and white pepper to taste
2 fresh tomatoes, diced
Lettuce leaves

PESTO

4 tablespoons chopped fresh basil
5 cloves garlic, chopped
2 tablespoons pine nuts
4 tablespoons freshly grated Parmesan cheese
2 tablespoons olive oil

First make the pesto, placing all the ingredients in the bowl of a food processor and blending until the mixture is smooth. Set aside.

Heat 1 tablespoon of the olive oil in a sauté pan. Add the shrimp and sauté for 1 minute, stirring frequently. Add the vermouth and cook for 30 seconds. Add the pesto and mix. Add the vinegars, sugar, and the rest of the olive oil. Bring to a simmer, season with the salt and white pepper, and remove from the heat. Add the tomatoes and serve on lettuce leaves.

What is now a chic bistro used to be the corner grocery store and then a neighborhood bar and sandwich shop owned by Ed and Betty Clancy. Their sign now hangs over the bar and ''Clancy's'' is written in large red script on the many windows that run along two sides of the restaurant. The décor is simple, letting the white linen tablecloths and tuxedoed waiters stand out. The clientele is varied and casual, however, and many regulars bypass the restaurant and head straight for the small bar area, where the TV is always tuned to the sports channel.

CLANCY'S

—

NEW ORLEANS

There is nothing new about pasta salads, but this one is an all-time favorite with Rebecca's customers — both for eating in and taking out.

ORIENTAL SHRIMP AND PASTA SALAD

Serves 6 to 8

1½ pounds baby shrimp, peeled and deveined
¾ pound linguine, cooked *al dente* and drained
1 bunch green onions, chopped
2 cups drained water chestnuts, rinsed, dried, and sliced
¼ cup sesame seeds, toasted
3 cups sliced radishes
¼ pound snow peas, blanched for 30 seconds and refreshed in cold water

DRESSING

1 tablespoon minced fresh ginger
1 tablespoon minced garlic
¼ cup sesame oil
¼ cup sake
Juice of 3 oranges
2 tablespoons honey
2 tablespoons white vinegar

First, prepare the dressing. Sauté the ginger and garlic in the sesame oil, add the sake, and reduce by half over high heat. Add the remaining ingredients and again reduce by half.

Blanch the shrimp in boiling water for 1 minute, refresh with cold water, and drain thoroughly. Com-

REBECCA'S

—

BOSTON

bine with the remaining ingredients and gradually add the dressing, tossing gently, until the mixture is well coated.

ITALIAN RICE SALAD

Serves 6 to 8

2 cups arborio rice
2 tablespoons butter
2 tablespoons olive oil
4 to 5 cups hot chicken stock
1 pound small cooked shrimp
1 14-ounce can artichoke hearts, quartered
3 tablespoons capers, drained
3 tablespoons chopped parsley
3 tablespoons coarsely chopped fresh basil, when available
Lettuce leaves
Tomato slices for garnish

DRESSING

¾ cup olive oil
¼ cup lemon juice
Salt and freshly ground pepper

Sauté the rice in the butter and oil until the color changes to white. Add 1 cup hot chicken stock and cook slowly, at a low temperature, stirring fre-

The trio behind this café are Susan Snider, Martha Johnson, and Nancy Bullock. Martha and Nancy are sisters, and Martha and Susan formerly owned a restaurant in Carmel, California. Before moving back to the city, they first spent some time in Europe, where they became familiar with the stand-up coffee bar–café. The concept was brought to Fillmore Street when Trio Café opened in May 1985.

TRIO CAFÉ

—

SAN FRANCISCO

quently, until all the stock is absorbed. Add more chicken stock, 1 cup at a time, until the rice is *al dente*. Stir occasionally but not too much (or the rice will become mushy). The rice should be sticky and a bit chewy. Cool.

Prepare the dressing by combining all the ingredients.

When the rice is cool, toss it with a fork and add the shrimp, artichoke hearts, capers, parsley, and basil. Gradually add the dressing while mixing the ingredients together. Serve on a bed of lettuce and garnish with tomato slices.

NOTE: The rice may be cooked a day ahead and refrigerated, but be sure to bring it to room temperature before mixing with the other ingredients.

SHRIMP AND WHOLE-WHEAT FETTUCCINE SALAD

Serves 6

12 shrimp (about ¾ pound)
3 ounces green beans (preferably *haricots vert*)
8 ounces whole-wheat fettuccine
1 tomato, peeled, seeded, and julienne-cut
1 large onion, diced
Salt and pepper to taste
12 leaves radicchio
12 leaves red lettuce
12 leaves Boston lettuce

DRESSING

1 teaspoon coarse-grain mustard
1 tablespoon chopped shallots
1 clove garlic, minced
6 tablespoons olive oil
2 tablespoons wine or champagne vinegar
1 tablespoon chopped fresh basil
Salt and freshly ground pepper to taste

Cook the shrimp in their shells in seasoned water until just done. Cool in ice water, peel, and devein. Cut each shrimp into four pieces, on the diagonal. Set aside. Blanch the beans in boiling water for 2 or 3 minutes (depending on their size), drain, refresh with cold water, and drain again. Set aside. Cook

A fifteen-minute drive from the center of Dallas, Café Pacific offers a pleasant alternative to bustling downtown lunch choices. In addition to businesspeople, the lunch crowd includes shoppers taking a break from Gucci, Laura Ashley, and similar emporia. At night frequent patrons include Highland Park residents and even students from Southern Methodist University in search of a special night out.

CAFÉ PACIFIC

—

DALLAS

the fettuccine in boiling salted water, drain, and cool in ice water. Set aside.

Prepare the dressing by combining the mustard, shallots, and garlic in a bowl. Slowly whisk in 2 tablespoons of the olive oil and a little of the vinegar. Continue adding the oil and vinegar until they are completely incorporated. Add the basil and salt and pepper.

Carefully dry the shrimp, beans, and fettuccine and place in a large mixing bowl. Add the tomato and red onion, mix well, and season with salt and pepper. Gradually add the dressing and mix carefully.

Divide the lettuce among individual serving plates and top with the salad.

MUSSEL SALAD WITH MANGO MUSTARD DRESSING

Serves 6

1 pound pasta (fusilli or small shells)
5 dozen mussels
1 cup vinaigrette (see page 334)
2 tablespoons mango chutney, chopped
1 tablespoon Dijon mustard
½ red onion, diced
1 cup diced celery
1 sweet red pepper, diced
Sliced green onion for garnish

Cook the pasta according to package instructions.
Drain and rinse under cold water. Set aside.

Scrub the mussels thoroughly under cold running
water. Steam them in a large heavy pot until the
shells have opened and drain. Remove the mussels
from the shells (reserving a few shells for garnish)
and snip off the beards with a pair of small sharp
scissors. Chill.

Combine the vinaigrette, chutney, and mustard in
a blender or food processor. Place the pasta, vegetables, and dressing in a large bowl and mix well. Just
before serving, add the mussels and toss. Garnish
with the green onion slices and mussel slices.

HARVARD
BOOK STORE
CAFÉ

—

BOSTON

Glenn Bergman, the executive chef at the Commissary, parent of USA Café, has the somewhat incongruous background typical of many of today's food professionals. Although his mother had a cooking school in New York, his own training was in the field of public health. During a career in the pharmaceutical industry, he began cooking Oriental food as a hobby and gradually migrated to the restaurant business.

LOBSTER MARGARITA

Serves 6

3 1½-pound lobsters
½ pound chilled poached fish or seafood
Seasonal fruits and vegetables for garnish

MAYONNAISE

3 egg yolks
1 teaspoon salt
½ teaspoon dry mustard
½ teaspoon freshly ground pepper
Juice of 1 lime
1 cup olive oil
¼ cup Triple Sec
¼ cup tequila
½ cup fresh basil leaves, coarsely chopped

Steam the lobsters in 3 quarts boiling salted water for 10 minutes. Remove and let cool.

While the lobsters are cooling, make the mayonnaise. In a mixing bowl, whisk the egg yolks with the seasonings and lime juice. Add the oil, drop by drop, whisking vigorously until the mixture begins to thicken. Add the Triple Sec, tequila, and basil.

When the lobsters are cool, split them from end to end, starting at the head. If you wish, retain the tomalley (green liver) and coral (roe) from the female lobsters. They can be added to the mayonnaise.

USA CAFÉ

—

PHILADELPHIA

Crack the large claws so that the meat can be removed easily at the table. Remove and dice the tail meat.

In a bowl, combine the lobster meat and the chilled poached fish and toss lightly with the mayonnaise. Return the seafood to the lobster shell. Place ½ lobster on each of six serving plates and garnish with the fruits and vegetables.

Apropos is a sleek city café that offered Philadelphia something new when it opened in September 1984 — a sophisticated setting for breakfast, lunch, and dinner, with dinner served until midnight. A glassed-in sidewalk area lets patrons observe the comings and goings on busy South Broad Street.

BAY SCALLOP, CLEMENTINE, AND BABY BANANA SALAD

Serves 4

2 tangerines
2 shallots, chopped
¼ cup extra virgin olive oil
Champagne vinegar to taste
3 clementine oranges *or* navel oranges
8 baby bananas *or* 4 red bananas
Unsalted butter, for sautéing
¾ pound bay scallops, muscles removed
1 head radicchio
Chopped fresh herbs (parsley, chervil, tarragon, chives, thyme) for garnish

Using a zester, remove the rind (orange part only) from one of the tangerines. Juice both tangerines and mix the juice and the rind with the shallots, olive oil, and champagne vinegar. Peel the oranges, making sure to remove all the white pith, and section. Peel the bananas and cut in two lengthwise (if you are using the larger red bananas, cut them in two crosswise as well).

Just before serving, quickly sauté the banana halves in the butter until browned. Remove from the pan, add the scallops, and sauté until just cooked through. Add the clementine sections at the end, to heat through. Place the scallops and clementines in a bowl and heat the tangerine dressing in the sauté pan, swirling to allow it to emulsify. Toss most of the dressing with the scallops and clementines.

Place a bed of radicchio on individual serving plates. Top with a mound of scallops and clementines and lay the banana halves around the edges. Sprinkle with a little extra dressing and the chopped fresh herbs. Serve immediately.

On the sidewalk in front of Trio stand two life-size cutouts of a waiter and a waitress, relics of the thirties. They hold the menu for the day and help draw people to this small gem of a café.

TUNA AND WHITE BEAN SALAD

Serves 6 to 8

8 cups cold water
2 cups dried small white beans
2 bay leaves
1 tablespoon salt
1 pound fresh albacore tuna *or* 2 tins albacore tuna
    packed in water
1 bunch green onions, chopped
3 stalks celery, chopped
2 teaspoons dill weed
Salt and pepper to taste

DRESSING

2 cloves garlic, pressed
1 teaspoon dry mustard
2 teaspoons Dijon mustard
4 tablespoons red wine vinegar

SALADS

TRIO CAFÉ

—

SAN FRANCISCO

4 tablespoons olive oil
8 tablespoons vegetable oil

Bring the water to a boil and add the beans. Return the water to a boil and boil for 1 minute. Remove the pan from the heat and cover it. Let stand for 1 hour. Return the pan to the heat, add the bay leaves and salt, and return the mixture to a boil. Simmer for approximately 45 minutes, until the beans are cooked but not mushy. Drain and cool.

If you are using fresh tuna, poach it in simmering water until it flakes when poked with a fork. Set aside.

To prepare the dressing, whisk together all the ingredients.

Break the tuna into bite-size pieces and mix it lightly with the beans. Add the green onions and celery, then blend in the dressing, dill weed, and salt and pepper. Serve at room temperature.

Cafe Med

NEW WAVE NIÇOISE

Serves 6

6 3-ounce fresh tuna steaks
1 red onion, thinly sliced
4 tablespoons tarragon vinegar
1½ tablespoons sugar
6 red-skin potatoes, cooked until still firm,
   and halved
1 cup green beans, blanched
1 sweet red pepper, julienne-cut
1 yellow pepper, julienne-cut
3 hard-boiled eggs, peeled and halved
6 leaves romaine
12 anchovy fillets, rinsed and halved lengthwise
1 lemon, cut in 6 wedges
3 tablespoons capers, drained

POMMEREY VINAIGRETTE

2 tablespoons Pommerey mustard
2 tablespoons tarragon vinegar
Juice of 1 lemon
Salt and pepper to taste
2 tablespoons chopped fresh thyme *or*
   1 teaspoon dried thyme
¾ cup olive oil

Wash the tuna steaks and pat dry with paper towels.
   Marinate the red onion in a mixture of the tarragon vinegar and sugar for 30 minutes. While the onion is marinating, prepare the vegetable gar-

"New wave" also describes the interior at Café Med. The dancing room features a desert mural that seems to be "part Salvador Dali and part Louis L'Amour," and elsewhere there are glass-block walls, silver draperies, bits of neon, and shadow boxes containing Day-Glo 1940s telephones, radios, and such. Though the décor may show some funkiness, the food is a thoughtful blend of nouvelle and classic, and every dish is painstakingly prepared.

CAFÉ MED
—
WASHINGTON, D.C.

nishes; make the vinaigrette by whisking together all the ingredients.

Just before serving, place a romaine leaf in the center of each serving plate and distribute the vegetables and eggs around the edge of the lettuce. Season the tuna steaks with salt and pepper and cook on an indoor or outdoor grill for 2 minutes on a side, until the fish is cooked but still translucent in the center.

To serve, place a tuna steak on each lettuce leaf and drizzle vinaigrette over the steak and the vegetables. Garnish with the strips of anchovy, the lemon wedges, and the capers.

PIRET M
BISTRO
GALLERY
™

BEAN AND BEEF SALAD

Serves 6 to 8

1 to 1½ pounds green beans
2 pounds cold cooked roast beef, julienne-cut
Salad greens
Chopped parsley for garnish

DRESSING

2¼ teaspoons red wine vinegar
1 tablespoon lemon juice
1 clove garlic, minced
¼ teaspoon drained horseradish
1 tablespoon Dijon mustard
Salt and freshly ground pepper to taste
3 tablespoons olive oil
2 tablespoons *crème fraîche* (see page 335)
  or sour cream

To prepare the dressing, whisk together the vinegar, lemon juice, garlic, horseradish, mustard, and salt and pepper. Slowly whisk in the olive oil and then the *crème fraîche*. Set aside.

Cook the beans in boiling, salted water for 5 minutes, until they are tender but still resist the bite. Plunge immediately into ice water to preserve the color and stop the cooking. Drain and toss with the beef and enough dressing to coat the salad generously. Serve on a bed of greens and sprinkle with the parsley.

The success of Piret and George Munger's business owes much to the variety of services they offer. Take-out food has always been an important feature, and the salad case contains several offerings each day. The restaurant part of the operation started as a way of introducing San Diegans to some of the unfamiliar foods available for take-out.

PIRET M
—
SAN DIEGO

NOTE: Snow peas or asparagus can be substituted for the beans, in which case the dressing should be changed to include 2 tablespoons olive oil and 1 tablespoon sesame oil. Garnish the salad with toasted sesame seeds.

For another variation, cut the beef into 1-inch dice and use broccoli flowerets instead of green beans.

In true café fashion, Rebecca's is available for full meals or just munching at almost any hour of the day. In addition to breakfast, lunch, and dinner, coffee and dessert or wine and cheese are offered in the afternoon and late evening. The menu changes every three weeks and there are always daily specials — salads in particular.

MEDITERRANEAN ANTIPASTO SALAD

Serves 6 to 8

½ pound thinly sliced hard salami, cut in
    ½-inch strips
⅓ pound Mozzarella cheese, cut in ½-inch cubes
1 zucchini, thinly sliced
1 yellow squash, thinly sliced
1 sweet red pepper, cut in ½-inch squares
1 green pepper, cut in ½-inch squares
½ Bermuda onion, sliced in thin half moons
1 cup pitted Greek olives
4 ripe tomatoes, cut in wedges and seeded

DRESSING

¼ cup red wine vinegar
¼ cup chopped fresh basil
1 cup olive oil
⅓ cup chopped parsley
Salt and pepper to taste

Combine all the ingredients for the dressing and set aside.

Carefully combine the salad ingredients and gradually pour over the dressing, tossing gently until the mixture is well coated. Serve immediately or refrigerate until ready to serve, adding the tomatoes at the last minute.

REBECCA'S
—
BOSTON

Petaluma

CHICKEN LIVER AND SPINACH SALAD

Serves 6

6 tablespoons butter
1½ pounds chicken livers, well trimmed
Salt and pepper to taste
3 tablespoons dry Marsala wine
6 ounces spinach, stemmed, washed, and dried

VINAIGRETTE

1 egg yolk
2 tablespoons red wine vinegar
1 tablespoon Dijon mustard
½ teaspoon salt
Pinch of freshly ground pepper
½ cup corn oil

Prepare the vinaigrette by placing the egg yolk, vinegar, mustard, and salt and pepper in a small bowl and slowly whisking in the corn oil. Set aside.

Place the butter in a heated sauté pan, add the chicken livers, and sauté over high heat until they are crisp on the outside and still pink inside. Season with salt and pepper. Pour the fat from the pan and add the Marsala. Reduce the liquid by half, add ¾ cup of the vinaigrette, and cook for a minute or two, stirring constantly.

Remove the livers from the pan and cut them in half. Divide the spinach among six individual plates and place the livers on top. Strain the sauce over the livers and serve the salad warm.

PETALUMA
—
NEW YORK CITY

BAY WOLF

RESTAURANT & CAFE

SPINACH SALAD WITH DUCK CRACKLINGS

Serves 6

Skin from 3 duck breasts
1 English cucumber
2 pounds fresh spinach, washed, thoroughly dried, and stemmed
⅓ cup unsweetened red or white grape juice or gamay verjuice
2 tablespoons fresh lemon juice
½ cup olive oil
3 tablespoons duck fat
1 shallot, minced
Salt and pepper to taste

Place the duck skin on a rack in a pan in a 375° oven for 45 minutes, until the skin is crisp and brown, being careful not to let it burn. (A convection oven works well for this.) Reserve 3 tablespoons of fat for the dressing and save the rest for another use. Crack the skin into small pieces and drain on paper towels.

Peel, seed, and julienne-cut the cucumber. Combine the spinach and cucumber and toss with a dressing made by combining the grape juice or verjuice, lemon juice, olive oil, duck fat, shallot, and salt and pepper. Sprinkle the salad with the cracklings and serve immediately.

One of the popular features of Bay Wolf are the theme dinners held every Monday night. Some have holiday motifs and others are built around a national cuisine or even an ingredient. This interesting variation on spinach salad was part of an all-duck menu devised by chef de cuisine Carol Brendlinger — the only part of the meal not using duck was the dessert.

BAY WOLF
—
OAKLAND,
CALIFORNIA

This dish is a favorite on the Northwest menu that Nick & Sully offers as part of its catering business. Tins or boxes of smoked salmon are one of the most popular culinary souvenirs for tourists traveling to the state of Washington and points north.

NORTHWEST POTATO SALAD

Serves 8

8 radishes, sliced
½ teaspoon salt
¼ cup mayonnaise
¼ cup sour cream
¼ cup yogurt
3 hard-boiled eggs, chopped
½ cup sliced black olives
2 cups ½-inch pieces smoked salmon
2 cups boiling potatoes, peeled, cooked, and cut
     into ½-inch dice
1 tart apple, peeled, cored, and cut into ½-inch dice
½ cup minced red onion
2 tablespoons chopped fresh dill
2 tablespoons chopped fresh parsley
Salt and pepper to taste

Toss the radishes with the salt. Combine the mayonnaise, sour cream, and yogurt and gently toss with all the other ingredients in a large bowl. Cover and chill for at least 1½ hours. Return the salad to room temperature before serving.

NICK & SULLY
—
SEATTLE

City Market is owned by Kathleen McDaniel and Lisa Courtin. Kathy, who is also a part owner of a wine bar called the Grape, is a native of Dallas who felt there were too few good places to eat in the downtown area. In spite of the café's location in an office tower, patrons include tourists and visitors to the Dallas Museum of Art, a stone's throw away.

TEXAS CAVIAR

Serves 6

1 15-ounce can black-eyed peas, drained
¼ cup red wine vinegar
½ cup thick picante sauce
⅓ teaspoon Maggi seasoning
1 small sweet red pepper, seeded and julienne-cut
1 small green pepper, seeded and julienne-cut
1 small yellow pepper, seeded and julienne-cut
1 tablespoon chopped cilantro
½ teaspoon salt
½ teaspoon pepper

Place the peas in a bowl and add the vinegar and picante sauce. Cover and refrigerate for several hours or overnight.

Add the remaining ingredients to the marinated peas. Taste and adjust the seasoning. Serve chilled with fried chicken or any Texas-style barbecue or picnic fare.

CITY MARKET

—

DALLAS

DESSERTS

Cakes, Pies, and Tarts
Fruit Desserts
Mousses, Puddings,
and Ice Cream

CAKES, PIES, AND TARTS

Semolina Cake
Almond Cake
Black Walnut Torte
Austrian Nut Roll
Bittersweet Chocolate Cake
Carrie Waldman's Chocolate Piñon Torte
Shortbread Apple Pie
Gingerbread
Cranberry-Almond Streusel Pie
Lime Mousse Pie
Hot Buttered Pecan Pie
Maple Walnut Pie
Chocolate Walnut Pie
Black-Bottom Pie
Chocolate Whiskey Pecan Pie
Fresh Lemon Tart
Pastry Shells with Chocolate and Fruit
Plum-Almond Tart

Bistro at Maison de Ville

SEMOLINA CAKE

Serves 12 to 16

4½ cups milk
1½ cups plus 2 tablespoons sugar
Scant 2 cups semolina flour
14 tablespoons butter, softened
3 whole eggs
10 eggs, separated
1 tablespoon vanilla

Rub the bottom and sides of a large heavy pot with butter; add the milk and half of the sugar and bring to a boil. Gradually stir in the semolina with a wooden spoon and cook over low heat, stirring frequently, until the mixture has thickened (about 5 minutes). Stir in half of the butter and the remaining sugar and remove from the heat.

Transfer the mixture to a large bowl, let cool for a few minutes, and stir in the remaining butter, the whole eggs, the 10 yolks, and the vanilla.

Beat the egg whites until stiff but not dry and fold them, a third at a time, into the semolina mixture. Pour the batter into a buttered and floured 10-inch springform pan. Cover the outside of the bottom and sides of the pan with foil and place in a larger pan. Fill the larger pan with water to about halfway up the sides of the springform and bake the cake at 325° for 45 minutes to an hour. Let the cake cool on a rack.

The ambience of this elegant bistro transports one to fin de siècle Paris. The space is long and narrow, with seating for only forty people. Polished mahogany walls are hung with Impressionistic paintings in gilded frames, and a red leather banquette backed by a wall of mirrors lines one side of the room. Waiters wearing black vests and floor-length aprons deftly make their way around the limited space.

THE BISTRO AT
MAISON DE
VILLE

—

NEW ORLEANS

NOTE: This cake is good plain, but it also may be served with a flavored *crème anglaise* (see page 336) or a berry or kiwi purée.

ALMOND CAKE

Makes 1 9-inch cake

10 ounces whole blanched almonds (about 2 cups)
1⅓ cups granulated sugar
8 egg whites
½ teaspoon salt
Grated peel of 1 lemon
6 tablespoons flour
Chopped toasted almonds for garnish
Confectioners' sugar for garnish

Grind the almonds with the sugar in a food processor. Place in a bowl and set aside. Beat the egg whites with the salt until stiff. Add the almond sugar and the lemon peel, a little at a time, mixing gently. Shake the flour through a wire sieve and add, a little at a time. Mix gently.

Pour the batter into a greased 9-inch springform pan and shake to level off the top. Bake at 350° for 45 minutes to 1 hour. Let the cake cool on a rack, remove from the pan, and top with the almonds and a sifting of confectioners' sugar. The cake will keep well for several days in a tin container.

This café has recently expanded to accommodate eight tables. Originally there was standing room only; and the patrons still gather at the attractive bar, with the scene resembling a lively cocktail party. Wine and beer are served in addition to several kinds of coffee.

TRIO CAFÉ

—

SAN FRANCISCO

BLACK WALNUT TORTE

Serves 8

6 large eggs, separated
1½ cups black walnuts, finely ground
1 cup fine breadcrumbs, processed from zweiback
   or toasted Italian bread
1 cup confectioners' sugar
1 teaspoon almond extract
¼ teaspoon mace
¼ teaspoon salt
2 cups heavy cream
2 tablespoons sugar
¼ teaspoon vanilla
½ cup black walnut pieces

Whip the egg whites to stiff peaks and set aside. Lightly beat the egg yolks. Add the ground walnuts, breadcrumbs, confectioners' sugar, almond extract, mace, and salt. Mix well and gently fold in the egg whites.

    Line a 13-by-9-by-2-inch baking pan with parchment or waxed paper and butter and lightly flour the paper and the sides of the pan. Pour in the batter, smoothing the top, and bake at 350° for 25 minutes, until a knife inserted in the center comes out clean. Cool the cake in the pan for about 20 minutes, invert on a rack, remove the paper, and let cool for another 30 minutes. Wrap the cake in plastic and chill for 3 hours.

Behind the scenes at Piret_M is a veritable family of dedicated staff. Ben Patterson was the Mungers' first chef in 1976 and now helps Piret with recipe development and testing. His Black Walnut Torte makes an elegant dessert without the need for complicated techniques. Black walnuts make the torte special, but common English ones can be used instead.

PIRET_M

—

SAN DIEGO

After about 2¾ hours, whip the cream and add the sugar and vanilla. Cut the cake into two 6½-by-9-inch rectangles. Split each rectangle into 2 layers. Place one layer on a serving plate and top with ¼ of the whipped cream. Repeat three times, ending with cream on the top (do not frost the sides). Sprinkle the top of the cake with the black walnut pieces and chill before serving.

brasserie

AUSTRIAN NUT ROLL

Serves 8 to 10

9 large eggs, separated
1 cup superfine sugar
1 teaspoon baking powder
1 cup finely ground toasted hazelnuts (or pecans or walnuts)
1½ cups heavy cream
1 tablespoon sugar
2 tablespoons Cognac
Confectioners' sugar for dusting cake

Before starting the cake, liberally oil a 14-by-18-inch jelly roll pan, line the bottom and ends with waxed paper (leave some overhang of paper at the ends, to help in removing the cake from the pan), and oil the paper. Next, tape together two lengths of waxed paper, making a single sheet that is about 3 inches larger than the pan on all sides. Set aside.

Beat the egg yolks, superfine sugar, and baking powder with an electric mixer until the mixture ribbons thickly. Beat the egg whites to the soft peak stage. Sprinkle the ground nuts over the egg whites and scrape the yolk mixture onto the nuts. Fold together. Transfer the batter to the prepared pan and bake in a 400° oven for about 25 minutes. The cake should be well risen, brown, and dry to the touch. Let the cake cool to warm in the pan, on a rack.

Whip the heavy cream with the sugar and the Cognac and set aside in the refrigerator.

While the cake is still warm, place the double sheet of waxed paper on the counter in front of you.

Dione Lucas, the doyenne of French cooking in this country, launched the Brasserie in 1968. Today the six or seven desserts regularly available are carefully prepared classics and include two of hers: the famous Roulage Léontine and this delicate Viennese specialty. The detailed instructions for rolling the cake are not meant to put you off but to make a relatively simple job easier.

Loosen the long edges of the cake with a paring knife and peel the waxed paper from the short edges. Dust the surface of the cake with confectioners' sugar.

Holding the waxed paper overlaps away from the cake at the ends, stand the long side of the cake pan down on the near edge of the large sheet of waxed paper. The pan should be perpendicular to the sheet of paper (the cake will not fall out!). In one smooth motion, bang the pan down as though you were closing a book, being careful that the "hinge" edge does not move off the counter.

Distribute the whipped cream evenly over the two thirds of the cake nearest you. Roll the cake as follows: Fold over two inches of the long edge nearest you, pressing a bit until the fold holds. Continue rolling by picking up the two end corners of the waxed paper, pulling it taut to support the cake, and leading with the palms of your hands, using a smooth motion. Cut the roll in slices and serve immediately, or refrigerate for an hour or two until ready to slice and serve.

CITY CAFE

The menu at City Café changes every Wednesday, and there is always a great emphasis on desserts. After all, that's the impression people take away. This is one of the richer choices, but it can be made lighter with a scoop of vanilla ice cream.

BITTERSWEET CHOCOLATE CAKE

Serves 12 to 16

11 eggs, separated
Pinch of salt
1¾ cups sugar
1 teaspoon vanilla
1½ tablespoons Grand Marnier
16 ounces bittersweet chocolate
1 cup unsalted butter

ICING

6 ounces semisweet chocolate
6 tablespoons heavy cream
Chopped nuts for garnish (optional)

Whip the egg whites until foamy; then add the salt, ¼ cup of the sugar, the vanilla, and the Grand Marnier. Continue beating until soft peaks form.

Melt the bittersweet chocolate with the butter over hot water. Beat the remaining 1½ cups sugar with the egg yolks until the mixture is lemon yellow. Fold in the chocolate mixture, then fold in the egg whites. Pour into a greased 10-inch springform pan and bake at 350° for 45 to 50 minutes. Remove the cake from the oven and let it cool.

To prepare the icing, melt the semisweet chocolate with the heavy cream over hot water. Whisk the mixture until smooth. Remove the cake from the pan and spread the icing on the top and sides. Press chopped nuts into the sides of the cake if you wish.

CITY CAFÉ
—
DALLAS

Ruth Bronz describes her grandmother as a fantastic "executive chef," managing a superb East Texas kitchen and training household help and grandchildren alike; however, the setup at Miss Ruby's is strictly democratic, and there is no fixed hierarchy in the kitchen. Ruth cooks four days a week and Carrie Waldman prepares most of the desserts.

CARRIE WALDMAN'S CHOCOLATE PIÑON TORTE

Serves 12

½ pound *piñones* (pine nuts)
7 ounces unsweetened chocolate, roughly chopped
1 cup butter, at room temperature
1 cup plus 1 tablespoon sugar
4 eggs, at room temperature, separated
Grated rind of 1 orange
Piñones for garnish
Whipped cream flavored with orange zest and
    Cointreau

In a food processor, blend the *piñones* and chocolate until they are finely ground. In a separate bowl, cream the butter, add the sugar, and beat until the mixture is fluffy. Add the egg yolks and beat again. Add the grated orange rind and the chocolate-*piñon* paste. In a separate bowl, beat the egg whites until stiff. Fold into the batter in three stages.

Cut a round of parchment or waxed paper to fit the bottom of a 9-inch springform pan. Place the round in the bottom of the pan and butter and flour it and the sides of the pan. Pile the batter into the pan and bake at 300° for 45 minutes. Turn the cake out of the pan while still warm and press whole *piñones* into the surface for decoration. Serve with whipped cream flavored with orange zest and Cointreau.

MISS RUBY'S
CAFÉ

—

NEW YORK CITY

SHORTBREAD APPLE PIE

Serves 6 to 8

2 large Granny Smith or Golden Delicious apples,
   peeled, cored, and sliced
¼ cup superfine sugar
¼ teaspoon cinnamon
1 egg yolk

CRUST

2 cups flour
¼ teaspoon baking powder
½ cup butter
1 cup sugar
4 egg yolks

To make the shortbread crust, sift the flour and baking powder together and set aside. Cream the butter and sugar until well blended; add the egg yolks and mix well. Add the dry ingredients and blend.

Press half of the dough into the bottom of a 9-inch round cake pan. Arrange the sliced apples on top of the dough and sprinkle with the sugar and cinnamon. Pat the remaining dough into a 9½-inch circle on waxed paper and lay over the apples. Lightly beat the egg yolk and brush it over the top. Make decorative lines in the crust with the back of a fork.

Bake the pie in a 375° oven for 45 minutes. (If the top begins to get too brown, cover it with foil.) Turn

According to Monique Hooker, being successful in the restaurant business takes ''the patience of a saint, the legs of an ox, the memory of an elephant, a sixth sense for trends, a feel for real estate, money — lots of money — and endless time and work.'' Her own training began at home in Brittany, where the family struggled for material goods and everyone had to work hard. ''But all the food around us was fresh and there was always a gâteau breton set out on the kitchen table.''

MONIQUE'S
CAFÉ

—

CHICAGO

off the oven and leave the pie inside for 10 minutes. Let the pie cool in the pan before unmolding it. Slice and serve, with or without ice cream.

GINGERBREAD

Makes 16 to 20 squares

1 cup butter, at room temperature
4 ounces fresh ginger, peeled and cubed
1 cup brown sugar
1 cup molasses
2 eggs, lightly beaten
½ teaspoon salt
2 teaspoons baking soda
3 cups whole-wheat flour
1 cup buttermilk

Cream the butter and ginger in a food processor until smooth. Add the brown sugar, molasses, and eggs and process until smooth. Pour the mixture into a large bowl. Sift the dry ingredients into the bowl and gradually add the buttermilk. Mix well. Pour the batter into a greased and floured 8-by-12-inch pan and bake in a 350° oven for 35 to 40 minutes, until a toothpick inserted in the center comes out clean.

NOTE: This batter rises considerably, so be sure that the baking pan is twice as deep as the batter line.

This neighborhood café is a few yards from the Dallas–Highland Park line, in an area of small commercial establishments, antiques shops, and apartment buildings. The many young single people who live in the area eat out a lot, and the simple décor and healthful fare of the Dream Café make it a comfortable choice for breakfast, lunch, or dinner.

THE DREAM
CAFÉ

—

DALLAS

CRANBERRY-ALMOND STREUSEL PIE

Serves 6 to 8

4 cups fresh or frozen cranberries
1 cup water
1 cup sugar
3 tablespoons minute tapioca
½ teaspoon cinnamon
¼ teaspoon coriander
Grated zest of 1 orange
1 Bartlett pear, peeled, cored, and coarsely chopped
1 Golden Delicious apple, peeled, cored, and
  coarsely chopped
1 unbaked 10-inch (or deep-dish 9-inch) pie shell

STREUSEL TOPPING

6 tablespoons butter
⅔ cup flour
½ cup sugar
1 cup sliced almonds

In a heavy saucepan, combine the cranberries and
the water. Simmer just until the berries burst (if you
are using frozen berries, merely thaw them and place
in a saucepan before proceeding with the recipe).
Add the sugar, tapioca, spices, and orange zest and
heat through. Add the chopped fruit, mix well, and
pour into the pie shell.
  Prepare the topping by cutting the butter into the

*Enoteca's menu advertises
"seasonal Northwest cuisine,"
and this dessert fills the bill
perfectly. Though New En-
glanders may think that the
Cape Cod area is the only pro-
ducer of cranberries, there is
an abundant annual harvest
in the state of Washington as
well.*

ENOTECA
WINE SHOP &
RESTAURANT
—
SEATTLE

flour with a pastry blender and then adding the sugar and almonds. Sprinkle on top of the cranberry mixture, being sure to cover the entire surface. Bake for 1 hour at 350°, until the crust and topping are brown.

LIME MOUSSE PIE

Serves 10

1 cup sweetened coconut
2 tablespoons butter
3 limes
1 envelope unflavored gelatin
1 cup sugar
6 eggs, separated, at room temperature
1 cup heavy cream
Pinch of salt
Toasted coconut for garnish

Sauté the coconut in the butter until it is lightly toasted and press onto the bottom of an oiled 9½-inch springform pan. Set aside.

Grate the rind of the limes and set aside. Juice the limes and combine with the gelatin in a small bowl over a hot water bath. Combine ½ cup of the sugar with the egg yolks in a stainless steel bowl and beat over simmering water for 1 minute. Add the lime juice mixture and continue whisking until the yolks

STAR TOP CAFÉ

—

CHICAGO

are thick enough to coat a spoon and a trail is left behind when a finger is run through the mixture. Set aside.

Whip the cream and set aside. In a clean bowl, whip the egg whites with an electric mixer until they are foamy; add the salt and gradually add the remaining ½ cup sugar. Continue beating at high speed until the whites are stiff and glossy.

Place the egg yolk mixture over a bowl of ice and stir until the mixture begins to set. Carefully and quickly fold the egg whites into the yolks; then fold in the grated rind and whipped cream. Gently turn into the springform pan and chill for at least 2 hours before serving. Garnish the top with more toasted coconut if you wish.

NOTE: The trick with this recipe is to combine the egg yolk mixture with the egg whites at just the right moment. The gelatin must not be overly set and the egg whites should just have reached stiff peaks.

HOT BUTTERED PECAN PIE

Serves 6 to 8

PASTRY

2 cups flour
⅓ cup sugar
¼ teaspoon salt
½ teaspoon baking powder

The way the menu is set up at Mr. B's reflects the Brennans' goal of presenting old New Orleans cooking as well as lighter adaptations. On the right are the daily specials, where inventiveness and seasonal ingredients prevail, and on the left is a page of traditional dishes, including this favorite dessert.

MR. B'S

—

NEW ORLEANS

½ teaspoon nutmeg
¾ teaspoon cinnamon
7 tablespoons cold butter, in small chunks
1 egg, lightly beaten

FILLING

1 cup dark corn syrup
1 cup sugar
½ teaspoon vanilla
½ cup butter, melted
4 eggs
1 cup pecans

To make the pastry, first combine the dry ingredients in a bowl, then add the butter and cut in with a pastry blender until the mixture resembles coarse cornmeal. Add the egg and blend well. Shape into a ball and refrigerate for 30 minutes.

Roll the dough out on a floured surface to a ⅛-inch thickness. Transfer to a 9-inch pie plate and trim and flute the edge. Set aside.

To prepare the filling, first combine the corn syrup, sugar, and vanilla in a bowl and mix for 2 minutes. Add the butter and mix for another 2 minutes. Add the eggs and mix well to incorporate. Sprinkle the pecans over the bottom of the pie shell and pour over the filling. Bake at 350° for 45 to 55 minutes, until the filling is set (do not let the pecans burn). Serve warm and accompany with whipped cream or ice cream if you wish.

MAPLE WALNUT PIE

Serves 4 to 6

½ cup dark or light brown sugar (or half of each)
1 cup grade A maple syrup
2¾ tablespoons melted butter
½ cup coarsely chopped walnuts
2 extra large eggs
1 8-inch pie shell, unbaked
Whipped cream and walnut halves for garnish
  (optional)

Combine the sugar, maple syrup, butter, walnuts, and eggs in a bowl and mix thoroughly. Pour into the pie shell. Place the shell on a baking sheet and bake in a 350° oven for 35 to 40 minutes. Cool slightly before serving. Serve with a dollop of whipped cream and top with a walnut half.

Maple desserts are a rarity in California, but Ian Barrington likes to hold on to favorite flavors from his Canadian boyhood. Barrington later moved to southern California and learned to cook in college, where his roommates "couldn't turn a tap on, much less boil water." After getting a Ph.D. in communications arts and teaching for several years, he made a full-time commitment to the restaurant business.

THE EGG AND
THE EYE
—
LOS ANGELES

The Erasmus Café is on Spring Street, one of two main shopping streets in this college town. The terrace at the front is a popular spot in the summer, when the Williamstown Theatre and nearby musical events bring large numbers of tourists to the area. The café serves continuously from nine in the morning until late in the evening and superb desserts are always available. This one is usually embellished with vanilla ice cream, crème de cacao, and chocolate shavings.

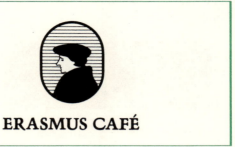

ERASMUS CAFÉ

CHOCOLATE WALNUT PIE

Serves 6 to 8

3 large eggs
1½ cups sugar
6 tablespoons unsalted butter, melted and cooled
2 teaspoons vanilla
¾ cup flour
1½ cups mini chocolate chips
1½ cups chopped walnuts
1 9-inch pie crust

Lightly beat the eggs and add the sugar, butter, and vanilla. Blend well. Gradually add the flour, mixing thoroughly. Stir in the chocolate chips and walnuts. Pour the mixture into the pie shell and bake on the center rack of a 350° oven for 50 minutes. Serve warm.

ERASMUS CAFÉ
AT THE COLLEGE
BOOKSTORE
—
WILLIAMSTOWN,
MASSACHUSETTS

BLACK-BOTTOM PIE

Serves 12 to 16

5 cups heavy cream
8 egg yolks
¾ cup sugar
2 vanilla beans, split open and seeds scraped out
6 ounces unsweetened chocolate
6 ounces semisweet chocolate
2 teaspoons (1 package) unflavored gelatin
⅓ cup dark rum
7 ounces almond paste
Shavings of white and bittersweet chocolate
   for garnish

CRUMB CRUST

1 8½-ounce package chocolate wafers, to make
   2 cups chocolate cookie crumbs
1 cup finely ground walnuts
¼ cup melted unsalted butter

First, prepare the crust by combining all ingredients and pressing the mixture firmly onto the bottom and sides of a 10-by-3-inch springform pan. Let it set in the freezer for several hours, then bake at 350° for 20 minutes and let cool.

    Make a custard by first scalding 3 cups of the heavy cream. Beat the egg yolks with the sugar and add the vanilla seeds. Add a little of the hot cream to

In true bistro fashion, Apropos is a place where people meet for an appetizer and a drink, an elaborate five-course meal, or a late coffee and dessert. Across the street from the Philadelphia Music Academy, the home of the Philadelphia Orchestra, it is a popular place for pre- and post-concert eating and drinking. A case of sumptuous desserts greets patrons as they enter. This one is an updated version of a southern classic.

        DESSERTS

the yolk mixture; then gradually add the remaining cream. Heat, stirring constantly, until the custard coats a wooden spoon. Remove from the heat.

Melt the two chocolates over boiling water and soften the gelatin in ¼ cup of cold water.

Divide the custard into two parts, 1½ cups and 3 cups. To make the black bottom, mix the larger part with the melted chocolate. Add the rum and allow the custard to cool until lukewarm. Pour into the cooled crumb crust and refrigerate.

To make the white top, heat the softened gelatin until it liquifies and whisk it into the remaining custard, making sure there are no lumps. Cream the almond paste in a food processor or mixer. When it is completely smooth, add a little of the custard at a time, processing after each addition until the mixture is creamy and smooth. Cool to room temperature. Whip the remaining 2 cups of cream and fold into the almond custard. Pour over the black bottom and allow to set in the refrigerator for several hours or, if possible, overnight. Decorate with the chocolate shavings.

North Star Bar

casual drinking & dining

CHOCOLATE WHISKEY PECAN PIE

Serves 8

3 ounces unsweetened chocolate
4 tablespoons butter
4 eggs
1 cup sugar
1¼ cups dark corn syrup
6 tablespoons whiskey
2 cups pecan halves
1 10-inch unbaked pie shell
Whipped cream

Melt the chocolate and butter together in a heavy saucepan or in a double boiler over hot water. Set aside to cool. Place the eggs in a medium-size bowl and beat with the sugar. Add the corn syrup and whiskey and blend well. Add the slightly cooled chocolate mixture to the bowl.

Sprinkle the pecan halves over the bottom of the pie shell. Pour the chocolate-whiskey mixture over the nuts. Bake at 350° for 40 to 50 minutes. (The top should jiggle slightly and the nuts should not be allowed to burn.) Serve cold with plenty of whipped cream.

Big yellow stars on its clapboard façade make the North Star Bar easy to spot from a distance. Inside, the typical Art Deco color scheme of pink, gray, turquoise, and black only partially masks the old-fashioned tavern lurking beneath. Changing art exhibits are an important part of the North Star's ambience.

NORTH STAR
BAR
—
PHILADELPHIA

DESSERTS

Although the menu at Suzanne's changes daily, regular customers insist that certain desserts be almost always available. This classic tarte citron *is one of the all-time favorites.*

FRESH LEMON TART

Serves 6 to 8

1 10-inch unbaked tart shell
5 eggs
5 small or medium lemons, grated zest and juice
1 cup sugar
4 tablespoons unsalted butter, melted
5 paper-thin lemon slices
2 tablespoons apricot preserves
1 tablespoon water

Bake the tart shell for 10 minutes at 350°. Remove from the oven and let cool.

In a bowl, lightly beat the eggs and add the lemon zest and juice, the sugar, and the melted butter. Mix well and pour into the cooled tart shell. Bake for 30 to 35 minutes at 350°, until the lemon curd has set.

When the tart is cool, arrange the lemon slices over the top and brush with a glaze made by melting the apricot preserves with the water over low heat until the preserves have dissolved.

NOTE: The tart can be presented more attractively if it is baked in a pan with a removable bottom and lifted out before serving.

SUZANNE'S CAFÉ
AT THE PHILLIPS
COLLECTION

—

WASHINGTON, D.C.

PASTRY SHELLS WITH CHOCOLATE AND FRUIT

Makes 6 to 8

PASTRY

2 cups flour
¾ cup butter or margarine
1 egg
¼ cup confectioners' sugar

FILLING

2 teaspoons unflavored gelatin
½ cup water
1 teaspoon lemon juice
1 teaspoon sugar
3 ounces semisweet chocolate
1 pint raspberries
Whipped cream for garnish

To make the pastry, place all the ingredients in the bowl of a food processor and blend just until the mixture forms a ball (do not overprocess). Refrigerate the dough for a half hour or more before rolling it to a thickness of ¼ inch. Cut the dough in circles to fit individual pastry tins and press against the bottom and sides of each tin. Poke holes in the bottom with a fork. Place the tins on a baking sheet and bake at 425° for 12 to 15 minutes.

Those who have studied the life of Robert Sterling Clark believe that he would like having lunch and tea served to visitors to his museum. Clark was something of a gourmand himself, and his diaries make frequent references to meals and menus. One of his favorite paintings was Renoir's still-life Onions, *which hung over the sideboard in his dining room for many years and is one of the thirty-seven Renoirs that are part of the museum collection.*

CLARK CAFÉ

—

WILLIAMSTOWN,
MASSACHUSETTS

To make the filling, first dissolve the gelatin in the water and heat it together with the lemon juice and sugar until it is fully melted. Let cool. Melt the chocolate in the top of a double boiler over hot water and brush it on the inside of each pastry shell. When the chocolate has set, fill each shell with the raspberries and cover with the gelatin just before it hardens. Garnish with a dollop of whipped cream.

NOTE: The pastry shells will keep for a week or more in an airtight container before being lined with chocolate and filled. Various kinds of berries and fruit or even a good jam may be used.

PLUM-ALMOND TART

Serves 6

8 ounces almond paste
3 tablespoons sugar
5 tablespoons soft butter
3 eggs
3 tablespoons flour
½ teaspoon grated lemon rind
1 9-inch unbaked tart shell
8 to 12 friar or Italian plums (depending on size),
   halved and pitted

Beat the almond paste until soft, then slowly add the
sugar and the butter. Lightly beat in the eggs until
they are incorporated. Add the flour and the grated
lemon rind. Spread the mixture in the tart shell and
arrange the plum halves, pitted side down, in a cir-
cular pattern to cover the filling. Bake at 350° for 30
minutes, until the crust is golden.

*Café Sport is across the street
from the north end of the Pike
Place Market, one of the country's finest and most extensive
food markets. Originally a
farmer's market featuring the
abundant fruits, vegetables,
wild mushrooms, and fish of
the region, the area became
the focus of an urban renewal
project, and restaurants, bakeries, and crafts displays of all
kinds have been added.*

CAFÉ SPORT

—

SEATTLE

FRUIT DESSERTS

Crêpes with Quince, Caramel, and Roasted Walnuts
Raspberry Cobbler
Raspberries with White Chocolate Mint Sauce
Pear Crisp
Blueberry Slump
Fresh Fruit with Sauternes Zabaglione
Bahamian Bananas

Cafe Med

CRÊPES WITH QUINCE, CARAMEL, AND ROASTED WALNUTS

Serves 6

CRÊPES

1 cup flour
3 eggs
⅔ cup water
⅔ cup milk
2 tablespoons sugar
2 tablespoons butter, melted and cooled
⅛ teaspoon ground cloves
2 tablespoons clarified butter (see page 335), melted

Place all the ingredients except the clarified butter in a blender or food processor and blend at high speed for 1 minute. Refrigerate for at least 1 hour.

Heat a crêpe pan or well-seasoned skillet over high heat and, when hot, brush with the clarified butter. Pour ¼ cup of the batter into the pan and swirl to coat evenly. Pour out any batter that does not immediately adhere to the pan. Cook the crêpe for 30 seconds, turn, and cook the other side. Cook the remaining batter in the same fashion, separating the finished crêpes with sheets of waxed paper once they are cooked. Set aside.

Though Café Med has been praised for its "winning examples of modern dessert making," this crêpes preparation is a combination of modern and classic. The innovative use of the old-fashioned quince proves that it is good for more than making jelly.

CAFÉ MED

—

WASHINGTON, D.C.

CARAMEL SAUCE

1 cup sugar
⅓ cup water
½ cup unsalted butter
⅔ cup heavy cream

Cook the sugar with the water in a heavy saucepan until the mixture is dark brown, washing down the sides of the pan with water to prevent crystallization. Remove from the heat and add the butter and cream, tilting the pan away from you — the mixture will bubble furiously. Stir the sauce until smooth, returning it to the heat to melt any lumps. Strain and set aside.

FILLING/TOPPING

2 tablespoons clarified butter
4 quinces, peeled, seeded, cut into ⅛-inch slices, and tossed in lemon juice
1 tablespoon sugar
1½ cups heavy cream, whipped
½ cup walnuts, roasted in a 350° oven for 5 minutes

To make the filling and assemble the crêpes, heat the clarified butter until it is smoking and sauté the quinces in two batches, cooking until the fruit has caramelized. Toss the quinces with the sugar. Place some of the fruit on one half of each crêpe and fold in half. Pour caramel sauce over the crêpe, add a dollop of whipped cream, and garnish with the roasted walnuts.

RASPBERRY COBBLER

Serves 6

PASTRY

1 cup softened butter
1 cup sifted flour
Pinch of salt
2 tablespoons ice water

Cut the butter into the flour and salt until the mixture is crumbly. Add enough ice water to let the mixture form a ball of dough. Let it rest in the refrigerator for at least 30 minutes before baking.

SAUCE

1 cup raspberries
½ cup superfine sugar
Liqueur to taste

Place all the ingredients in a blender or food processor and mix until smooth. If you want to get rid of the seeds, pass the sauce through a fine sieve.

ASSEMBLY

2½ pints raspberries
1 cup dark brown sugar

This intimate café is perched on a mezzanine overlooking the gift shop of the Craft and Folk Art Museum. Peach walls, dark green tablecloths, and track lighting designed to highlight the fresh flowers on every table provide a restful setting interrupted only when one of the chefs happens to be performing (albeit silently) at the omelette bar. Desserts are another specialty, and this unusual cobbler is spectacularly presented on a large service plate.

THE EGG AND
THE EYE

—

LOS ANGELES

1 cup chopped walnuts
1 cup toasted slivered almonds
4 tablespoons butter
1 cup heavy cream, whipped and sweetened
   to taste
6 sprigs mint for garnish

Place the raspberries in a buttered 8-by-10-by-3-inch baking pan. Roll the pastry as thin as possible to fit the top of the baking pan. Sprinkle with the brown sugar, walnuts, and almonds and dot with the butter. Place on a cookie sheet and bake in a 350° oven for 35 to 40 minutes, until the top is golden.

When the cobbler is cool, spoon some of the sauce onto a dinner plate. Cut a square of the cobbler and place it on top of the sauce. Add a dollop of whipped cream and garnish the plate with a sprig of mint.

NOTE: Blackberries or blueberries may be substituted for the raspberries.

RASPBERRIES WITH WHITE CHOCOLATE MINT SAUCE

Serves 6

8 ounces white chocolate
¼ cup milk
6 sprigs fresh mint
2 cups heavy cream
1 quart raspberries

Break up the chocolate and melt it in the top of a double boiler over hot water. Bring the milk to a boil and steep the mint in it for 5 minutes. When the chocolate has melted, pour in the cream, whisking until the mixture is well blended. Pour the milk and mint through a fine sieve and discard the mint. Add the milk to the chocolate, whisking well. Chill the sauce and serve under or over the raspberries, divided among six plates.

Chef Andrew Thomson's office is lined with framed letters from fellow chefs and several pictures of one of the restaurant's favorite celebrity patrons, Larry Hagman. Another regular customer is Governor Mark White, whose meal is served on an official plate bearing a picture of the state capitol.

CAFÉ PACIFIC
—
DALLAS

Although the cuisine at Nick & Sully originally represented state-of-the-art gourmet cooking, the clientele has gradually influenced the chefs back to a middle ground. Seasonal ingredients are the guiding force, and the berries and fruits of the Northwest are a popular feature. This pear crisp is a delicious variation on a familiar dessert.

PEAR CRISP

Serves 6

5 Bartlett pears, peeled, cored, and sliced
2 teaspoons fresh lemon juice
1 cup brown sugar
1 cup flour
2 teaspoons cinnamon
½ teaspoon salt
8 tablespoons butter
Pinch of clove
Pinch of nutmeg

Butter a deep 8-inch cake pan or gratin dish. Place a layer of sliced pears in the pan and sprinkle with lemon juice. Repeat, using all the pears and lemon juice. Press down gently.

Combine the remaining ingredients in a food processor until the mixture resembles coarse meal. Spread over the pears and press down, making sure the topping reaches the edges of the pan. Bake at 350° for 45 minutes to 1 hour, until the top is golden. Serve warm or cold.

NICK & SULLY

—

SEATTLE

BLUEBERRY SLUMP

Serves 6

2 pints blueberries, washed and picked over
1½ cups sugar
½ teaspoon ground cloves
1 lemon, sliced
1 cup flour
1 tablespoon baking powder
¼ teaspoon salt
Sprinkle of sugar
1 egg
⅓ cup milk, more or less
Heavy cream

Place the first four ingredients in a wide, 3-quart glass or enamel saucepan and simmer gently until the berries begin to be soft and juicy. Remove from the heat and discard the lemon slices.

Meanwhile, sift the flour with the baking powder, salt, and sugar. Break an egg into a measuring cup and fill to the ½-cup mark with milk. Beat well and stir into the dry ingredients. Return the blueberry mixture to a simmer and drop the dough by teaspoonfuls onto the surface without covering it entirely. Cover the pan tightly and cook gently for 12 to 15 minutes. Serve warm with heavy cream.

Ruth Bronz thinks of herself as a missionary for American regional food. This dessert is an old New England recipe (sometimes called Blueberry Grunt, because of the sound the blueberries make as they cook) that is enjoying a comeback, along with many other old-fashioned desserts. A variation on shortcake, in this case the dough forms dumplings.

MISS RUBY'S
CAFÉ
—
NEW YORK CITY

Although the preparation of food at Café Med has been deemed "reminiscent of lace making," fine, close work demanding a great deal of time, some of the dishes require more creativity and imagination than time. This refreshing approach to zabaglione is one of those dishes. The fruit may vary with the season.

Cafe Med

FRESH FRUIT WITH SAUTERNES ZABAGLIONE

Serves 6

1 pint strawberries
2 ripe pears
2 ripe mangoes
Grated lemon rind for garnish

ZABAGLIONE

½ cup sugar
8 egg yolks
1 cup Sauternes
½ teaspoon ground cardamom
1 cup heavy cream

Wash and slice all but 6 of the strawberries; peel, core, and dice the pears (sprinkle with lemon juice if they are not being served immediately); and peel and dice the mangoes. Set aside.

Whisk the sugar and egg yolks together in the top of a double boiler until the mixture is thick and lemon-colored. Place over simmering water and add the Sauternes and cardamom. Whisk constantly until the sauce thickens; do not let it boil or the egg yolks will curdle. Let cool.

In a chilled bowl, whip the cream. Fold into the cooled sauce and chill until ready to serve.

Divide the mixed fruit among six wineglasses and generously spoon over the sauce. Garnish with a whole strawberry and some grated lemon rind.

CAFÉ MED
—
WASHINGTON, D.C.

BAHAMIAN BANANAS

Serves 4

4 tablespoons butter
4 bananas, sliced lengthwise
⅓ cup turbinado sugar
1 cup heavy cream
3 tablespoons Key lime juice or regular lime juice
2 tablespoons turbinado sugar for garnish
Wedges of lime for garnish

Heat the butter in a sauté pan until it is bubbling. Sprinkle the bananas with half of the turbinado sugar and sauté in the butter until they are brown on both sides and the sugar is beginning to caramelize. Set the bananas aside and keep warm.

In another pan, bring the cream to a boil and reduce by one third. Add the rest of the sugar, reduce the heat, stir, and simmer until the sugar is incorporated. Add the lime juice, continue stirring, and cook until the sauce is as thick as you like.

Transfer the bananas to warmed plates and drizzle over the sauce. Sprinkle with the 2 tablespoons turbinado sugar and place a wedge of lime on each plate.

Alix Kenagy Carson describes chef Mitch Manoloff's fare as "vacation food, the kind of food you eat when you're having a good time, sailing and sunning in the islands." And that usually means quick and easy to prepare, too, as is true of this island dessert that can be fixed at the last minute in front of guests.

INDIGO COASTAL
GRILL
—
ATLANTA

MOUSSES, PUDDINGS, AND ICE CREAM

Lemon Pudding Cake with Berry Coulis
Crème Caramel with Orange and Rosemary
Chocolate Amaretto Banana Trifle
Almond–Brown Rice Pudding with Raspberry
   Coulis
Apricot-Raisin Bread Pudding
Ginger Mousse with White Chocolate
Poppyseed Parfait with Blueberry Coulis
Frozen Amaretto Soufflé
Strawberry Frozen Yogurt Mousse
Adobe Pie
Mountain of Snow
Coupe Clancy
Lemon-Almond Ice Cream
Mandarine Napoleon Sorbet
Sorbetto allo Spumante (Champagne Sherbet)

All the desserts at *Pacific Heights Bar & Grill* are made on the premises by chef Lonnie Williams. This familiar pudding — didn't your grandmother make it? — is brought up to date by the underliner of berry coulis.

LEMON PUDDING CAKE WITH BERRY COULIS

Serves 6

1 cup sugar
⅛ teaspoon salt
¼ cup flour
4 tablespoons butter, melted
⅓ cup lemon juice
Grated zest of 1 lemon
3 eggs, separated
Pinch of nutmeg
1⅛ cups milk

BERRY COULIS

2 1-pint baskets fresh raspberries *or* 2 10-ounce
   packages frozen raspberries, thawed
2 tablespoons fresh lemon juice
Sugar to taste

In a mixing bowl, combine ¾ cup of the sugar, the salt, and the flour and stir. Add the melted butter, lemon juice, lemon zest, and egg yolks. Mix until well blended. Stir in the nutmeg and milk. In a separate bowl, beat the egg whites with the remaining ¼ cup sugar until they are stiff but still moist. Fold into the lemon mixture.

Pour the batter into a buttered 8-inch-square baking pan. Set in a larger pan and pour hot water into

PACIFIC
HEIGHTS BAR &
GRILL
—
SAN FRANCISCO

the larger pan to come halfway up the sides of the baking pan. Bake at 350° for 40 to 45 minutes, until the top is lightly browned.

While the pudding is baking, prepare the berry coulis. Place the raspberries, lemon juice, and as much sugar as you wish in the bowl of a food processor and purée. Strain through a fine sieve, taste, and adjust the seasoning.

Spoon the pudding cake, warm or cold, onto individual serving plates that have been lined with the berry coulis. Pass any extra coulis.

C A M P A G N E

CRÈME CARAMEL WITH ORANGE AND ROSEMARY

Serves 6

¾ cup sugar
¼ cup water
2¼ cups half-and-half
1 teaspoon vanilla
Rind from ½ orange, removed with a potato peeler
1 sprig fresh rosemary
3 eggs plus 2 yolks
⅓ cup plus 1 tablespoon sugar

To make the caramel, place the ¾ cup sugar and the water in a straight-sided saucepan over medium heat. Stir to dissolve before the cooking begins; from then on, do not stir. When the mixture is the color of strong tea (or weak coffee), remove from the heat. Holding the pan at arm's length, add 1 or 2 table-spoons of cold water. When the caramel stops splut-tering, immediately pour it into six 5- or 6-ounce molds so that the bottom of each mold contains about ¼ inch caramel.

While the caramel is cooling, make the custard. Put the half-and-half in a saucepan with the vanilla, orange rind, and rosemary and scald the mixture. In a large bowl, combine the eggs, yolks, and the re-maining sugar and whisk until the eggs pale a bit. Pour the hot half-and-half over the egg mixture in a steady stream, beating continuously. Strain into a pitcher and pour into the molds.

Set the molds in a baking pan and add enough lukewarm water to the pan to come halfway up the

Chef Ted Furst does not merely rely on inventive combinations of ingredients to make his cooking interesting but also pays close attention to tech-nique, hoping to reveal subtle-ties that otherwise would not be noticed. When you make this refreshing variation on the classic crème caramel, the tech-niques involved are important.

CAMPAGNE

—

SEATTLE

sides of the molds. Cover the pan or molds with foil or a baking sheet and place in a 300° oven. The cooking time can vary as much as an hour, depending on the shape and thickness of the molds, the temperature of the water bath, the depth of the caramel, and even the quality of the half-and-half. Start checking the molds after 30 or 40 minutes and continue periodic checks until the custard bulges somewhat when you tilt the mold at a 60° angle. The consistency should be exactly like that of Jell-O.

Remove the molds from the water bath and refrigerate for at least 2 hours (up to three days). Unmold onto individual serving plates, first running a thin-bladed knife around the edges. Pour the liquified caramel over and around the custard and serve.

Star Top has become well known among adventuresome and discriminating Chicago diners. Since the café is open until five o'clock in the morning on weekends, it attracts people who work in other restaurants and clubs and need somewhere to have a proper meal after their own places have closed.

CHOCOLATE AMARETTO BANANA TRIFLE

Serves 10

CHOCOLATE GENOISE

7 eggs, at room temperature
1 cup sugar
1 cup flour
¾ cup cocoa
4 tablespoons butter, melted and cooled
1 teaspoon vanilla

Combine the eggs and sugar in the bowl of an electric mixer and whip for 7 minutes. Sift together the flour and cocoa and fold into the sugar and egg mixture. Quickly fold in the melted butter and vanilla. Divide the batter between two greased 9-inch round cake pans lined with waxed paper and bake at 350° for 20 to 25 minutes, until the cake springs back to the touch. Let the cakes cool on racks.

CRÈME ANGLAISE

2 cups milk
6 egg yolks
½ cup sugar

Scald the milk. Whip the egg yolks with the sugar until the mixture forms a ribbon when the beaters

STAR TOP CAFÉ

—

CHICAGO

are lifted. Continuing to beat, slowly pour half the hot milk into the egg yolks in a steady stream, then pour the egg mixture into the rest of the hot milk. Cook over boiling water, stirring constantly, until thickened, but do not let the mixture boil.

ASSEMBLY

½ cup Amaretto
5 very ripe bananas, sliced
½ cup candied citrus peel
1 cup heavy cream, whipped
Fresh mint leaves for garnish

Assemble the trifle in a bowl about 9 inches in diameter. Cut one of the rounds of genoise into 2 layers (save the other for another occasion; the recipe cannot be cut in half) and cut one of the layers into three strips. Spoon one third of the *crème anglaise* into the bottom of the bowl. Place the center strip of cake over the custard, drizzle with one third of the Amaretto, add a layer of sliced bananas, and top with one third of the candied citrus peel and one third of the whipped cream.

Repeat the layering two more times, using the two remaining strips of cake for the second layer and the whole layer for the third. The layering should end with whipped cream. Chill until ready to serve. Garnish with mint leaves if you wish.

NOTE: This recipe can be varied and lightened in several ways. Other fruits and liqueurs may be used and the whipped cream may be omitted.

Union Square Cafe

ALMOND–BROWN RICE PUDDING WITH RASPBERRY COULIS

Serves 4

½ cup long-grain brown rice
1¼ cups water
1 tablespoon butter
4 egg yolks
¼ cup confectioners' sugar
2 cups heavy cream
1 teaspoon vanilla
1 teaspoon almond extract
1 cup Sauternes (or any good dessert wine)
½ cup dried apricots
½ cup whole blanched almonds, toasted in a 300°
    oven for about 10 minutes

RASPBERRY COULIS

1 8-ounce package frozen raspberries, thawed
¼ cup sugar

Place the rice, water, and butter in a covered pan and bring to a boil. Reduce the heat and continue cooking for about 40 minutes, until all the water is absorbed and the rice is tender. Let the rice cool.

To prepare the custard, place the egg yolks in a mixing bowl and whip vigorously for about 2 minutes. Add the sugar and whip until the mixture is thick and light yellow. Bring the cream to scalding

A popular feature of this café is the list of little-known wines offered at attractive prices, especially a comprehensive selection of dessert wines. The menu also recommends special wines of the day, available by the glass as well as the bottle. This dessert uses Sauternes and was devised by chef Ali Barker for the American Rice Council.

UNION SQUARE
CAFÉ
—
NEW YORK CITY

DESSERTS

and slowly add it to the egg yolk–sugar mixture, stirring continuously. Add the vanilla and almond extract.

In a saucepan, bring the Sauternes and apricots to a simmer and poach the apricots for about 15 minutes, until they are completely soft. Remove the apricots with a slotted spoon and reduce the Sauternes by half. Add the reduced Sauternes to the custard.

Combine the rice, custard, apricots, and almonds, and pour into a buttered 8-inch-square pan. Set the pan in a larger pan, fill the outer pan with hot water until it reaches halfway up the square pan, and bake at 325° for about 1 hour, or until a knife inserted in the center comes out clean.

To make the raspberry coulis, purée the raspberries and sugar in a blender or food processor and strain to remove the seeds. Serve the pudding cool or warm. Line each plate with the coulis and top with a mound of the pudding.

APRICOT-RAISIN BREAD PUDDING

Serves 12 to 16

2 24-inch loaves day-old French bread
¼ pound dried apricots, chopped
¼ pound golden raisins
2 quarts half-and-half
6 large eggs
1½ teaspoons orange extract
1½ teaspoons cinnamon
2½ cups sugar

SAUCE

1 cup butter, at room temperature
2 cups confectioners' sugar, sifted
1 large egg
1½ teaspoons orange extract

Thinly slice the French bread. Butter a 9-by-13-by-2-inch pan and put a layer of bread slices in the bottom. Sprinkle with the apricots and raisins. Repeat the layering until the pan is full, making sure the top layer is bread, decoratively arranged.

Combine the remaining ingredients in a large bowl. Pour the liquid over the bread and fruit, reserving a small amount. (The pudding can stand for up to an hour before baking.)

Place a baking sheet in the oven and put the pan on top. Pour the remaining liquid over the pudding

CITY MARKET

—

DALLAS

and bake at 350° for 1½ hours, checking after 45 minutes to be sure the top is not too brown; if it is, cover with foil. The pudding is done when a small knife inserted in the center comes out clean.

To make the sauce, cream the butter, add the sifted sugar, and mix well. Add the egg and orange extract. Brush over the top of the pudding in a thick layer. The pudding is best served hot or warm.

GINGER MOUSSE WITH WHITE CHOCOLATE

Serves 12

12 ounces white chocolate
4 tablespoons melted butter
6 egg yolks
6 tablespoons sugar
1 quart heavy cream
1 tablespoon ground ginger
1 tablespoon Cointreau

Melt the chocolate in the top of a double boiler. Fold in the melted butter and let cool. Beat the egg yolks with the sugar until the mixture is thick and pale. Fold the chocolate mixture into the egg yolk mixture. Beat the cream with the ginger and Cointreau until just stiff. Fold into the chocolate mixture. Chill the mousse until it is set, about 4 hours.

The food at West End Café has a reputation for being inventive without being quirky. This dessert on a bed of crème anglaise *is laced with raspberry purée.*

WEST END CAFÉ
—
WASHINGTON, D.C.

POPPYSEED PARFAIT WITH BLUEBERRY COULIS

Serves 4

2 egg yolks
4 tablespoons sugar
1½ teaspoons honey
1 teaspoon vanilla
2 tablespoons Grand Marnier
1 ounce poppyseeds, toasted in a 350° oven for
   1 minute
2 cups heavy cream

Place the egg yolks, sugar, honey, vanilla, and Grand Marnier in a bowl and whip vigorously until the mixture turns white, about 3 minutes. Add the poppyseeds. In a large bowl, whip the cream to soft peaks and gently fold in the egg mixture. Pour the mixture into 4 5-ounce molds (such as timbales or baba au rhum molds) and freeze for 8 hours. To unmold, dip the molds into warm water for 1 minute. Serve on a bed of Blueberry Coulis (recipe follows).

Blueberry Coulis

1 pint blueberries
¼ cup sugar
¼ cup water

56 EAST

—

ATLANTA

DESSERTS

Place all the ingredients in a saucepan, bring to a boil, and boil for 2 minutes. Remove from the heat, let cool, purée in a food processor, and strain. Chill before serving.

FROZEN AMARETTO SOUFFLÉ

Serves 12 to 16

10 egg yolks
⅔ cup superfine sugar
⅓ cup Amaretto
3 cups heavy cream
1⅓ cups confectioners' sugar
10 egg whites
Pinch of salt
Pinch of cream of tartar
1⅓ cups coarsely crushed amaretti cookies
⅓ cup finely chopped toasted almonds

Beat the egg yolks with ⅓ cup of the superfine sugar until thick. Stir in the Amaretto and set aside. Beat the heavy cream with the confectioners' sugar until stiff peaks form. Beat the egg whites, salt, cream of tartar, and the remaining ⅓ cup superfine sugar until glossy and stiff. Combine the amaretti and almonds and stir all but 4 tablespoons into the egg yolks. Fold in the whipped cream and then the egg whites.

Spoon the soufflé into a 10-inch springform pan that has been greased with vegetable oil and drained.

There is a lively after-theater business at West End Café, with full meal service available until eleven-thirty or midnight and pianist Burnett Thompson on deck five nights a week.

WEST END CAFÉ
—
WASHINGTON, D.C.

Freeze until it is set through (at least 5 hours). Unmold and sprinkle the remaining crumbs over the top. Cut into 12 to 16 wedges.

STRAWBERRY FROZEN YOGURT MOUSSE

Serves 8

2 cups fresh strawberries
1 cup sugar
1⅓ cups low-fat yogurt
4 egg whites
Additional strawberries for garnish

Place the strawberries, sugar, and yogurt in the bowl of a food processor and process until the fruit is chopped fine but not puréed. Pour the mixture into a bowl, cover, and place in the freezer until it begins to thicken. Meanwhile, beat the egg whites until stiff peaks form. Fold the egg whites into the thickened fruit mixture and return the bowl to the freezer until the mousse is firm (at least 4 hours). Scoop onto plates or into bowls, like ice cream, and garnish with fresh strawberries.

One of the fringe pleasures of visiting the Clark Art Institute is the surrounding landscape, visible from the gallery windows. The majestic Berkshire Hills are a backdrop for rolling meadows and lawns — a perfect setting for band concerts in the summer and cross-country skiing in the winter. An extensive herb garden, including signs in Braille, has been planted on the front terrace of the original main building.

CLARK CAFÉ

—

WILLIAMSTOWN,
MASSACHUSETTS

Isabelle Moya's son D.J. named this pie for the adobe bricks that are still used to construct houses in Santa Fe. Any premium ice cream — or, better yet, your own home-made — will make this simple dessert a big success.

ADOBE PIE

Serves 6 to 8

1¾ cups Famous Chocolate Wafer cookie crumbs
¼ cup melted butter
1 teaspoon Amaretto
1 pint vanilla ice cream
1 pint coffee ice cream
2 ounces semisweet chocolate, grated

Combine the cookie crumbs, melted butter, and Amaretto and press the mixture onto the bottom and sides of a buttered 9-inch pie pan. Bake in a 350° oven for 5 minutes. Allow the crust to cool, then place in the freezer for 15 minutes.

Let the vanilla ice cream soften at room temperature and spread it evenly over the chilled crust. Return the pan to the freezer for another 15 minutes, while the coffee ice cream is softening. Spread the coffee ice cream over the vanilla, sprinkle with the chocolate shavings, and return to the freezer until about 10 minutes before serving.

GUADALUPE
CAFÉ
—
SANTA FE

ERASMUS CAFÉ

MOUNTAIN OF SNOW

Serves 8

12 meringues (recipe follows)
4 ripe bananas, sliced
2 cups heavy cream, whipped
1 quart premium dark chocolate ice cream, slightly
   softened
6 ounces semisweet chocolate bits
6 ounces (¾ cup) butter

Using a 10-inch serving platter as a base, build the mountain as follows: Place a layer of the meringues on the platter and top with sliced bananas, leaving a bit of empty space around the edge. Cover the bananas with whipped cream, top with a mound of the ice cream, and cover with the remaining bananas. Cover the mound with the remaining meringues and spread whipped cream over the entire surface. Place in the freezer for 5 to 10 minutes.

Make a glaze by melting the chocolate bits and butter together in a heavy saucepan or double boiler. Let the glaze cool until it is warm instead of hot and drizzle from the top of the "mountain" in all directions. Serve immediately, cut in wedges, or hold in the freezer for up to 30 minutes.

NOTE: Chocolate mousse may be used in place of the ice cream.

Scott Van Hensbergen's menu includes homemade soups, salads, crêpes, and several sandwiches as well as various ethnic dishes. There is something for everyone, including a peanut butter and banana sandwich, and at prices suitable even for student budgets. Van Hensbergen has done catering for many years, and this dramatic dessert is always a hit at parties as well as at the café.

ERASMUS CAFÉ
AT THE COLLEGE
BOOKSTORE
—
WILLIAMSTOWN,
MASSACHUSETTS

DESSERTS

Meringues

Makes 12 3-inch meringues

4 egg whites, at room temperature
1 teaspoon vanilla
⅛ teaspoon cream of tartar
1 cup sifted confectioners' sugar

Using an electric mixer, beat the egg whites until foamy, then add the vanilla and cream of tartar. While continuing to beat, add the sugar, 1 tablespoon at a time. Beat until the mixture holds stiff peaks (do not overbeat). Form the meringues with a spoon and a spatula and drop onto a baking sheet covered with parchment paper. Bake at 225° for 1 hour. Turn off the oven, open the door, and leave the meringues inside for at least 5 minutes. Remove from the oven and let cool gradually. When cool, remove from the baking sheet and immediately place in an airtight container to store.

Clancy's

COUPE CLANCY

Serves 6

½ cup sugar
½ cup hot water
½ cup butter
½ cup Cappella or Frangelico liqueur
4 tablespoons chopped hazelnuts, toasted
1 quart homemade or premium vanilla ice cream

Mix the sugar with the hot water over medium heat until the sugar dissolves. Continue cooking until the mixture turns caramel in color. Remove from the heat and add the butter and liqueur. Immediately pour over individual servings of ice cream and top with the chopped hazelnuts.

NOTE: If the caramelized sugar forms a ball once the liqueur has been added, return the pan to the heat and let the sugar melt.

Part of the simple décor at Clancy's is a collection of pencil drawings by local artist George Schmid, portraits of the "guest maître d's" who are pressed into service from time to time. The system is this — one of the regular patrons serves as maître d' for the evening and invites his friends to the restaurant. The receipts go to his favorite charity. On the most memorable occasion, the director of the nearby New Orleans Zoo was host and his colleagues led over an elephant, hoping to have him sit at the bar. Though the beast failed to fit through the doorway, the publicity was unbeatable.

CLANCY'S

—

NEW ORLEANS

At Michela's, the meal begins with foot-long homemade breadsticks artfully laid on the linen tablecloths when guests arrive and ends with numbers of delectable desserts — tortes, puddings, and of course *sorbetti* and *gelati*. *This popular ice cream is the creation of Martha Burgess, the pastry chef.*

LEMON-ALMOND ICE CREAM

Serves 6

1 pint heavy cream
1 pint light cream
1 vanilla bean, split open
Zest from 1 lemon, removed with a potato peeler
8 egg yolks
1 cup sugar
Juice and grated zest of 1 lemon
¼ cup light corn syrup
1 cup toasted almonds, coarsely chopped

In a heavy saucepan, combine the heavy and light creams, the vanilla bean, and the lemon zest. Heat until steam rises from the surface. Strain to remove the zest and seeds. In a large bowl, whisk the egg yolks with the sugar and lemon juice. Slowly add the steaming cream mixture to the yolk mixture, stirring constantly with a wooden spoon. Return the mixture to the saucepan and add the corn syrup.

Stir constantly over medium heat until the mixture begins to coat a wooden spoon. Strain into a container set in a bowl of ice. When the mixture is cool, add the lemon zest and the almonds. Place in an ice cream maker and proceed according to the manufacturer's instructions.

MICHELA'S

—

CAMBRIDGE,
MASSACHUSETTS

MANDARINE NAPOLEON SORBET

Serves 4 to 6

1 cup sugar
¾ cup water
3 cups tangerine juice
2 tablespoons finely chopped tangerine rind
Juice of 1 lemon
¼ cup Mandarine Napoleon or orange liqueur

Place the sugar and water in a saucepan and stir over high heat with a clean wooden spoon until the sugar dissolves and the syrup comes to a full boil. Remove from the heat and pour into a bowl to cool.

When the syrup is cool, stir in the tangerine juice and rind, the lemon juice, and the liqueur. Add more lemon juice if the mixture seems too sweet. Freeze in an ice cream maker according to the manufacturer's instructions.

Maison de Ville is a small, elegant hotel with a rich history. Tennessee Williams wrote much of A Streetcar Named Desire *in the courtyard, just a few blocks from the streetcar line, and in the nearby cottages that are part of the hotel, John James Audubon created many of his famous bird paintings.*

THE BISTRO AT
MAISON DE
VILLE

—

NEW ORLEANS

DESSERTS

Petaluma is a great place for people watching. The writers Peter Maas, Lally Weymouth, and Ed Epstein can often be found near the open kitchen, while Richard Avedon, the photographer, prefers the center of the front room. Angie Dickinson makes a point of stopping in for crème brulée *when she's in New York, and Dr. Lee Salk comes over from New York Hospital around the corner.*

Petaluma

SORBETTO ALLO SPUMANTE (CHAMPAGNE SHERBET)

Serves 8

2 cups noncarbonated mineral water
¾ cup sugar
Finely grated rind from 1 lemon
Finely grated rind from 1 orange
2 cups Spumante

Bring the mineral water and sugar to a boil and continue boiling for 10 minutes. Add the grated lemon and orange rind to the hot syrup and place in the refrigerator. When the mixture is thoroughly chilled, add the Spumante. Pour into an ice cream maker and proceed according to the manufacturer's instructions. Just before serving, drizzle a small amount of Spumante into each dish.

` PETALUMA

—

NEW YORK CITY

BREAKFAST AND BRUNCH

BREAKFAST AND BRUNCH

Red Flannel Hash with Béarnaise
Louisiana Chicken Hash
Polenta with Poached Eggs and Sauce Arrabbiata
Eggs St. Bernard
Benedict Mexican with Con Queso Sauce
Migas
Huevos Pamul
Breakfast Burritos
Frittata Genovese
Grillades and Grits
Ginger Pancakes
Corn Cakes with Crème Fraîche and Caviar
Poppyseed Muffins
Banana Pecan Muffins
Orange-Walnut Muffins
Oat Bran Muffins
Creole Muffins
Strawberry Coffee Cake
Almond Danish Pastry

THE·EGG·AND·THE·EYE

RED FLANNEL HASH WITH BÉARNAISE

Serves 6

2 cups diced Spanish onion
4 tablespoons butter
⅓ cup flour
2 cups diced cooked potatoes
2 cups diced cooked beets
2 cups diced cooked corned beef
Salt and pepper to taste
6 eggs
2 cups Béarnaise Sauce (recipe follows)
Chopped parsley and freshly grated Parmesan
　　cheese for garnish

In a 10-inch cast-iron skillet or sauté pan with a cover, cook the onion in the butter. When the onion is transparent, sprinkle the flour over it and cook, stirring, for 2 or 3 minutes. Add the potatoes, beets, and corned beef and mix again gently (so as not to make the mixture overly beet pink). Cover and bake in a 375° oven for 30 minutes.

Remove from the oven and flip the hash (in sections, if other attempts fail) so that the crusty bottom is now on top. Cover and continue to bake for 15 to 20 minutes, until the bottom forms a crust.

While the hash is baking, poach the eggs and keep

Because the Craft and Folk Art Museum is in the same building and the newly expanded Los Angeles County Museum is across the street, weekend brunch at the Egg and the Eye is a popular occasion. One of owner Ian Barrington's favorite brunch dishes is this red flannel hash he remembers having at his family's summer house in Huntingdon, Québec.

THE EGG AND
THE EYE
—
LOS ANGELES

them warm in lukewarm water. Make the Béarnaise Sauce.

To serve, place approximately ½ cup of the sauce on a dinner plate and mound a serving of hash over it. Place a poached egg on top and sprinkle with the parsley and/or Parmesan.

Béarnaise Sauce

3 sprigs tarragon, chopped
3 sprigs chervil, chopped
3 small shallots, minced
¾ cup dry vermouth
Salt and freshly ground pepper to taste
3 egg yolks
1 tablespoon lemon juice
1 cup softened butter

In a small saucepan, combine the herbs, shallots, vermouth, and salt and pepper and bring the mixture to a boil. Continue cooking until the mixture is reduced to about 2 tablespoons. Set aside.

In the top of a double boiler over simmering water, whisk the egg yolks and lemon juice together and slowly add the softened butter, whisking constantly. Add the reduced herb mixture, blend well, and correct the seasoning, adding lemon juice or salt and pepper as needed.

KRAMERBOOKS
& afterwords
A café

The kitchen at Afterwords is small and visible from many of the café tables, so food preparation must be fairly simple. This popular Sunday brunch dish is made ahead and then heated and topped with freshly poached eggs just before serving.

LOUISIANA CHICKEN HASH

Serves 6

2 tablespoons butter
2 tablespoons flour
½ teaspoon salt
½ teaspoon white pepper
½ teaspoon freshly ground black pepper
½ teaspoon thyme
½ teaspoon paprika
½ teaspoon cayenne pepper or less
1 quart milk
2 pounds poached chicken meat, cut up
6 to 12 eggs, poached

Melt the butter in a heavy saucepan, add the flour, and cook, stirring constantly, until the mixture is a light brown color, about 5 minutes. Add the seasonings and cook for 1 minute, to toast the spices. Add the milk and heat; stir until the sauce is thick. Adjust the seasoning and add the chicken. Place the hash in individual baking dishes and heat for 10 minutes in a 350° oven. Top with 1 or 2 eggs and serve immediately.

KRAMERBOOKS
& AFTERWORDS
CAFÉ
—
WASHINGTON, D.C.

Sports is a major theme at *Washington Square Bar & Grill*, which is clear the moment you walk through the door. Facing the entrance is a pair of stadium seats from the old Navin Field in Detroit, given a champagne dedication by Hank Greenberg the day they were installed. The saloon fields its own softball team, Les Lapins Sauvages, which plays local teams but has been known to travel—to Paris, for example, where the Wild Rabbits played a team from the restaurant Moulin du Village in the Bois du Boulogne in 1979. Closer to home have been two contests with an East Coast media team — Tom Brokaw, Peter Jennings, and friends — during the 1984 Democratic National Convention in San Francisco and again in May 1987 in New York's Yankee Stadium.

Washington Square Bar & Grill.

POLENTA WITH POACHED EGGS AND SAUCE ARRABBIATA

Serves 6

1 quart milk
3 cups chicken broth
4 tablespoons unsalted butter
1 cup plus 2 tablespoons finely ground cornmeal
Salt and pepper to taste
6 eggs

SAUCE ARRABBIATA

2 tablespoons plus 1 teaspoon extra virgin olive oil
2¼ ounces pancetta (Italian bacon), sliced thin and julienne-cut
6 cloves garlic, minced
1 large onion, chopped fine
2 cups pear tomatoes crushed in purée
3 tablespoons minced fresh basil
1 teaspoon black pepper
1 teaspoon crushed red pepper
Salt to taste

First, make the sauce. Heat the olive oil in a wide enamel skillet and add the pancetta. Cook until the bacon is transparent. Add the garlic and onion and cook slowly until translucent. Add the tomatoes, basil, and seasonings. Cook over medium-high heat, stirring with a wooden spoon from time to time, until the sauce has thickened, about 20 minutes.

In a 4-quart pot, bring the milk and chicken broth to a boil. In a small skillet, cook the butter until it is light brown over gentle heat and add to the milk and broth. Stir the polenta into the boiling liquid; season to taste. Cook the polenta, stirring constantly, until the mixture thickens into porridge. Keep warm, covered with a piece of buttered waxed paper.

Bring the sauce to a simmer and poach the eggs in it. Divide the polenta among six serving bowls, place an egg in each, and spoon the sauce over all.

EGGS ST. BERNARD

Serves 4

4 whole-wheat English muffins
8 eggs
1 1-pound bunch broccoli, flowerets and 2 inches of
   stem only
½ pound country ham, thinly sliced

BRANDIED HOLLANDAISE SAUCE

1 cup brandy
4 tablespoons finely chopped shallots
4 egg yolks
1 pound unsalted butter, melted
Juice of 1 lemon
Coarse (kosher) salt and freshly ground pepper
   to taste
1 tablespoon chopped fresh thyme, if available
   (do not used dried)

In rare instances, the pervasive theme at White Dog Café even makes its way onto the menu. This delicious variation on an old standby is easy to make, once the brandied hollandaise is out of the way, and is enhanced by the quality of the components one is able to find. Aliza Green uses homemade English muffins, farm fresh eggs, and country ham.

WHITE DOG
CAFÉ

—

PHILADELPHIA

To prepare the hollandaise, first warm and flame the brandy in a saucepan (making sure the area is clear). Once the flames have died down, add the shallots. Simmer for several minutes, until ½ cup liquid remains (add water if the mixture has reduced too much). Strain into a stainless steel bowl. Add the egg yolks and whisk the mixture over a pan of simmering water. Whisking constantly, gradually ladle in the melted butter as the mixture begins to thicken. When all the butter has been incorporated, add the lemon juice to taste, the salt and pepper, and the thyme. If the sauce seems too thick, add a little hot water. Set aside in a warm place.

Just before serving, toast the muffins, poach the eggs, and blanch the broccoli in boiling water for 1 or 2 minutes. Place the muffins on four warmed plates. Arrange the ham slices over the muffin halves in an X. Place the eggs over the ham, arrange the broccoli next to the muffins, and cover the eggs and broccoli with the brandied hollandaise. Serve immediately.

NOTE: There will be hollandaise left over, but it is difficult to make the sauce in smaller quantities.

BENEDICT MEXICAN WITH CON QUESO SAUCE

Serves 6

1 pound Velveeta cheese
½ cup Green Chile Sauce (see page 155)
Dash of Worcestershire sauce
6 English muffins, toasted
12 slices ham, sautéed in a little butter
12 eggs, poached

To make the sauce, combine the cheese, chile sauce, and Worcestershire in the top of a double boiler and place over simmering water until the cheese has melted.

Place a toasted English muffin on each of six plates and top each half with a slice of ham and a poached egg. Spoon the sauce over each egg and serve immediately.

Isabelle Moya feels that people keep coming back to the Guadalupe Café because the chili is hot, the portions are large, and family dining is encouraged. Children's plates and hamburgers share the menu with New Mexican classics, and many All-American favorites are given a southwestern twist.

GUADALUPE
CAFÉ
—
SANTA FE

One of the good things about breakfast at the Dream Café is that it is available until two P.M. Several of the items on the menu are Tex-Mex dishes, and the Migas, served with black beans, brown rice, and whole-wheat tortillas, are among the most popular.

MIGAS

Serves 4

8 corn tortillas, cut in triangles and baked until
   crisp
¼ cup olive oil
2 cups cooked salsa (commercial salsa may be used)
8 eggs, lightly scrambled
1 cup grated Cheddar or Monterey Jack cheese

In a heavy cast-iron skillet or sauté pan, cook the tortilla triangles in the oil over high heat. Add the salsa and stir to soften the tortillas. Add the scrambled eggs and stir to mix. Sprinkle the cheese on top, cover the pan, and remove from the heat. Serve as soon as the cheese has melted.

NOTE: For a dish with less cholesterol, substitute tofu for the scrambled eggs: just crumble it into the skillet after the tortillas have been softened with the salsa.

THE DREAM
CAFÉ

—

DALLAS

HUEVOS PAMUL

Serves 1 or 2

½ cup refritos
1 flour or corn tortilla
½ cup grated Cheddar cheese
3 eggs
¼ cup sliced green onion
3 tomato slices
Salt and pepper to taste
¼ cup diced tomato
2 tablespoons sour cream
¼ cup salsa

Spread the refritos on the tortilla and sprinkle with the grated cheese. Place in a 400° oven for 5 minutes.

While the tortilla is in the oven, lightly scramble the eggs and spoon them into an omelette pan over medium heat. Sprinkle with half of the green onion, and place the tomato slices in the eggs. Sprinkle with the salt and pepper. (It should look like an egg pancake.)

Remove the tortilla from the oven and transfer it to a serving plate. Slide the eggs onto the tortilla and garnish the top with the remaining onion, the diced tomato, sour cream, and salsa. Serve immediately, with additional salsa if you wish.

This recipe is evidence that regional cooking has become popular all over the country, both in and away from its own region. Although this dish technically serves one person, that person needs to have a Paul Bunyan appetite. You can present it whole, for aesthetic purposes, and then cut it in half.

NICK & SULLY

—

SEATTLE

The Guadalupe Café has been called ''as comfortable and friendly as one's favorite pair of shoes.'' The clientele is mostly local and the décor is simple, with a wood stove at the ready for those moments after sundown when the high mountain air turns chilly. Breakfast and weekend brunch are busy times at the Guadalupe; this popular dish is served with pan-fried new potatoes seasoned with basil.

BREAKFAST BURRITOS

Serves 6

4 cups sliced mushrooms
2 tablespoons butter
3 10-ounce packages frozen chopped spinach, thawed, drained, and squeezed dry
6 medium flour tortillas
Green Chile Sauce (see page 155)
2 cups grated Monterey Jack cheese

Sauté the mushrooms in the butter until they are barely cooked. Add the spinach and continue cooking until the mixture is hot. Spread each tortilla evenly with the mushroom-spinach mixture. Roll the tortillas tightly and place them, seam side down, in a buttered shallow baking dish. Spread the Green Chile Sauce over the top and sprinkle with the grated cheese. Bake in a 450° oven for about 5 minutes, until the cheese has melted.

GUADALUPE
CAFÉ

—

SANTA FE

FRITTATA GENOVESE

Serves 2

4 large eggs
½ cup chopped green onion
½ cup diced ham
½ cup grated Swiss cheese
½ cup sautéed sliced mushrooms
½ cup freshly grated Parmesan cheese
¼ cup chopped fresh basil
¼ cup chopped parsley
2 tablespoons clarified butter (see page 335)

Whisk the eggs thoroughly in a bowl. Combine the remaining ingredients, except the clarified butter, and blend into the eggs. Place the clarified butter in an 8- to 10-inch omelette pan and heat until the foaming subsides. Pour the egg mixture into the pan. As it cooks, lift the edges and allow the uncooked egg to flow underneath. When the top is set, flip the frittata and allow the other side to brown. Slide from the pan, cut in half, and serve immediately.

NOTE: If you wish to keep two pans going at once, just double all the ingredients and serve 4.

The original menu at The Egg consisted of fifty different omelettes, two soups, and bread. Although the current menu offers a range of bistro fare, one can still choose among fifty omelette fillings — everything from Lorraine (bacon, Swiss cheese, and chives) to African (diced beef, dried apples, prunes, raisins, curry, and dried apricots). A few of the choices are made as frittatas, with the filling mixed into the eggs.

THE EGG AND
THE EYE

—

LOS ANGELES

Fine food is not the only attraction at Mr. B's bistro. The good times do roll, especially at Sunday brunch when the Original Crescent City Jazz Band performs. A popular choice on the brunch menu is Grillades and Grits, a traditional New Orleans breakfast. In some versions the veal is broiled, thus "grillades." The sauce contains the browned roux basic to many Creole dishes.

GRILLADES AND GRITS

Serves 6

½ cup vegetable oil
½ cup flour
4 cups beef stock (see page 331)
1 medium green pepper, chopped
1 medium onion, chopped
1 bunch green onions, chopped
2 cloves garlic, minced
1½ pounds veal cutlets
2 tomatoes, peeled, seeded, and chopped
Salt and pepper to taste
Flour for dredging
3 tablespoons butter
3 cups cooked grits

Heat the oil in a skillet and add the flour. Whisk together and cook until the mixture is golden brown. Add the stock and, whisking continuously, bring to a boil; boil for 5 minutes. Strain the mixture through a sieve and return it to the skillet.

In another large skillet sauté the pepper, onions, and garlic until they are tender but not brown. Add the stock mixture and simmer for 10 minutes. Add the tomatoes and salt and pepper.

Cut the veal into strips 2 inches wide, season with salt and pepper, and dredge with flour. Heat the butter in a sauté pan and lightly brown the veal on both sides. Add the veal to the sauce and simmer for ½ hour. Serve with buttered grits.

MR. B'S
—
NEW ORLEANS

GINGER PANCAKES

Serves 4

2½ cups whole-wheat flour
½ teaspoon salt
1½ teaspoons baking soda
1 teaspoon ground cloves
1 tablespoon cinnamon
3 eggs, lightly beaten
¼ cup brown sugar
2 cups buttermilk
¼ cup brewed coffee
1 tablespoon melted butter
2 tablespoons grated fresh ginger

Combine the dry ingredients in a bowl and mix well with your hands (sieve the baking soda if it is lumpy). In another bowl, or a pancake pitcher, stir together the remaining ingredients. Add the dry ingredients to the wet ingredients, blending until just incorporated. Cook the pancakes on a lightly oiled, sizzling pancake griddle or in a cast-iron skillet for approximately 5 minutes on the first side and 1 minute after flipping.

The menu at the Dream Café includes a note about the O'Briens' philosophy of cooking and eating: "We believe in using whole grains and the freshest vegetables and fruits in the creation and preparation of our food. . . . We think you'll agree that the results are worth it." It is no surprise, then, that these delicious whole-wheat pancakes are served with fresh creamery butter and real maple syrup.

THE DREAM
CAFÉ
—
DALLAS

The menus at West End Café have catchy theatrical sub-heads: appetizers are Over-tures, desserts are Grand Finales, Liqueurs are Curtain Calls. In keeping with today's emphasis on offering light al-ternatives to standard entrées, there are sections of Light Fare as well as Splendid Fare. This recipe comes from the Short Subjects segment of the Sunday brunch menu.

CORN CAKES WITH CRÈME FRAÎCHE AND CAVIAR

Serves 6

2 eggs
¼ cup Wesson oil
½ cup cornmeal
½ cup flour
½ teaspoon baking soda
½ teaspoon salt
Generous pinch of cayenne pepper
1½ to 2 cups orange juice
Clarified butter
1½ cups *crème fraîche* (see page 335)
Selection of caviars

Combine the eggs and oil. Sift the dry ingredients and add to the eggs (the mixture will be very dry). Gradually add the orange juice until the mixture re-sembles thin pancake batter. Heat the clarified but-ter in a skillet. Ladle the batter into the pan, using a 1-ounce ladle to form 2½-inch corn cakes. When the bottom of each cake has browned, flip and finish cooking the other side. Serve with a dollop of *crème fraîche* and pass a selection of caviars.

WEST END CAFÉ

—

WASHINGTON, D.C.

POPPYSEED MUFFINS

Makes 14 to 18

1¼ cups sugar
3⅓ cups flour
4 teaspoons baking powder
1 teaspoon salt
⅓ cup plus 1 tablespoon poppyseeds
1 cup plus 2 tablespoons vegetable oil
1½ cups milk
1½ teaspoons vanilla
3 eggs
Grated rind of 2 lemons

GLAZE

Juice of 1 lemon
½ cup water
¼ cup sugar

Combine the first five ingredients in a bowl and blend well. In the bowl of an electric mixer, combine the oil, milk, vanilla, eggs, and lemon rind. Add the dry ingredients and mix for 2 minutes, until the batter is smooth. Bake at 325° for 30 to 40 minutes, until a toothpick inserted in the center of a muffin comes out clean. While the muffins are warm, poke holes in the top and liberally brush on the glaze.

There seems to be an almost equal emphasis on food and fun at the White Dog Café. Most evenings there is live music, and "special events" are held throughout the year — among them a Bastille Day celebration, when the staff dresses up like white dogs, sporting red berets; a Halloween party, complete with costumes, skits, and judges; and a Brides' Brunch, for which patrons wear their old wedding or bridesmaid's dresses and all participants join in cutting the cake.

WHITE DOG
CAFÉ
—
PHILADELPHIA

Rebecca's is on Charles Street at the foot of Beacon Hill, the home of business and professional people of all ages, many of whom stop in for a quick breakfast on the way to work. Freshly squeezed fruit juices, homemade pastries, and the morning papers are all strong attractions.

BANANA PECAN MUFFINS

Makes 18 to 20

½ cup unsalted butter
1¼ cups sugar
2 eggs
2 cups flour
½ teaspoon salt
2 tablespoons baking powder
½ teaspoon vanilla
½ cup plus 2 tablespoons milk
2 ripe bananas, chopped
1 cup chopped pecans

Cream the butter and sugar and add the eggs, beating after each one is added. Sift the dry ingredients together and add to the creamed mixture, blending just until the ingredients are combined (do not overmix). Add the vanilla and milk and blend. Fold in the bananas and pecans. Spoon the batter into greased and floured muffin tins and bake at 300° for 40 minutes or until the tops are golden brown and spring back to the touch.

REBECCA'S

—

BOSTON

At Trio the same menu is served from eight in the morning until six at night, which means that these muffins are not just for breakfast. Though the café makes bite-size muffins, the yield given here is for regular-size tins.

ORANGE-WALNUT MUFFINS

Makes 1 dozen

½ cup butter, at room temperature
⅔ cup brown sugar
1 teaspoon baking soda
½ cup sour cream
2 eggs, beaten
1½ cups flour
1 cup chopped walnuts
1 teaspoon vanilla
1 heaping tablespoon grated orange zest (1½ large oranges)

Cream the butter and sugar. In a separate bowl, mix the soda with the sour cream. Add the eggs and sour cream mixture to the butter-sugar mixture. Fold in the flour, nuts, vanilla, and orange zest. Fill greased muffin tins two-thirds full and bake at 350° for 25 minutes, until the tops of the muffins are lightly browned.

NOTE: The batter may be refrigerated overnight.

TRIO CAFÉ
—
SAN FRANCISCO

Irresistibly named, the Dream Café is a family operation run by Mary O'Brien and her sister and three brothers. The O'Briens were raised in Indiana, but all have made their way to Dallas, their mother's hometown. Mary and her brother John do the cooking, and the results are natural foods that make you forget you're eating healthfully. The bonus in these muffins is that oat bran is thought to be helpful in lowering cholesterol levels.

OAT BRAN MUFFINS

Makes 18 to 24

2 cups whole-wheat flour
1½ cups oat bran
2 teaspoons baking soda
1 teaspoon salt
¼ cup butter, melted
½ cup brown sugar
2 eggs
3 cups buttermilk
½ cup currants

Combine the flour, oat bran, baking soda, and salt in a large bowl. Mix the butter, brown sugar, eggs, and buttermilk in a separate bowl. Combine the two mixtures and blend (do not overmix). Add the currants and spoon the batter into buttered muffin tins. Bake at 350° for 20 to 25 minutes.

THE DREAM
CAFÉ

—

DALLAS

CREOLE MUFFINS

Makes 10 to 12

1 large egg
¼ cup vegetable oil
1¼ cups milk
⅓ cup mixture of half chopped onion and half
  finely diced sweet red pepper
⅓ cup chopped parsley
2 cups flour
1 tablespoon sugar
1 tablespoon baking powder
1½ teaspoons salt
⅔ teaspoon white pepper
⅔ teaspoon thyme
½ teaspoon garlic powder
½ teaspoon oregano
¼ teaspoon cayenne pepper
¼ teaspoon freshly ground black pepper

In a small bowl, combine the egg, oil, milk, onion and red pepper, and parsley. Sift the remaining ingredients into a large bowl. Add the liquid mixture to the dry mixture and stir with a wooden spoon until just blended. Do not overmix.

Grease a muffin tin and fill the cups two-thirds full. (Fill any empty spaces with water.) Bake at 400° for 15 minutes, until the tops are light brown.

Although these muffins are perfect for breakfast or brunch with simple scrambled eggs, they may also be served with such Texas favorites as barbecue, gumbo, or red beans and rice. Or bake the muffins in bite-size tins and serve them as an hors d'oeuvre with beer.

CITY MARKET
—
DALLAS

Nick & Sully is a popular spot for a quick coffee before work, a business breakfast, or a leisurely weekend brunch. Copies of all manner of newspapers and magazines hang on library racks along the wall — everything from Paris Match *to* Food & Wine *— and in good weather the outdoor patio provides a special setting.*

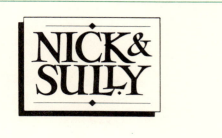

STRAWBERRY COFFEE CAKE

Serves 8

½ cup butter
½ cup sugar
1½ cups flour
1½ teaspoons baking powder
1 egg, lightly beaten
1 teaspoon vanilla
1½ cups sliced strawberries

TOPPING

2 cups sour cream
2 egg yolks
½ cup sugar
1 teaspoon vanilla

GARNISH

½ cup sliced strawberries
½ cup sliced almonds
Confectioners' sugar

Cream the butter and sugar. Combine the flour and baking powder. Add to the butter-sugar mixture; add the egg and vanilla. Pat the mixture into a greased 9-inch springform pan and sprinkle the sliced strawberries on top.

Combine all the ingredients for the topping, blend well, and pour over the strawberries. Bake at 350° for approximately 1 hour. Before serving, sprinkle

NICK & SULLY
—
SEATTLE

the garnishes over the cake, ending with confectioners' sugar.

ALMOND DANISH PASTRY

Makes 36 pieces

The menu at the Clark Café owes its special quality to Jytte Brooks and her Danish heritage. Though she has been in this country since she was a graduate student, regular visits to family and friends in Denmark give her a chance to pick up new ideas. Cooking is just one of Jytte's talents; she is also a silversmith and teaches creative movement and dramatics.

DOUGH

1 tablespoon dry yeast (1 ¼-ounce package)
1 cup cold milk
3 tablespoons sugar
2 large eggs
½ teaspoon salt
1 teaspoon cardamom
2 tablespoons margarine or butter
4 cups flour (must be unbleached)
1 pound cold margarine or butter

In a large bowl, dissolve the yeast in the milk and stir in the sugar. Add the eggs, salt, cardamom, the 2 tablespoons margarine, and the flour. Mix together and knead lightly. On a floured pastry cloth, roll out the dough 1 inch thick and about 12 inches square. Place the remaining margarine in the center of the square (lay the sticks flat, in a row) and fold the sides of the dough over the margarine so that it is completely covered. Press the dough gently with the

CLARK CAFÉ

—

WILLIAMSTOWN,
MASSACHUSETTS

palm of your hand to flatten the margarine.

Roll the dough into a rectangle, about 12 by 18 inches, and fold it twice as you would a piece of paper meant for an envelope. Wrap the pastry cloth around the dough and let it rest in the refrigerator for 10 minutes. Roll the dough (with the narrow end facing you), fold it, and let it rest two more times, increasing the rest to ½ hour the last time.

FILLING

1 8-ounce package almond paste
1 cup sugar
1 cup margarine or butter
1 tablespoon vanilla
1 cup raisins
1 cup sliced blanched almonds

Mix all the ingredients except the raisins and almonds in a food processor. Stir in ¾ cup each of the raisins and almonds, reserving the rest. Refrigerate until ready to use.

CUSTARD

2 tablespoons sugar
2 egg yolks
1 cup milk
1 tablespoon cornstarch
1 tablespoon vanilla

Beat the sugar and egg yolks until the mixture is nearly white. In a heavy saucepan, bring the milk to a boil and whisk in the egg mixture and the cornstarch. Whisk constantly until the custard thickens. Remove from the heat, add the vanilla, and let cool. Refrigerate until ready to use.

NOTE: A vanilla bean may be used in place of the vanilla extract to flavor both the filling and the custard. For the filling, use the seeds scraped from the inside of the bean; for the custard, place the empty bean in the milk before it is scalded and discard it once the custard has thickened.

ASSEMBLY

Roll the dough into a rectangle ½ inch thick. Cut the rectangle lengthwise into three strips. Place one of the strips on a baking sheet and refrigerate the other two until you have finished filling the first. Mentally divide the strip into three sections lengthwise and spread a thick layer of the filling on the center section. Spread a layer of cold custard over the filling and sprinkle with some of the almonds and raisins and a touch of sugar.

Fold the empty sides toward the center, leaving 1 inch of filling visible. Let the dough rise for about 20 minutes. Fill the remaining strips of dough, one at a time. Brush the top of the pastry with an egg wash made by beating 1 egg with 1 tablespoon water and bake in a 425° oven for about 20 minutes, until nicely brown. Cool and cut into individual servings.

NOTE: This recipe has a high yield, but the finished pastries freeze well (after baking), and the dough may be frozen before the custard and filling are added.

THE CAFÉ PANTRY

THE CAFÉ PANTRY

Chicken Stock
Beef Stock
Veal Stock
Fish Stock
Vinaigrette
Mayonnaise
Clarified Butter
Crème Fraîche
Crème Anglaise
Pizza Dough

CHICKEN STOCK

Makes about 2 quarts

4 pounds chicken backs, necks, wings, and feet, fat
  removed
4 quarts cold water
10 white peppercorns
1 bay leaf
1 teaspoon thyme
4 whole cloves
⅓ cup coarsely chopped parsley
1 medium onion, quartered
1 carrot, roughly chopped
3 stalks celery, diced
1 clove garlic, minced

Place the chicken parts in a large stockpot, cover
with cold water, bring to a boil, and blanch for 5
minutes. Pour off and discard the water, add the 4
quarts cold water, and slowly bring the water to a
boil. Reduce the heat and simmer, uncovered, for
about 30 minutes. Remove the scum and add the
remaining ingredients. Continue to simmer, partly
covered, for 3 hours, until the liquid is reduced by
half. Strain the stock and cool, uncovered, before
refrigerating. Remove the coagulated fat from the
top of the stock before using.

BEEF STOCK

Makes 2 to 3 quarts

3 pounds beef shinbone
2 marrow bones
3 pounds chuck, cut in three pieces
3 quarts water
1½ tablespoons salt
6 peppercorns
1 large onion, peeled, studded with 4 whole cloves
1 large leek, trimmed and washed well under
   running water
1 bay leaf
½ teaspoon thyme
2 carrots, trimmed
2 sprigs parsley
2 stalks celery

Remove the meat from the shinbone and set aside. Place the shinbone and marrow bones in boiling water, cook for 5 minutes, and drain well. Place the bones and all the meat in a large kettle. Cover with the water and bring to a rolling boil. Reduce the heat. Skim the surface to remove the scum and continue skimming until the foam ceases to rise.

Add the remaining ingredients, cover the kettle loosely, and simmer for 4 to 5 hours. Strain the stock through a double thickness of cheesecloth. Taste the stock and reduce over high heat if a stronger flavor is desired. Chill until the fat has solidified on top. Lift off the fat.

VEAL STOCK

Makes about 2 quarts

4 pounds veal knuckles or cracked hock or shank
    bones in pieces 2 to 3 inches long
4 quarts cold water
1 medium onion, quartered
2 carrots, roughly chopped
3 stalks celery, chopped
1 clove garlic, minced
1 bay leaf
4 whole cloves
8 white peppercorns
⅓ cup roughly chopped parsley

Place the veal bones in a large stockpot, cover with
water, bring to a boil, and blanch for 5 minutes. Pour
off and discard the water and add the 4 quarts cold
water to the pot. Bring the water to a boil, reduce to
a simmer, and cook, uncovered, for about 30 minutes. Remove the scum and add the remaining ingredients. Simmer, partly covered, for about 3 hours,
until the liquid is reduced by half. Strain the stock,
cool (uncovered), and refrigerate. Remove the coagulated fat from the top before using.

FISH STOCK

Makes about 2 quarts

Butter
1 medium white onion, sliced thin
2 shallots, sliced
2 pounds fresh fish bones and trimmings (do not use bones and heads from oily fish, skin, or any part of the entrails or gills)
¾ cup white wine
About 2 quarts water
2 bay leaves
10 white peppercorns
1 teaspoon thyme
2 sprigs parsley
1 teaspoon lemon juice

Smear a small amount of butter over the bottom of a nonreactive stockpot (stainless steel, enamel, glass, or anodized aluminum). Add the onion and shallots and place the fish bones on top of them. Set the pot over medium heat and let the ingredients sweat for a few minutes. Add the wine and raise the heat; let the wine boil for 3 or 4 minutes.

Add enough cold water to cover the bones by ½ inch and bring it to a boil, removing any scum that rises to the surface. When the stock begins to boil, lower the heat until the liquid is barely moving, then add the remaining ingredients. Let the stock simmer for 30 minutes and strain through a fine sieve.

MAYONNAISE

Makes about 2 cups

2 egg yolks
1 teaspoon dry mustard
½ teaspoon salt
Pinch of cayenne pepper
¼ cup wine vinegar or lemon juice
1 cup olive oil
1 cup vegetable oil

Using a whisk or electric mixer, beat the yolks until they are thick and lemon-colored. Add the seasonings and half the vinegar or lemon juice. Combine the oils and add, while beating, drop by drop at first, then in a gradually increasing amount as the mixture thickens. Slowly add the remaining vinegar or lemon juice and beat well. Chill. The mayonnaise will keep, covered, in the refrigerator for at least a week.

VINAIGRETTE

Makes 1 cup

¾ cup olive oil
¼ cup tarragon vinegar
1 teaspoon Dijon mustard
Salt and pepper to taste

Whisk together all the ingredients or shake in a covered jar.

CLARIFIED BUTTER

Clarified butter is less likely to burn during frying and sautéing than regular melted butter. To prepare it, place any amount of butter in a saucepan and heat slowly until it begins to froth and the white milk solids sink to the bottom. Skim off the foam and carefully pour out the clear yellow liquid (the clarified butter), leaving the white residue in the pan. Clarified butter will keep for a few days, refrigerated.

CRÈME FRAÎCHE

Makes 1 cup

1 cup heavy cream
2 tablespoons buttermilk *or* 1 tablespoon plain
   yogurt

Place the cream and buttermilk or yogurt in a glass jar, cover tightly, and shake well. Let the mixture sit in a warm place for about 8 hours, until it has thickened. Refrigerate overnight before using. *Crème fraîche* will keep for a week or so, refrigerated.

CRÈME ANGLAISE

Makes 2 cups

2 cups milk
5 egg yolks, lightly beaten
4 tablespoons sugar
Pinch of salt
1 teaspoon vanilla

Scald the milk in the top of a double boiler. Slowly stir in the egg yolks, sugar, and salt. Place the pan over boiling water and stir the mixture constantly with a wooden spoon until it begins to thicken and coat the spoon. Remove from the heat and add the vanilla. Strain the custard through a sieve into a bowl and let cool.

NOTE: A variety of flavorings may be used instead of the vanilla. Sherry, a liqueur, or grated lemon rind may be added, to taste. For a coffee flavor, add 1 tablespoon of instant coffee granules to the hot custard and stir until they dissolve.

PIZZA DOUGH

Makes 2 pounds

¼ cup lukewarm water
1½ teaspoons honey
¼ ounce (1 package) active dry yeast
3 tablespoons olive oil
4 cups flour
4 tablespoons whole-wheat flour
1½ teaspoons salt
1 to 3 cups water (see Note)

Place the lukewarm water, honey, yeast, and olive oil in a bowl and whisk together until the yeast and honey are dissolved. Let proof for 10 minutes. Mix the flours and salt in a large bowl and add the yeast mixture. Mix and gradually add the water. Work the dough with a dough hook or by hand until it is smooth, soft, and elastic. Let it rise at room temperature for 1 to 2 hours, punch down, and refrigerate until ready to use.

NOTE: The amount of water needed will vary according to the humidity of the surroundings. Less water will be needed where there is high humidity.

THE CAFÉS AND
THEIR
ADDRESSES

———

INDEX

THE CAFÉS AND THEIR ADDRESSES

APROPOS BISTRO
(215) 546-4424

211 South Broad Street
Philadelphia, Pennsylvania 19107

BALBOA CAFÉ
(415) 921-1113

3199 Fillmore Street
San Francisco, California 94123

BAY WOLF
(415) 655-6932

3853 Piedmont Avenue
Oakland, California 94611

THE BISTRO AT MAISON DE VILLE
(504) 528-9206

733 Toulouse Street
New Orleans, Louisiana 70130

THE BRASSERIE
(802) 447-7922

324 County Street
Bennington, Vermont 05201

CAFÉ BA-BA-REEBA!
(312) 935-5000

2024 North Halsted
Chicago, Illinois 60614

CAFÉ MED
(202) 338-0417

3065 M Street, N.W.
Washington, D.C. 20007

CAFÉ PACIFIC
(214) 526-0318

24 Highland Park Village
Dallas, Texas 75205

THE CAFÉ PETITTO
(202) 462-8771

1724 Connecticut Avenue, N.W.
Washington, D.C. 20009

CAFÉ SPIAGGIA
(312) 280-2764

980 North Michigan Avenue
Chicago, Illinois 60611

CAFÉ SPORT
(206) 443-6000

2020 Western Avenue
Seattle, Washington 98121

CAMPAGNE
(206) 329-4650

1812 Summit Avenue
Seattle, Washington 98102

CHIANTI & CUCINA
(213) 653-8333

7383 Melrose Avenue
Los Angeles, California 90046

CITY CAFÉ
(214) 351-2233

5757 West Lovers' Lane
Dallas, Texas 75209

CITY MARKET (214) 979-2696	2001 Ross Avenue Dallas, Texas 75201
CLANCY'S (504) 895-1111	6100 Annunciation New Orleans, Louisiana 70118
CLARK CAFÉ (413) 458-8109	Sterling and Francine Clark Art Institute 225 South Street Williamstown, Massachusetts 01267
DESERT CAFÉ (505) 984-3100	Sanbusco 540 Montezuma Street Santa Fe, New Mexico 87501
THE DREAM CAFÉ (214) 522-1478	3312 Knox Dallas, Texas 75205
THE EGG AND THE EYE RESTAURANT (213) 933-5596	5814 Wilshire Boulevard Los Angeles, California
EL FAROL (505) 983-9912	808 Canyon Road Santa Fe, New Mexico 87501
EMPIRE DINER (212) 924-0011	210 Tenth Avenue New York, New York 10011
ENOTECA WINE SHOP AND RESTAURANT (206) 624-9108	414 Olive Way Seattle, Washington 98101
ERASMUS CAFÉ (413) 458-5007	76 Spring Street Williamstown, Massachusetts 01267
56 EAST (404) 364-WINE	56 East Andrews Drive Atlanta, Georgia 30305
GUADALUPE CAFÉ (505) 982-9762	313 Guadalupe Street Santa Fe, New Mexico 87501
HARVARD BOOK STORE CAFÉ (617) 536-0097	190 Newbury Street Boston, Massachusetts 02116
INDIGO COASTAL GRILL (404) 876-0676	1397 North Highland Avenue Atlanta, Georgia 30306
KRAMERBOOKS & AFTERWORDS CAFÉ (202) 387-1462	1517 Connecticut Avenue, N.W. Washington, D.C. 20036
MARABELLA'S (215) 545-1845	1420 Locust Street Philadelphia, Pennsylvania 19102
MICHELA'S (617) 494-5419	245 First Street Cambridge, Massachusetts 02142
MISS RUBY'S CAFÉ (212) 620-4055	135 Eighth Avenue New York, New York 10011
MR. B'S BISTRO (504) 523-2078	201 Royal Street New Orleans, Louisiana 70130

MONIQUE'S CAFÉ
(312) 642-2210

213 West Institute Place
Chicago, Illinois 60610

NAPOLEON HOUSE BAR &
    CAFÉ
(504) 524-9752

500 Chartres Street
New Orleans, Louisiana 70130

NICK & SULLY
(206) 325-8813

2043 Eastlake Avenue East
Seattle, Washington 98102

NORTH STAR BAR
(215) 235-STAR

2639 Poplar Street
Philadelphia, Pennsylvania 19130

OUISIE'S TABLE
(713) 528-2264

1708 Sunset Boulevard
Houston, Texas 77005

PACIFIC HEIGHTS BAR & GRILL
(415) 567-3337

2001 Fillmore Street
San Francisco, California 94115

PETALUMA
(212) 772-8800

1356 First Avenue
New York, New York 10021

PIRET$_M$
(619) 943-7515

763 Second Street
Encinitas, California 92024

REBECCA'S
(617) 742-9510

21 Charles Street
Boston, Massachusetts 02108

STAR TOP CAFÉ
(312) 281-0997

2748 North Lincoln Avenue
Chicago, Illinois 60614

SUZANNE'S CAFÉ AT THE
    PHILLIPS COLLECTION
(202) 483-7779

1600 21st Street, N.W.
Washington, D.C. 20009

TAPAS
(617) 576-2240

2067 Massachusetts Avenue
Cambridge, Massachusetts 02140

TRIO CAFÉ
(415) 563-2248

1870 Fillmore Street
San Francisco, California 94115

UNION SQUARE CAFÉ
(212) 243-4020

21 East Sixteenth Street
New York, New York 10003

USA CAFÉ
(215) 569-2240

1710 Sansom Street
Philadelphia, Pennsylvania 19103

WASHINGTON SQUARE BAR &
    GRILL
(415) 982-8123

1707 Powell Street
San Francisco, California 94133

WEST END CAFÉ
(202) 293-5390

One Washington Circle, N.W.
Washington, D.C. 20037

WHITE DOG CAFÉ
(215) 386-9224

3420 Sansom Street
Philadelphia, Pennsylvania 19104

INDEX

Hot dogs (pigs in blankets), 30
Huevos pamul, 312

Ice cream, 293–99
    adobe pie, 293
    champagne sherbet, 299
    coupe Clancy, 296
    lemon-almond, 297
    mandarine Napoleon sorbet, 298
    mountain of snow, 294
Insalata di bistecca, 9
Italian olive salad, 103
Italian rice salad, 224

Jade and ivory chicken, 8
Jalapeño cheese soup, 75
Jambalaya, 195
Jerked chicken with salsa, 152

Lamb
    chops with port wine and tarragon, 139
    and fig kebabs with cucumber salad, 138
    and spinach in phyllo, 136
    turnovers, Caribbean, 34
Leek soup, chilled, 92
Lemon
    -almond ice cream, 297
    pudding cake with berry coulis, 280
    tart, fresh, 265
Lime mousse pie, 257
Linguine with spicy mussel sauce, 206
Liver, chicken, and spinach salad, 239
Lobster and green tomato sauce, penne with, 204
Lobster Margarita, 229
Louisiana chicken hash, 306

Mahi-mahi with tomato sauce, 185
Mandarine Napoleon sorbet, 298
Maple walnut pie, 260
Marabella's famous sweet and hot peppers, 6
Marigold mint chicken salad, 214
Marinade, seafood, 218
Marinade for prawns, 50
Marinated filet mignon of tuna, 177
Marinated monkfish, grilled, 187
Master potter's lunch, the (caponata sandwich), 100
Mayonnaise, 188, 229, 334
    green peppercorn, 96
    jade dressing, 8
    sorrel, 212
Mediterranean antipasto salad, 238
Meringues, 295
Mexican B.L.T., 104
Mezzo ditale with eggplant, 43
Migas (egg-tortilla), 311
Mint yogurt sauce, 35
Monkfish, grilled marinated, 187
Montrachet calzone, 118
Mountain of snow, 294
Mousse
    ginger, with white chocolate, 289
    lime, pie, 257
    strawberry frozen yogurt, 292
Muffins
    banana pecan, 319
    Creole, 322
    oat bran, 321
    orange-walnut, 320
    poppyseed, 318
Muffuletta, 102
Mushrooms. *See* Wild mushrooms
Mussel(s)
    baked smoked, with spinach, 54

Pie(s), 254–64. *See also* Tart(s)
    adobe ice cream, 293
    black-bottom, 262
    chocolate whiskey pecan, 264
    cranberry-almond streusel, 256
    lime mousse, 257
    maple walnut, 260
    pecan, hot buttered, 258
    shortbread apple, 254
Pigs in blankets, 30
Pimiento cheese sandwiches, 98
Pissaladière (a snack from Provence), 108
Pizza, 112–23. *See also* Calzone
    dough, 337
    fig, 117
    garlic, 114
    with goat cheese, sun-dried tomatoes,
      and black olives, 116
    primavera, 112
    al quattro formaggi, 113
Plum-almond tart, 268
Poblano butter, 194
Polenta with poached eggs and sauce
    arrabbiata, 307
Polenta and porcini, braised rabbit with,
    146
Pollo limonese, 153
Poppyseed muffins, 318
Poppyseed parfait with blueberry coulis,
    290
Porcini and polenta, braised rabbit with,
    146
Pork
    loin chops stuffed with sausage, 135
    cold roast, with marinated papaya, 12
    roast with prunes, 134
    tenderloin sandwich, roasted, 107
    and veal, terrine of, 10
Potato(es)
    grilled red, with rouille, 40

    new, stuffed with three cheeses, 41
    Ouisie's spud, 42
    salad, Northwest, 241
Poussin with Cabernet sauce and curried
    corn fritters, 168
Prawns. *See also* Shrimp
    in brandy sauce, 52
    grilled, with black beans, chili, and
      garlic, 50
    red chili pasta with salsa, cilantro, and,
      202
Pudding
    almond-brown rice with raspberry
      coulis, 286
    bread, apricot-raisin, 288
    cake, lemon, with berry coulis, 280

Quesadillas fritas, 31
Quince, crêpes with, and caramel and
    roasted walnuts, 270

Rabbit, braised with porcini and polenta,
    146
Raspberry(ies)
    cobbler, 272
    coulis, 286
    pastry shell with chocolate and fruit,
      266
    soy dressing, 13
    with white chocolate mint sauce,
      274
Red flannel hash with béarnaise, 304
Red snapper baked in corn husks, 180
Red snapper with melon sauce, 182
Redfish, cayenne, with garlic sauce,
    184
Redfish Nantua, 183
Rémoulade, 61

coulis. *See* Coulis
crème anglaise, 336
garlic, creamy, 184
green chili, 155
herb, 19
hollandaise, brandied, 308
mayonnaise. *See* Mayonnaise
mint yogurt, 35
mustard, 36
mustard, Creole, 193
pizza, 115
rémoulade, 61
rosemary beurre blanc, 179
rouille, 40
spiced pear, 33
tapenade, 5
tomato cream, 190
tomato salsa, 152
tomato, roasted, salsa, 26
vinaigrette. *See* Vinaigrette
yellow tomato, 20
Sausage
  andouille, and shrimp with Creole
    mustard sauce, 192
  hoagie with peperonata, 110
  Syrian, in pita, 109
Scallop(s)
  bay, clementine, and baby banana
    salad, 231
  ceviche with mint, 24
  fisherman's salad, 218
  hot and spicy, 57
  sea, with mint, Montrachet, and
    cappelini, 56
  seafood salad, Thai, 220
Seafood, 188–95. *See also name of seafood*
  chowder, Down East, 80
  gazpacho, 87
  marinade, 218
  salad, 23

salad, Thai, 220
seasoning, Creole, 192
Semolina cake, 246
Sherbet, champagne, 299
Shiitake, sweetbread, and shrimp sauté, 36
Shortbread apple pie, 254
Shrimp. *See also* Prawns
  and andouille sausage with Creole
    mustard sauce, 192
  Gulf, with poblano butter, 194
  jambalaya, 195
  Mykonos plate, 49
  and pasta salad, Oriental, 223
  salad, warm, 222
  seafood salad, Thai, 220
  sweetbread and shiitake sauté, 36
  and whole-wheat fettuccine salad, 226
  and wild mushrooms with lemon, 16
Slats (tomato topping), 29
Small courses. *See* Tapas and small
  courses
Smoked
  cheese, tomato, and barbecued onion
    sandwich, grilled, 99
  chicken and ham salad, 216
  duck breast with pears and
    persimmons, 170
  fish chowder, 79
  fish, trout fritters, 62
  mussels, chicken fricassee with, 165
  mussels baked with spinach, 54
  salmon with mozzarella and yellow
    tomato sauce, 20
Snack from Provence, a (pissaladière),
  108
Snapper. *See* Red snapper
Snow pea soup with pickled ginger, sake,
  and maguro, 88
Softshell crabs with tomato cream sauce,
  190